Fore-play, Fair-play & Foul-play:

Emotional Assertiveness, the Happiness Equation

By John Parr MSc, CMT, CQSW

Published by: Emotional Assertiveness International Ltd

Cover artwork and design by Tina Scahill

Paperback ISBN: 978-1-947635-55-5
Ebook ISBN: 978-1-947635-56-2

Praise for John Parr and *Fore-play, Fair-play & Foul-play*

"Before my husband and I met, life had presented both of us with some pretty stressful events which triggered deep emotions. As I got to know my future husband and listened to his life stories, I also witnessed how he had disconnected from authentic emotions related to some past experiences. John had played a pivotal role in my own life a couple of years earlier and I knew, if there was one person who would be able to help transition my husband from unconsciously suppressing deep pain towards accepting and fully embracing his emotions, it was John. I proposed to my husband that we do John's emotional assertiveness seminar together.

"Through John's loving being, his clarity and transparency, he authentically and easily creates an incredibly safe environment that allows every individual in the room to go deep and explore. As we went through John's program, my husband opened up to a 40-year-old deep emotional wound and allowed himself to feel, accept, make peace and fully embrace his authentic emotions. Unlocking this one particular moment in his life has liberated his emotional world, which has enriched our relationship in a beautiful way.

"For me, as an Executive Coach, coaching high-performing CEOs and Executives, John's work is priceless in my business. The brilliance of John's model makes it easy for high-performing CEOs and executives to re-connect with their authentic emotions, with love, and become transformational and influential leaders."

—Nicole Heimann, Co-CEO, Heimann Cvetkovic & Partners AG,
Author of *How to Develop the Authentic Leader in You*
and multi award-winning CEO-Coach

"John distils his decades of experience as a psychotherapist and makes it accessible to us in simple language. The exercises are easy to follow. If you want a practical tool that can change the way you look at and do relationships, look no further. Come prepared with a pen and paper and be ready for some intense wow moments!"

—Parul Banka, Career Coach, Speaker and Author.

"I recommend this book to you. It summarises the model John used in my successful recovery from Crohn's disease over thirty years ago now. John's model of Emotional Assertiveness was instrumental in my learning to recognise and use my emotions to achieve psychological, emotional, and physical wellbeing. I now no longer need medications to treat my symptoms, rather when I experience a pain in my gut, I use it to alert me to apply what I know. The pain then goes, it is my barometer."

—Julie Guest MSc Psychotherapy

"I have attended an Emotional Assertiveness seminar led by John. There I learned a lot about how to identify my authentic emotions, instead of resorting to unhealthy cover-up emotions, that lead to unproductive conflict. Thanks to the solutions offered on the seminar I now practice using my emotions in a healthy way. Within just a week, the results in my personal life were positive, I am unlocking myself. Additionally, the model benefited me in my role as a people manager. I highly recommend the training and the description of the model in this book. Both you and the people you connect with will gain from the skills you learn."

—Fanny Carouge, Director of Commercial Data and Insights, Immediate Media

Table of Contents

Part III
Emotions on Stage:
The Model in Action

Acknowledgments

I am grateful to many people for their patience, help, encouragement, and support while I wrestled with writing this book. I name some here and regret that I cannot name you all. First, I wish to thank my supervisor, Biljana van Rijn, who read the first draft of my MSc thesis and encouraged me to rewrite it. I also want to thank Joseph LeDoux for his willingness to exchange e-mails about his work on fear and for his supportive comments about my work. Special thanks go to Dr Liz Chye for helping me get past the finish line. Her skill in managing the written word is outstanding and much appreciated. I appreciated the input from Kim Payne, my son's English tutor. I listened to their sessions in awe and learned more about English grammar from her in a few hours than I had from my schoolteachers back in high school. She also encouraged me to write this book.

My dear friend and colleague Dr Kalman J Kaplan was a great support. Kal edited Chapter 13, graciously allowing me to paraphrase his words to fit the topic. He also permitted me to reproduce his diagram and conceptualise his work to illustrate the many ways different theories can be cross matched to provide new insights.

My daughter Sarah, who volunteered to read the prepublication proof of the book, went through it with a fine-tooth comb, and helped with corrections, questions, and clarifications. This was a great act of love; thank you Sarah.

I also owe a debt of gratitude to my colleagues in the Transactional Analysis (TA) community for listening to my early ideas, particularly as I explained them with such excitement! Their support, feedback, and questioning have been invaluable in developing my theories and inspiring me to write this book.

To my certified trainers and those who have attended my workshops, I thank you for your feedback, sharing and questioning of my hypothesis. Your probing questions often inspired me to think deeper and ask questions about my ideas and assumptions. I am happy to say that with each seminar I run, I still learn from my students.

Thanks to my therapy clients, who were willing to experiment with the material and who gave me permission to use their work as examples. Their generosity has allowed me to include real life case study examples.

Finally, I thank my wife, children, extended family and friends for their love, relationships and commitment. They are living proof that communication, willingness to share intimacy and openness about our emotions are the most effective means to being close, connected and alive.

Prologue

"The Circle of Life"
By Elton John from the Lion King (Elton John and Tim Rice)

I began my journey into the field of Emotional Intelligence when I was in training to be certified as a Transactional Analyst psychotherapist. Entering the field of Emotional Intelligence in the mid-1990s, as the focus of my studies for a MSc in psychotherapy, motivated me to dig deeper. I noticed that all the books I read on the subject clearly indicated the importance of Emotional Intelligence whilst offering no clear indication about how to develop these skills. It seemed to me important to develop practical tools to change that and as a therapist I was already discovering these tools.

Noticing how important it is to be in touch with our emotions, I began developing techniques to facilitate my clients' finding solutions, by using their thinking and feeling together. As a tease, I call this using joined up thinking and feeling, as sometimes being playful can bypass defensiveness.

This book is based upon my quantitative and qualitative research about emotions, their function and expressions and how this links to cognitive processes. The contents span over thirty years of application of my theories as a therapist, consultant, coach and trainer.

The formal research was for the purpose of testing my hypotheses regarding emotional intelligence. This was an in-depth examination to clarify, test, and if possible, to validate my theories, towards gaining a MSc in psychotherapy that I submitted in 2003.

As well as drawing from my master's thesis, it contains updates on my work since then. There will be some case studies taken as real-life examples of my practice as a psychotherapist. I add to this some examples from my personal life experiences. I will share feedback and examples of how the theory has been applied based upon the experiences of my therapy clients as well as delegates in my seminars. All the real-life vignettes offered demonstrate the application and efficacy of my Emotional Assertiveness model and are intended to introduce you to the methodology and offer you some practical tools. Wherever case study material or testimonials are used, the identity of the individual is protected by altering personal details, without changing the theoretical aspects.

I now run seminars on the practicalities of understanding emotions and their healthy application within relationships. The objectives of the seminars and workshops are to improve communication, develop healthy relationships, and build trust through applied emotional intelligence. The model works. It is simple to grasp and apply and is based upon building trust through respect. The therapeutic case studies demonstrate the model can be applied in a therapeutic relationship and everyday life.

I see life as a journey that our emotional experiences escort and transport us through. The model portrays emotions as energy ebbing and flowing and revealing the circles of life. We will, therefore, be looking closely at these ebbs and flows, and our emotional cycles and movement. This is not intended as a static or rigid model, but something we can adapt to our own life experience. When recognised and regulated, emotions are the threads that weave through our personal tapestry, our circle of life.

Here is the good news about emotional intelligence; unlike IQ, you can grow your capacity for it and learn to apply your emotions in a healthy and assertive way. Emotional intelligence is an attribution, whilst emotional assertiveness is the behavioural application of that attribute.

Introduction

"Getting to Know You"
Rogers and Hammerstein from The King and I

The Fore-play

Why the title *Fore-play, Fair-Play, and Foul-Play*? I hate to break it to you, but before we go any further, I should tell you the term fore-play in this book has no sexual connotations. For me, all relationships have some aspects of these three experiences of human connection. Two are bonding behaviours, fore-play and fair-play, whilst foul-play are behaviours that lead to the breaking of relationship bonds.

Generally, we enter all of our relationships tentatively with behaviours I call fore-play. We meet and begin to discover each other by unconsciously following the exchange of socially and culturally understood behaviours. These culturally programmed exchanges are almost ritualistic in nature. Through these explorations we slowly and tentatively reconnoitre the terrain before deciding whether this person is OK to spend time with. This is an informal, and largely unconscious, stocktaking to measure risks against advantages. We are dealing with tricky issues such as how much of my real self is it safe to show them?

The Fair-play

Eventually, we move past this fore-play phase of involvement as we come to respect each other as equals and move into a relationship of fair-play. Mutual respect is essential for this, and we return to this topic later in the book.

As we spend more of our interpersonal relationship time showing fair-play, i.e., treating each other with respect, being willing to listen, making compromises and being mutually supportive, then the relationship grows and develops. Fair-play includes behaviours as diverse as returning the borrowed lawn mower on time to offering a meal to someone who is dealing with a sick relative and unable to provide so easily for themselves. It is about having clear agreements and keeping them, sharing deeper and more personal information, and being as good as your word. Such acts of human kindness help in building trust and deepening emotional bonds. Eventually, we begin to share deep and meaningful information with each other. These are our close friendships, as opposed to the more superficial friendships established during fore-play. In real terms, many of us have very few deep friendships, but may have many people we may call friends or acquaintances, i.e., people we get along with, socialise with, or work with. Nevertheless, these more superficial relationships all call for regular meaningful acts of fair-play. Just so long as we keep the relationship balanced by staying win-win, cooperative and respectful towards each other, our relationships will prove to be satisfying and mutually gratifying. These are the relationships we need in the workplace, where teamwork needs to be based upon trust and commitment towards shared goals and objectives. Some of these acquaintances develop deeper into long term committed friendships and partnerships. Fair-play is, therefore, central to creating bonds and attachments.

Foul-play

If, on the other hand, we experience foul-play in our relationships with others, i.e., where we treat each other with disrespect, do not tolerate difference or diversity, show prejudice, break trust, are rude, manipulative or aggressive, then the relationship is unlikely to survive. Not only do we fail to show fair-play, we will probably step into negative forms of fore-play, where we unconsciously seek to prove negative beliefs. This inevitably leads to a disconnect from the relationship. Foul-play is at the heart of negative, unproductive human conflict and disease. Conflict of itself is not harmful and does not necessarily lead to acts of disrespect. So long as we remain in the zone of fair-play, conflict can be very productive as well as lead to creativity or stronger bonds of friendship. When we actively remain OK with each other, listen and look for workable compromise, we use the energy in conflict to drive our quest for cooperation.[1] In any well-adjusted relationship, there will be conflict, as we discover our personal needs are not always compatible. However, when conflict is not dealt with through emotional assertiveness, it descends into foul-play. It is therefore important to notice foul-play and to develop strategies to avoid using it ourselves, and manage it effectively when others offer it to us.

This book looks at the emotionally assertive components of each of these forms of social interactions; fore-play, fair-play, and foul-play. I offer some tools to analyse and regulate our behaviours in each stage. In this way, we can proactively manage our human relationships to achieve more satisfying interactions with others and minimise those times when things go pear-shaped.

Because this material is drawn from my research over years of application as a psychotherapist, I have tested it in practice and know it works. I have, therefore, verified the clinical validity of my hypotheses and the efficacy of Emotional Assertiveness. I trust that you will also find they work for you. I will include material from seminars I developed and run, which are designed to help people grow their capacity for applied emotional intelligence.

Theorists will see that I draw links between the Emotional Assertiveness Model and several other concepts, including Transactional Analysis (TA) (Dr Eric Berne); the Process Communications Model, (Dr Taibi Kahler); Teaching Individuals to Live Together, (Dr Kalman Kaplan); The Drama Triangle (Dr Stephen Karpman); and child developmental theorists like Erickson, Mahler and Bowlby. Where I draw upon theory from others, I present it in lay terms to keep the material accessible for all. Where I refer to theoretical constructs, I will point you to other reading for those who may wish to delve deeper. Where the use of some jargon is inevitable, I offer explanations and make footnotes. I see no need to complicate this subject, and this book is not directly aimed at therapists and psychologists. Rather, I want

---

1. Workable compromise is a term coined by Manuel J Smith. It is about conflict resolution based upon assertive behaviour and indicates seeking not for any old compromise, but rather compromise where individuals feel OK about making concessions, with no loss of self-esteem. For more on his book, see *When I Say No, I Feel Guilty*. It is an excellent read.

to communicate with anyone who seeks hints, tips and hacks to processing emotions. I trust that any professionals who read it will find it helpful in dealing with their ailing clients. I know from experience how many of my clients found this material valuable and used it to assist their cure.

I shall present my model and sometimes discuss its application in casework terms to bring the subject to life. When I do this, I intend to present the material in everyday terminology to communicate with a wider audience.

I invite the reader to remember all psychological descriptions of human behaviour are merely models and not the truth. The model I present is no different in this respect. It is intended as a guide into the inner world of our emotions and the external world of communication and relationships. Emotions are complex and I could never capture their full colours and subtle nuances in a few hundred pages. However, I hope to throw some light on the topic so you glean some useful information and insights[2] by using the book, much like a prism—splitting white light into its components. The book splits the complexity of emotion into easier-to-grasp flavours, or the basic components of emotion. You will discover that emotions present us with little gems of information, explaining what ails us and what we need to do to regain equilibrium. This will usually be in connection with human relationships, and it is in the context of our relationships where emotional assertiveness can help us the most.

---

2. I use the term information to denote an exchange of data. The term insight refers to gaining awareness of some internal information, previously overlooked. An insight comes from processing information in ways that create a new understanding. For example, by linking my thoughts and data, to my emotional responses, I blend thinking and emotions to take myself to deeper levels of understanding.

Behind the Curtain of Emotions: The Groundwork

CHAPTER 1

Why Are we Cursed with Emotions?

"I'd Rather Go Blind"[3]
*by Fleetwood Mac, written by Billy
Foster and Ellington Jordan*

"The world is a tragedy to those who feel,
but a comedy to those who think."
Horace Walpole (1717 – 1797)

The Universality of Emotion

Why are we cursed with emotions, and why do we have emotions? I open all my emotional assertiveness seminars with this question, and I find the delegates' responses interesting. For the most part, I see a wall of blank faces, as if this question has come from left field. Few seem to ponder this matter. It's a good question though, isn't it? Apart from researchers, it seems few people have ever asked or thought about it—we just have them.

At face value, this many sound an odd question, but over the years many people have told me how they felt life would be better for them if they had no emotions. They say, "My emotions get in the way and just cloud my perspective." They believe they could think clearly without being overwhelmed by their emotions. This theme has often been central to the issue that brought them into the therapy consulting room. Logic is the high card that sometimes gets trumped by emotionality.

In the twentieth century, characters like Spock from *Star Trek*, and Data from the next generation of *Star Trek*, were offered as

---

3. Something deep down in my soul said "Cry boy", when I saw you and him out walking
   I would rather, I would rather go blind girl, than to see you walk away from me child.

models of individuals with pure thought. These individuals were not cluttered with emotion, instead working and problem solving with pure logical thought. This model began to gain favour as if it were something to aspire towards. Interestingly, in the first *Star Trek* series, the character Spock came from a race that had previously been unable to manage their destructive anger and had learnt to subdue all of their emotions to protect themselves. For them, survival became a matter of suppressing emotions until eventually they felt none.

In a later series of *Star Trek*, we find the android Data, again possessed only of pure thought. However, unlike Spock, Data longs to be human and experience emotions. From the admiration many showed these characters, it seems many experience difficulty thinking clearly whilst experiencing and expressing our emotions. This seems to apply especially to emotions we label as negative, like anger, sadness, and fear. As you read on, you will find it is not the emotion that is either positive or negative, but how we express the emotion. Emotions can be expressed in either healthy or unhealthy ways. If the same emotion can be applied or communicated either positively or negatively, it therefore indicates the emotion is neutral.

So, what are they for?

Okay, so why on the USS Enterprise from *Star Trek*, or Earth, for us humans, do we have emotions? What purpose do they serve? To help answer the first question, I ask another question that delegates find easier to answer: "Why do we have physical sensations? Would it not be great never to feel pain?" People have clear awareness about this and tell me, "Pain protects us; it tells us when something is wrong with our body." We know that without pain, we are at high risk of death from many causes, like untreated infections, because without pain, the disease goes unnoticed and can prove fatal. For example, an untreated wound can lead to loss of limbs or even death. Physical pain tells us to avoid using damaged parts of the body to allow the organism time to heal. A broken limb that has not been immobilised is extremely painful, and could lead to complications that may in turn be life threatening if left untreated. We have sensations to facilitate our navigation in the physical world. Our nerve endings give us input to walk, taste, smell, hear and feel sensations, and so to move through our physical environment in relative safety.

When we experience pleasant sensations, the body releases many brain chemicals that lead to wellbeing, and so we are encouraged to continue experiencing pleasure. When we experience pain, we also release brain chemicals that help to manage pain and calm us, and prepare us for healing. If we think in terms of the process of evolution, those who did not function well with their sensory organs simply did not survive. Darwin described the capacity to have active and functional sensations as survival of the fittest, and the survivors passed this capacity on to their offspring. Survival of the individual is all about their health and resilience, and the ability to experience a range of sensations is essential for this. As an organism seems to be programmed to seek health and to heal if damaged, it is not too far-fetched to say that health and wellbeing are our default conditions and physical sensations exist to promote health and healing. We can therefore hypothesise that the default condition for our body is to continually seek out these states of being. While pain tells us to stop and allow time to heal, pleasurable sensations tell us to carry on, as this is good for us.

It is similar with emotions. They have a comparable function. However, they are more about navigating our emotional landscape or interpersonal relationships rather than our physical ones. Emotions tell us when something is unhealthy and needs healing in our relationships, or if all is well, to enjoy the moment.

Is this also connected with evolution and survival? I think we can say from circumstantial evidence the answer is yes! As a species, we have reached the top of the food chain, yet how did we achieve this? Yes, we are certainly smarter than other creatures, even though some human behaviours lead me to question this premise. However, our intellect alone will not be the deciding factor if we come face to face with a large predator while we are out hunting for lunch. Many predators are stronger, faster, and better armed with tooth and claw than we are. I cannot use my verbal coping skills to negotiate with a tiger: "Don't eat me, let's talk it through instead." This verbal coping skill in negotiation will not work. Alone, I am fresh meat for the many powerful predators our ancestors faced daily.

Our species learned to be effective by working together in cooperative groups. We have evolved to make attachments and bonds as we work together to achieve outcomes for the survival of the group. Therefore, I conclude emotions are all inseparably connected with survival as we manage relationships through emotions. By forming groups, the members of which efficiently communicate and effectively work together for the good of the whole, we become survivors and even create food surplus in times of plenty. In this way, the species is more likely to survive for long enough to raise offspring. Forming tribal groups and working together in teams was how we achieved our high status in the food chain. To work together, to recognise other members of the group, and be willing to make self-sacrifice for the good of the group, we need some means to establish and maintain attachment.

Most pack animals, like wolves, dogs, meerkats, horses and ruminants, use scent and territorial marking to form attachments. They also use other attachment behaviours such as touch and ritualistic greetings. For humans, emotions provide additional sophisticated tools for this; we can empathise, care for each other, share childcare duties and support those who need help. The whole group benefits from this form of cooperative lifestyle. We also have learned the skill of enjoying learning from each other, passing on knowledge and discovery, and copying the successful behaviours of our colleagues. We build upon our successes and develop at an exponential rate. We have moved away from hunting and gathering into farming, managing the environment, and laying down provisions for winter and hard times. All of this depended upon our capacity to work together cooperatively.

Emotion is the bedrock of this human evolutionary story. We see from the earliest archaeological and paleoanthropological evidence that humans not only learned to live together, but our earliest ancestors developed an interest in activities not directly related to survival. They drew intricate pictures on the walls of caves, made jewellery, used body make up and cared for their dead. All these activities clearly showed the role of emotion, attachment and bonding from the very beginnings of the time of Homo-sapiens. The evidence for emotion in our ancient history is preserved in many forms.

Clearly, not only humans form attachments and live in groups. Horses, elephants, wolves, dolphins, whales, meerkats and apes all live in groups and all display behaviours indicating attachment, bonding and emotion. The old belief that animals differed from humans because they do not have emotion is now debunked. A great deal of research clearly shows that many animals do indeed have emotions and form emotional attachments. Whilst we cannot ask an animal what it's feeling, we can observe behaviour and draw conclusions from this. The existence of emotion in animals is a well-debated topic and until recently has been difficult to prove. However, anyone who has owned a dog will be aware how empathic the creatures can be and how they sense your mood and show support and care for you. They also show you what they are feeling through their gestures, postures and general behaviour. Because of the central role that attachment and bonding plays in our survival and emotional stability, we will investigate this topic further in Chapter 3.

More recent research clearly indicates apes have emotions similar to humans; they grieve, they play, they cooperate and they even understand fair-play,[4] so what separates us from them? It appears humans have some capacities these animals lack, and the more important differences are found in impulse control, rather than the experience of emotions themselves. Apes seem unable to learn to refrain from simply grabbing what they want, whereas we have learned to hold back, tame our emotional urges, and gain rewards as a result. Also, we have acquired the ability to teach and learn through our capacity to draw the attention of others to what is important to us. Scientists call this the triangle. If I want you to look at something, I point to it. You look and we share an experience, hence the term triangle. Humans look to where we are pointing, whilst animals, like dogs, will look at the pointing finger.

---

4. de Waal, F. (2012) *Moral behavior in animals* [Online]. Available at: https://youtu.be/GcJxRqTs5nk

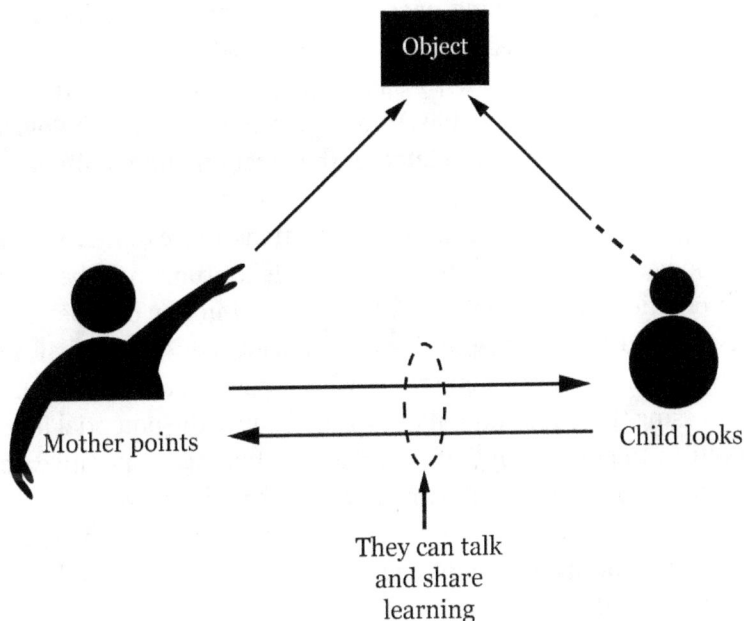

Figure 1: Attention triangle

Mothers teach their children these skills through play. Our emotions provide the compass that helps us to belong to kinship and tribal groups and, when moderated by impulse control, we grow wiser and more effective as individuals and in groups. Just as physical sensations help us navigate our physical environment, emotions help us find our way around our relationship environment and that also provides an important survival function.

In one of his TED Talks, Frans de Waal mentions the Pillars of Morality. These are the key to the healthy attachment behaviours, reciprocity (fairness) and empathy (compassion). He explains humans are not the only animals that demonstrate these two pillars, but we are clearly the group that most consistently acts upon these traits. Emotional assertiveness revolves around empathy and reciprocity and both are at the heart of respect for self and others. Respect is the core of civilisation, cooperation, partnership, productive conflict, conflict resolution and teamwork. Without respect, we quickly descend into unproductive conflict. Lack of respect is the mechanism for losing energy through fighting, for failure to work together and eventually for failure of the relationship itself.

As I unpack my model, I show how each of our emotions is uniquely connected to basic interpersonal and psychological needs. In turn, these are related to the creation and maintenance of emotional bonds.

In general terms, pleasurable sensations tell us all is well in our body, whilst pain announces there is a problem to be fixed. The emotion of happiness tells us all is well in our interpersonal relationship. The other emotions, like anger, sadness and fear, tell us we need to address something within a relational context, and addressing the issue authentically will enhance the potential for us to return to being happy. It is about maintaining cooperative and effective connections to the important others in our life.

Grasping this concept, and running with it, you will gain insights into why relationship maintenance is essential for your wellbeing and success. If you want to develop your understanding at a deeper level, I suggest you read more about the role of Mirror Neurons i.e., structures in the brain that allow us to identify with others and sympathise with them when they are in distress or happy and excited. Also, look at the work of Dr Jaak Panksepp PhD, a pioneer in affective neuroscience, who revealed the close link between human emotions and animal emotions in the process of bonding and wellbeing.

There is now plenty of experimental evidence to show that human beings are hard-wired for conforming to socially accepted norms, and there are centres in the brain that cause us to feel good when we conform, and to feel bad when we break with social norms. These mechanisms are behind group pressure and the tendency to go with the flow, sometimes even against our better judgement. For example, one experiment in conformity was to have a small group standing in the street and looking up into a tree. When others came by, they also looked up into the tree. Then the experimenters told the newcomers they were observing a snake; soon, the newcomers saw the snake when in fact there was no snake in the tree.

Another experiment had people in a museum following a red line that obviously led nowhere, including following it around in circles. Groups of people just fell in line and followed the crowd. Why do we sometimes feel compelled to follow the herd? Because in evolutionary terms, our survival may once have depended upon this behaviour and we have not lost these primal instincts. Whilst I think it probable that over thousands of years we may override these ingrained behaviours, I think it unlikely we will totally eradicate the genetically embedded group behaviours. Attachment is so deeply a part of our species' developmental processes and an integral part of healthy parenting that I think we will always have an attachment at the core of our being. Research on the human need for connectivity to others shows that being in proximity with other people is very important to us all. Even the toughest inmates in maximum security prisons fear solitary confinement. It is true there are people who can adapt to survive in solitary situations for years, for example, forced by circumstances to live or survive on a deserted island or those who choose a lifestyle of solitude. However, these are the exceptions that prove the rule. For most of us, we simply need to have others around us. That we need others is not a new concept. English poet John Donne (1572-1631) dean of St. Paul's Cathedral, London, wrote:

No man is an island entire of itself; every man
is a piece of the continent, a part of the main;
if a clod be washed away by the sea, Europe
is the less, as well as if a promontory were, as
well as any manner of thy friends or of thine
own were; any man's death diminishes me,
because I am involved in mankind.
And therefore, never send to know for whom
the bell tolls; it tolls for thee.

A good example of the effects of long term enforced living alone was portrayed in the Tom Hanks film, Castaway. The key character was marooned on a desert island for three years following an air crash into the ocean. During his time alone on the island, Hanks' character, Chuck Noland, created a companion from a basketball and named him Wilson. Each day, Chuck had long conversations with Wilson, and when he was eventually able to escape on a raft, he even took Wilson with him. Wilson was eventually washed from the raft and drifted away. At first, Chuck risked his life to save Wilson, but then admitted defeat. He grieved as the wind and waves carried Wilson away. This fictional piece is an illustration of how we can become attached to inanimate objects and we will return to this example when we examine the grief cycle later in the book.

In relationship with others, we blossom. Healthy relationships add to the quality of our life, offering a dimension immeasurably important to our health and wellbeing. We find deeper meaning in life, and we have the gift of trustworthy feedback, of reassurance, of recognition and acceptance. Research shows that people who live together with a committed partner live approximately five years longer than people who live alone. Sadly, however, mankind has a generalised history of failure of relating to others in healthy ways. From local tribal warfare to global cataclysmic conflicts like the last two world wars, we seem incapable of managing respectful and productive relationships. Why do we reach the point where, rather than cooperate with others, we enter unproductive and destructive conflict? We will see later that humans don't kill other humans, and that before we get to that stage, first we dehumanise them. Perceiving them to be unworthy, we then justify getting rid of them. It seems we can easily find limitless reasons to dehumanise and demonise others and then seek to destroy them. Dehumanising can be based upon race, skin colour, religious differences, sexual preference differences, territorial arguments and greed, but the list is seemingly endless. At the root of all killing is this process of making others not OK, i.e., somehow less human. Examples from armed conflicts are the British calling the Germans Krauts, and the Germans calling the British Tommies. We are not killing people who have mothers, wives and children, but bad people branded a de-humanising name such as Tommies or Gooks, as the Americans called the North Vietnamese.

However, modern genetic research shows just how closely we are all related to one another. Humankind is just one large extended family. Yes, we come in all shapes and sizes, and yes, we have different coloured skin and there are often huge differences in how we develop our societies and cultures. But we all came out of Africa and are distant relatives, connected through a single female, Lucy. However, cultural differences can be almost 180 degrees out of sync. For example, European culture is largely based upon the concept of the importance of the individual, and of personal rights and freedoms, whilst the Japanese culture is founded upon the premise that each person exists for the good of the whole. Therefore, in one culture, people are encouraged to stand up for their rights and put self first, and in the other, self-sacrifice is the norm. In both cultures, children are cared for, people fall in love and bonding and attachment remain central issues. If we are smart, we learn how to respect cultural differences, even to learn from them and get along with others, irrespective of the minor differences.

We can therefore liken war to family feuds; we are cousins, yet we fight to the death rather than negotiate for win-win outcomes and the sharing of resources. It seems we have lost sight of the importance of emotional intelligence, empathy and simply being friends and working together to build a better world for all. Yet emotional intelligence is really all about that; the survival of the species. Is it not time for a change? Deepak Chopra said,

Every time you are tempted to react in the same old way, ask if you want to be a prisoner of the past or a pioneer of the future. The past is closed and limited; the future is open and free.[5]

Reacting in the same old way will inevitably bring the same old results. Yet if we act upon our patterns, we will continue to walk down paths of emotional expression that lead us nowhere. In couples' therapy, the most common presenting problems always seem to follow this pattern: "I do this, and he/she does that, and then, and then and then and finally this is the bad outcome." When the pattern is revealed, and the question is asked, "When he/she says that, why not do something different?" both partners say, "Well,

---

5. Deepak Chopra (1998) *The Path to Love: Spiritual Strategies for Healing*, p. 170

it can't be that simple." The reality is that often it is that simple; when we follow patterns, we ultimately reach the same outcome.

We really must begin to change our patterns, or we will eventually kill off humanity.

What if, rather than having a war when Argentina invaded the Falkland Islands, the UK and Argentina simply agreed to give the people living on the islands the choice to remain a part of the UK or become Argentinian citizens? This would have allowed the Falkland Islanders self-determination and would have saved the lives of many hundreds of British and Argentinian young men. Instead, we had a conflict where both sides lost soldiers, airmen and sailors. Millions of pounds were spent by both sides to fund aircraft, ships, ammunition, oil and so on. That money could have been put to better use in both countries. For example, what if the two countries had made an alliance to help each other build hospitals, schools or research for curing disease? What an utter waste of human life and resources, and this is just one recent conflict. Look at the failure of communication all over the world today and the utter failure to use our innate skills to form attachment. We do not need more bombs; we need more bonding.

More recent examples of this include the civil war in Syria that seems to be grinding on with a pitiless disregard for human life, or for the safety of women and children. The conflicting inputs of the superpowers seem to be exacerbating this conflict, and the bloodshed and hatred seems to show no signs of letting up. From this conflict, we are presented with daily images of children living in squalor in the areas where fighting continues. Advertisements for charity organisations invite us to feel empathy for these children and donate funds to buy them blankets and so on. I understand the drive to want to help, but the adverts attempt to manipulate our emotions so we feel guilty and donate to their cause. Aid may help to offer some comfort to the needy, but will not really help bring about the kind of change required. As we feel sad for them and scared about how we may feel about our children in that situation, we can easily lose sight of what we can do to make a difference. I believe what is really needed is for the citizens of the world to say, "Enough!" We should persistently lobby our respective governments to abandon their quest for influence and power in the region, demand all governments unite and work together to deny the combatants weapons and bring them to the negotiation table, and encourage an active and honest desire to establish tolerance and peace. When I listen to the key players talking about the issues, it seems clear each side is seeking to prove they hold the moral high ground. In all the talking, where is the listening? Where is the voice of sanity drawing clear and non-negotiable lines in the sand to collectively act to protect the children and to find cooperative solutions?

Such conflicts are clear examples of how we fail to use our emotions to find healthy relationship outcomes and turn to displays of non-authentic emotion leading to self-destruction. The way of peaceful relationship is not easy, however if we are to survive on this earth, we need to seriously change our behaviours. Emotional assertiveness is therefore about all relationships; the personal, commercial, and international.

CHAPTER 2

Child Development: Parenting and Impulse Control

Later in the book, we will dive deeper into the world of emotions and their relationship to communication, cooperation, and attachment. However, at this point I think it is important to say something about parenting and impulse control. Impulse control seems to be an important differentiation between us and our cousins, the apes. When an ape is angry, it will quickly express this emotion aggressively and often violently. Humans have the capacity to learn to manage this emotion and express it in more sociably acceptable and helpful ways. This is not something that simply develops in us; we learn it in our childhood when we observe our caretakers managing their expression of anger in a rational and balanced way. If in childhood we saw anger expressed in a healthy way, without attack, blame or retreating into the victim position, we too will have learned to put some limits upon how we express our anger. We learn this not only as a function of observation of how our caretakers manage anger, but also by how they help us manage the expression of our own anger. Babies are essentially pattern recognition machines; they learn more from observation and emotional experiences than from being told something. However, unlike adults, they have little contextual information about how the world works. They also lack experience of human interactions and their meanings. It is as if they are newly arrived aliens from another planet who are attempting to piece together a map of their world as they go along. The consistency of their emotional experiences depends largely upon how well adjusted their primary caretakers are. However, what patterns we lay down in our formative years depends largely upon how our parents or caretakers helped us to internalise healthy messages. One important thing we have to learn is how to gain impulse control.

Observing other people and learning from them is more a

function of how they behaved rather than what they said. Parental modelling is many times more important than the rules they teach us. Sadly, when we become parents, we tend to depend upon the models we saw when we were children. We often fail to discern if the patterns are helpful or not, and so pass on some good information to our children and some that is less so. Either way, these deeply engrained patterns, often in our subconscious, have a powerful influence upon how we behave as adults and parents to our children. Even if we read books that provide us with other models, the pull of the early parental behaviours is strong. It is not a matter of parents deliberately sending us unreliable messages; it is just driven by our belief systems.

How do we as parents manage our own emotions, and how do we model this to our offspring? Let us start this exploration by addressing anger. Anger is the emotion that is most misrepresented, misunderstood, and therefore mis-communicated. Managing anger is central to impulse control. Learning to manage their anger, which often presents as rage in small children, is an essential first step. They become aroused when they have a problem, and this arousal is equivalent to anger. They express their emotion spontaneously, and the longer the problem remains, the more aroused or angry they become. They have not yet learned how to regulate their expression of the energy they have from arousal in a way that will help them communicate to invite cooperation. Can you recall how angry your small baby became if they were hungry and were kept waiting? Or if they had a tummy ache, and it did not respond quickly to parental care? I have seen small babies literally go red in the face with rage if not attended to appropriately. They have to learn control from somewhere, but how and when? Well, the first step is from the beginning. As parents of small babies, we have to be the ones who remain calm, patient, and attentive. This is not so easy when you are woken from your sleep every night by a baby who is not happy about your delay in providing a feed or nappy change. However, by learning to stay calm, we communicate that anger can be dealt with healthily. As they get older, about the time they start to speak, we can tell them it is OK, ask them what they need, and interact with them to encourage them to manage the emotion.

Helping Children Control Their Anger

With my own children, when they were small and very angry, I aimed to teach them how to manage this emotion. This cannot be achieved by ignoring them, sending them to their room, punishing them, or escalating my anger over theirs. These are crude attempts to be intimidating or manipulative, and it invites them to become compliant.

Rather, when they threw a paddy kicking and screaming, I simply held them at arm's length, firmly but safely.[6] I looked at them attentively, and let them kick and scream whilst constantly providing protection whereby neither they nor I got hurt. My first message was that it was OK they were angry, and that that required control. I spoke to them calmly, assuring them it was OK to be angry and when they were ready, I would ask them to tell me what they were angry about. I emphasised I would listen to them when they told me about why they were angry and what they needed.

When they appeared to have finished kicking, wriggling, and screaming, I asked them if they were done. If they said no, I would tell them, "It's OK to be angry, you are safe. I need you to speak to me and I will listen, so I can help." If they said yes, I would hold them close, and tell them I was ready to listen to them using a gentle tone of voice. I emphasised that it was important for me to hear what they were angry about so we could fix it together. They would tell me, and we would talk about it. I regularly reassured and let them know that what I wanted from them was to talk to me rather than to scream, kick and shout. Over time, they learned to control their rage and address their needs by asking to talk. They began to negotiate assertively for what they wanted, i.e., to say what their problem was and what they needed. They also learned, we cannot always get what we want, although we can usually discuss things

---

6. The arm's length technique I devised was intended to let them see I was not afraid of their anger. Nor was I mad at them for being angry. However, when angry, it was important to be safe and that no one was hurt.

and work out something we can both accept. I also explained to them that sometimes there are things we just have to do. We do not have to like this, and it is OK to be angry about it. However, we still have to do them.

This is how we can train our children to be assertive. The downside is that having assertive children can be quite challenging for a parent, but it is what we want them to be when they grow up. The learning must start in their childhood developmental years and these lessons will prove invaluable to them in their adult lives. Children do not have impulse control—they must be taught it. Impulse control is an important skill. Adults who failed to incorporate this learning in their childhood can also learn how to react differently, gain impulse control and manage their emotions appropriately. One of the key messages we need to incorporate is that anger expressed authentically and assertively is a potent force for building healthy relationships.

However, it is also a destructive force if we do not manage our aggressive impulses appropriately. Because so many people struggle with expressing anger authentically, the emotion has gained a bad name. You will see later that I view anger as the most creative and healthy force when expressed with respect.

You're Not to Blame

In defence of parents, parenting is not easy and does not come naturally. What most of us experience is a natural love and pride for our children. Also, we generally all want the best for our children. However, children are complex with multifaceted needs and few of the how-to books are very reliable. We also come with our own baggage from the learned patterns from how our parents brought us up. Sadly, wanting the best and meaning well does not reduce the potential traumas our children may experience when our attempt to help fails.

What will children learn if their parents do not teach them these important lessons? Some examples from confusing parenting include messages such as:

"Go to your room until you decide to behave properly."

The message that the parents intend to convey approximates

to: "I feel angry with you because of your behaviour. I want you to reflect upon what you just did and talk to me about what you will do about this." However, this is not likely to be the message the child actually receives with the "go to your room" intervention. The parent's motives were good, that is, they wanted to help the child cool down and act in a more rational and socially acceptable way. The outcome, however, is likely to differ somewhat from the intention. The child will probably learn an unhealthy way of expressing anger, especially as it is likely their parent has modelled unhealthy behaviours. This then begs the questions, how is this parental response unhealthy?

First, there is no direct expression of their emotion, we see only a reaction. Second, we do not hear what the parent actually wants, e.g., for their child to think about their behaviour, understand the impact of it, accept their responsibility and make amends. The message probably conveyed is more likely: "Unless you behave how I want you to, you will be rejected." Sending a child away for not behaving how the parent wants is tantamount to saying some behaviour can get you excluded from this relationship. "Go away" offers a win-lose outcome and invites the child to experience guilt, over-adapt and become pleasing or rebellious. In other words, the child will create a defence against their discomfort of experiencing rejection. When parents express their anger explosively, passively, indirectly or suppress it, each child will learn something negative from this. They, in turn, are likely to grow up without having incorporated healthy learning or how to use their anger in the most effective way. The modelling process is important not only for anger, but for all emotions. Children learn from their parents, though they do not always copy them. Sometimes a child will reject the parental behaviour and create an alternative, however, this is not generally any healthier. The pattern the child develops is likely to be driven to follow unhelpful parental modelling and this will not facilitate their autonomous development. Rather they may have difficulty in selecting the appropriate response for the situation. Ineffective modelling results in children growing up to be programmed to use the behavioural responses they created in their past.

"Tell your brother/sister that you are sorry" (said in a loud and intimidating voice.)

When children have angry conflicts, we parents often want to step in and "pour oil on troubled water". However, when we hear the fight, we may become frustrated and angry ourselves. We want the distress to go away. We make ourselves the police, the judge and jury, deciding who is right and who is wrong. (Note this is a huge trap. It is often impossible to get to the bottom of who started it, and in any event, this is not the issue. Both children need to learn how to negotiate, rather than how to gain the moral high ground.) We catch the culprit, if we guess correctly, and force them to apologise. However, what is the subliminal message that this child hears? "I am angry with you for disturbing the peace. If you apologise, you will be forgiven." The problem is solved. However, is it? More often than not, the child concerned, or both if you see them both as guilty, will apologise, but only to get you off their back. They are sorry you are mad at them, not for what they have done.

Potential lesson: It is not important for me to regret my behaviour and make amends. It is just important to satisfy the authorities and to get off the hook.

The following section includes an example of how I avoided the courtroom game with my daughters.

From Foul-Play to Fair-Play

My two daughters were aged eleven and nine when this incident occurred. They were good children and, as in most sibling relation-ships with this age difference, they showed sibling rivalry from time to time. Their mother and I had separated and still shared parent-ing. The girls came to me every other weekend, during holidays, and I spoke to them each day on the telephone. Back in those days, we did not have internet, or the opportunity for meeting online as we do today. The girls shared some electronic equipment, for example, the computer and VCR, and this was where their rivalry often came to the fore.

On this day, I received a distressed telephone call from their mother, who told me the girls had entered a deep conflict and were fighting. She could not manage their behaviour and asked me to intervene. I therefore collected the girls and took them back to my house. Sitting them on the sofa, side by side, I told them, "I am not interested in hearing who started it, who did what to whom. This behaviour is not OK, and we will manage it." Naturally, they wanted to tell their version of the story and attempted to draw me into being the judge and jury, deciding who was right and who was wrong. I persisted in saying, "I am not interested. I am angry that you have reached the point of fighting. This will stop. It is not negotiable; I expect you both to get along together." They sat and looked sulky.

This was the visual evidence that they were still in the realm of foul-play. Had I accepted the roles of the judge and jury, I would also have accepted deciding who was the winner and who was the loser. In effect, I would enter foul-play as there was no way to judge who started it. Each would have their own version, in which they were right, and the other was wrong. I was not willing to join in with this. I therefore told them there would be no courtroom, no judgement for and against. They were both responsible and would both be expected to take responsibility for their part. What they were to do was to sit and discuss calmly what they each wanted from the other. This was an invitation to leave foul-play and begin looking for win-win outcomes. It also invited them to focus their anger on me for "not being fair."

As I could manage dealing with their anger, it took the heat off each of them, allowing their primitive brains to calm down and make room for clear thinking. I gave them half an hour together, without me in the room. Their task was to discuss what they needed and to make a contract about the behaviours they wanted from each other. The contract was to be written up, signed, and finally witnessed by me. It would then be kept for them to return to, should they again get into conflict over managing their possessions and personal space. This would facilitate their future cooperation. I left the room and stayed nearby to listen for sounds of arguing; there were none, and they were discussing the matter calmly. This is effectively a return to fore-play, where they could explore each other's boundaries, and look respectfully at how best to cooperate in order to make a contract. Their problem was now between each of them and their dad; the focus was how to manage that relationship and, in the process, manage their own.

After thirty minutes, I returned to the room, and they had drafted a contract covering their needs. I read it, spoke to them about each clause, and appraised their demeanour during this phase of the discussion. Here, I checked the validity of their reformed relationship, to ensure they were not simply complying with dad's demands and over adapting to me. Finally, they signed their contract, and I signed as a witness. A copy of the document appears in figure 2 and 3 on the following pages. I have left their names in as they were both OK with me sharing this without protecting their identity. The girls discovered the benefits of engaging in fair-play, they had a better relationship, spent less time in unproductive conflict and had more fun, both together and when they had their own friends around. They are now in their mid-thirties, and each has two children. The girls are very close and see each other regularly. Even today, I receive occasional calls from them asking questions about how best to manage their children's behaviour. By establishing clear interpersonal boundaries, they have discovered that they can have satisfying relationships.

My role was to show that conflicts are not a problem, so long as they are managed from a win-win position. They learnt to negotiate to cooperate and help each other get their needs met. I also showed them that when their behaviour was not OK, they were not personally rejected. Instead, they were asked to find ways to realign their behaviour to maintain respect.

Rules

1. If you need to use the video or computer then as always you must knock and wait. (and the door will be answered)
2. When using the video or com-puter you are only to touch the absolute nessicery
3. Sarah must be quiet when using the computer.
4. If Sarah is sent into Suzys room when she needs to do her HW then when the video is finish-ed she shouldn't be sent back until she has completed that piece because it is disruptive (from experience)
5. If Sarah and Suzy are argueing before the TV and computer is mentioned then they arn't allowed to use the equipment in each others room.
6. If one of us is out the other can use the equipment in that persons room.
7. If you are doing something that you obviously need your room for then after this has been explained the other person must wait until called (up to ½ an hour)

Figure 2: Rules 1–7

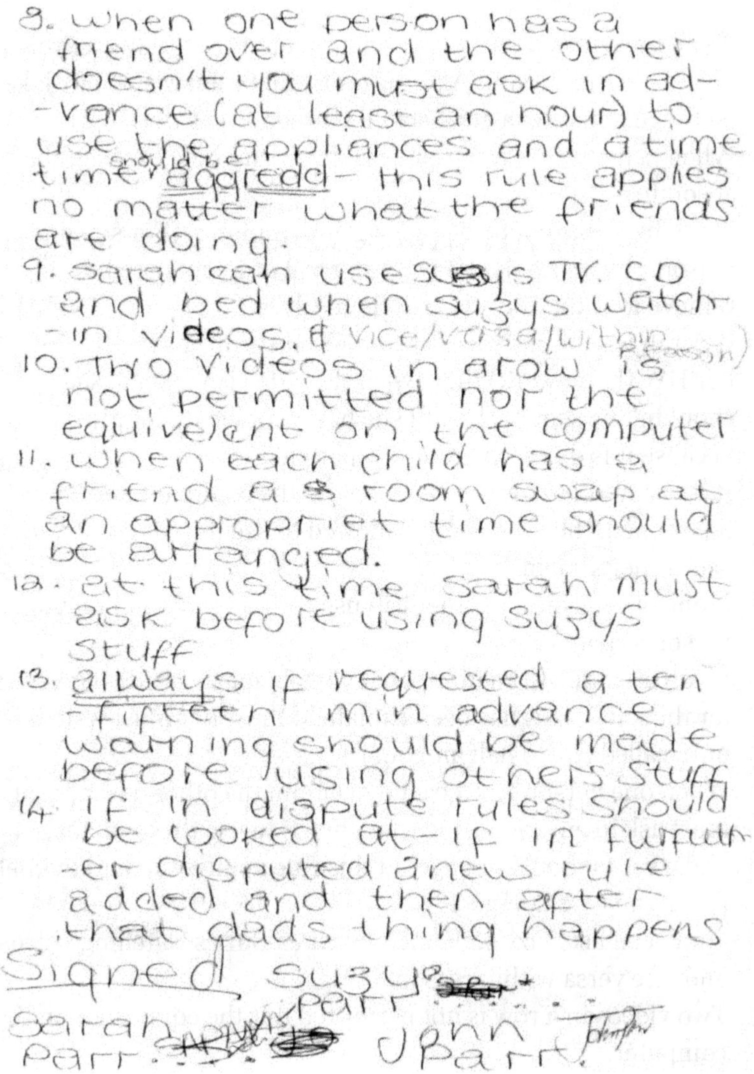

8. When one person has a friend over and the other doesn't you must ask in ad--vance (at least an hour) to use the appliances and a time time agredd- this rule applies no matter what the friends are doing.
9. Sarah can use suzys TV. CD and bed when suzys watch -in videos. & vice/varsa (within reason)
10. Two videos in arow is not permitted nor the equivelant on the computer
11. When each child has a friend a & room swap at an appropriet time should be arranged.
12. at this time sarah must ask before using suzys stuff
13. always if requested a ten -fifteen min advance warning should be made before using others stuff
14. If in dispute rules should be looked at - if in furfuth -er disputed a new rule added and then after that dads thing happens

Signed, Suzy Parr
Sarah Parr.   J Parr.

Figure 3: Rules 8–14 and signatures

Note: I transcribed this without altering their grammar or spelling to respect their work and age at the time of writing.

Rules:

1. If you need to use the video or computer, then as always, you must knock and wait. (And the door will be answered.) (A joke on the first clause; a good sign the process was working.)
2. When using the video or computer, you are only to touch the absolute nessicery.
3. Sarah must be quiet when using the computer. (For some reason, this was deleted. I do not recall if I negotiated to remove it or they decided for themselves.)
4. If Sarah is sent into Suzy's room when she needs to do her HW (homework) then when the video is finished, she shouldn't be sent back until she has completed that piece because it is disruptive (from experience)
5. If Sarah and Suzy are arguing before the computer and TV is mentioned, then they aren't allowed to use the equipment in each other's room.
6. If one of us is out the other can use the equipment in that person's room.
7. If you are doing something that you obviously need your room for then after this has been explained the other must wait until called (up to half an hour)
8. When one person has a friend over and the other doesn't you must ask in advance (at least an hour) to use the appliances and a time (should be) agreed this rule applies no matter what the friends are doing.
9. Sarah can use Suzy's TV and bed when Suzy's watching videos and vice versa within reason.
10. Two videos in a row is not permitted nor the equivalent on the computer.
11. When each child has a friend a room swap at an appropriate time should be arranged.
12. At this time Sarah must ask before using Suzy's stuff.
13. Always, if requested a 10–15 minutes advance warning should be made before using others stuff.
14. If in dispute rules should be looked at. If in further disputed a new rule added and then after that dad's thing happens.

Follow-up 1

Some years later, the younger of the girls came to live with me and we had quite an emotional ride for a few months whilst we realigned parental boundaries. She was, by then, well into the period of teenage rebellion. One day, at the dinner table, she said, "You know, Dad, I like living with you. You are a lot tougher on me than Mum was, but you respect me." This brought tears to my eyes. She had highlighted the essence of healthy child-parent relationships: respect for each other. (Note: This is also how all human relationships work best.)

Follow-up 2

On another occasion, my elder daughter invited me to a meal in her new apartment. This was a big occasion; she had prepared her first meal for her dad. It was roast chicken with all the trimmings. Sitting together at the table, she spoke to me in a voice I recognised to indicate that this was going to be a tricky question.

She said, "Dad, I am puzzled. When we were kids, you never shouted at us and never smacked us. Mum would go ballistic at us, but we were never really bothered when she got angry. But we would quickly do whatever you told us. You just spoke to us firmly, and if we didn't do as we were told, you would count, one, two ... You never ever got to three, we just did as we were asked."

"Yes, that's true, and what is your question?" I asked.

"Well, what would have happened if you got to three and we had still not done as we were asked?" she went on.

"Well, I don't know; I would probably have said four, but a little more firmly."

She laughed and said, "Damn!"

Together, we rocked with laughter.

I am sure that as parents, if we are firm and reasonable, we do not need to shout or use power plays[7] to manage our children. We just have to be calm, clear, direct, and yet non-threatening, and

---

7. A power play is a manipulative use of power. Power of itself is not an issue because as parents, we must have authority in order to discharge our parental duty. However, the misuse or abuse of power is harmful to relationships.

believe they will respond to the boundaries we establish. Sometimes we need sanctions, like for example, the naughty step. I used that measure occasionally. When they sat on the step, in silence, they were tasked with thinking about what behaviour caused them being there. They were also asked to think about whether they regretted their behaviour and, if so, what they would do to make amends. During their short stay on the step, I stayed with them, avoiding giving a message that they were only loved when they were good. Rather, I wanted them to understand that our behaviours have an impact upon the people we are in a relationship with; to take responsibility for our behaviour and to find ways to cooperate together. This includes how I, as a parent, cooperate with them and am willing to be responsible for my behaviour as a role model.

Both of the girls grew up understanding the importance of respect in their relationships and I still love the closeness we three share. Now they are adults, I believe it important not to interfere in their lives; they are no longer children and are responsible people with their own children. They know I am here for them if they need me and when they feel the need, they still tap into Dad's life experience for guidance.

CHAPTER 3

Bonding and Attachment

"Where Angels Fear to Tread"
written by Bryan Adams, composed by
Bryan Adams and Gretchen Peters

Relationships: Real Self, False Self and Relationships

Most of the words and sentiments expressed in the song introducing this chapter suggest a relationship where the singer is over-dependent upon the other. However, there is an important rationale for this swooning message. At a very deep level, we are emotionally attached to the notion that the best relationships are deeply intimate.[8] Bryan Adams believes that the object of his affection can "see right through" him and accept him for who he is. In this chapter, we will look at the myth that people can see through us and debunk it. In its place, we will offer a more rational approach to healthy relating. This will be based upon our ability to be open and vulnerable and permit people to see who we really are.

The Emotionally Assertive way to find intimacy is to spend time with people with whom we feel safe to be open with and to be real with them. These others also need to be willing and comfortable being open with us in turn. When we take this hard road to being intimate, we discover many benefits. However, in the process of being open, we must also make ourselves vulnerable to feeling hurt, misunderstood and even rejected. This is something many of us are afraid of, either consciously or unconsciously. Below are some simple drawings to illustrate the healthiest and most rewarding style of relating. The diagram represents our real self, as a circle in the centre. This is a mix of how we perceive ourselves, and things about ourselves, that may be more or less hidden, even

---

8. In this context, intimacy relates to being close, open and meaningful as opposed to having sexual connotations.

from our own consciousness. It is that part of us that can spontaneously reveal our desires, values, beliefs, etc. without censorship.
It includes those parts of us that could be described as light, as well
as shady and dark. No one is all light; we all cast a shadow, and,
despite our shadow, we are all OK. However, experience has taught
us to hide our shadow for fear of being rejected. It is our shadow,
or what we perceive as our shadow, that makes deeply honest and
intimate relationships so difficult to achieve and why they are so
scary. In the diagram, we see a simplified representation of our real
or core self in the centre. Our defence mechanisms surround this,
and are referred to as the life script in TA.

Real self with
authentic feelings

Defend self with
cover-up feelings

Figure 4: Diagram of real and false self

A life script, according to Dr Eric Berne, founder of TA,[9] is "a
set of childhood decisions made unconsciously by a person in
response to parental messages about self, others and the world."
Some of these unconsciously held beliefs are based upon misunderstanding and confusion. They are a child's attempt to make
sense of their world. As we live these primitive beliefs out we create

9. Transactional Analysis is a theory of personality developed by Dr
    Erik Berne. He was a psychiatrist in the USA and used his theories to
    support his therapy with individuals and groups. He is best known for
    his first book, *The Games People Play*. Today, TA is a widely known and
    respected form of psychotherapy.

patterns of behaviour we carry into adulthood. These patterns act much like the script of a play, telling us what to say and do next. Eric Berne said the aim of TA is autonomy, and broke this down into three components: awareness, spontaneity and the capacity for intimacy.[10]

The area of defence i.e., the space between the two circles, is full of messages such as, "Be careful what you say or, they will think you are a fool." "It is best not to get too close to people, because you know you can easily be hurt." "People are not to be trusted; they seem friendly now, but later they will reject you." "You are not loveable; don't fool yourself." "Don't listen to what they say; pride comes before a fall." "That thought is disgusting. Do not let people know you think that way." I am sure you could add to this short list. Some of the above may apply to your beliefs, some not, but it is highly likely that everyone will have some awareness of messages about their relationships and how to behave.

Some are helpful and reality based, but it is sadly those that are unhelpful and unrealistic that form the negative systems preventing us from being free to be ourselves. These negative messages hold us back from fully engaging with others. This lies behind much of our need to keep our darkest secrets hidden. This is how we prevent ourselves from taking our relationships deeper. It is often the defective beliefs that we are less aware of, and that most drive us to attempt to project a socially acceptable persona. It is this process that we use to prevent ourselves from being fully aware, spontaneous, and intimate. This mechanism interferes with our capacity to be autonomous. Instead, our unconscious script belief drives us. Following our script, we unconsciously engineer negative outcomes, that in turn reinforce the negative beliefs. It is a self-ceiling system that we use to keep ourselves stuck.

---

10. For those who may want to learn more of this, I recommend the book, *TA Today*, by Ian Stewart and Vann Joines Lifespace Publishing: ISBN: 9781870244022.

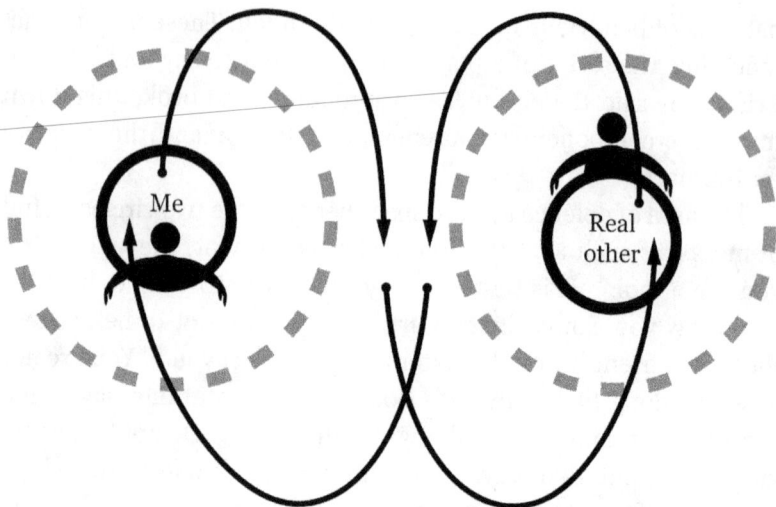

Figure 5: Diagram of healthy emotionally assertive interactions.
Two open people sharing intimacy, real self to real self. Emotionally
assertive interactions are based upon relatively uncensored
communication utilising spontaneity and awareness.

In this diagram, depicting mutual openness and intimacy, we
see each person is willing to be vulnerable and to offer and accept
friendly overtures from the other. We can experience this even with
strangers if we have self-confidence and are not afraid of being
invaded, misunderstood, invalidated, or rejected.

This is an example from my own experience. One morning near
Geneva, I was taken from my hotel to hold a seminar for a client
company in another hotel out of town. The drive to the venue took
us past a range of mountains covered with snow. It was mid-winter
and the sun was rising low in the sky across the lake. It was a bril-
liant orange and the snow on the mountains glistened and glowed
brightly, a soft pastel shade of pink, reflecting the light. The sky
was a bright clear blue, contrasting the orange reflections from the
mountainside. I had never seen such a beautiful sunrise and just let
out a loud, "Wow." The taxi driver asked me, "What is wrong? You
sound as if you are shocked. Is there a problem?" I explained to
him how I was moved by the sight of the sun on the mountain and
that I felt joyful at such a wonderful gift, freely given by nature. He

too was struck by the beauty and said, "I will turn off the meter and take you to a place where we can look at this for a while." Together we shared a moment of intimacy, watching this beautiful sight in awe. As I reflect upon this event, I can still recall and experience the feeling of sheer joy of sharing this moment with a total stranger.

Thinking about this event, I can imagine how it could have gone had either of us, or both of us, operated from a position of insecurity or block to intimacy. If just one of us was afraid of seeming to be overemotional, not manly, pathetic etc., this moment could have been lost. (See the following diagram for a block to the flow.)

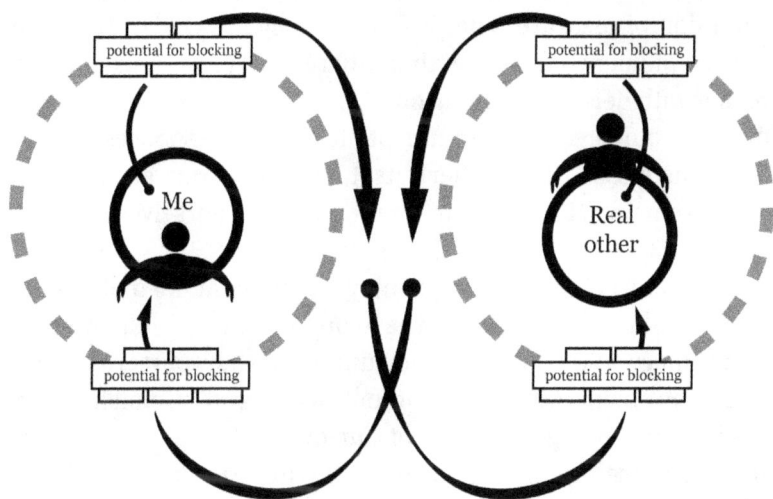

Figure 6: Diagram of two defensive people struggling to be intimate due to blocks. Interactions based upon censored communication (dashed line barriers) utilising cover-up emotions rather than authentic emotions

Again, I provide an example of a block from my own experience. On another occasion, on the first day of a stay in Maui, I was in the hotel breakfast room. The dining area looked out across the bay, and I was gazing out, taking in the magnificent seascape. Suddenly, I saw a whale breach in the middle of the bay. It was spectacular as the whale left the water, scribing an arc over the sea, and then falling back into the ocean, making a huge splash. It took my breath away. The whole scene was over in just a few seconds, yet it had a huge impact on me. As is my wont, I exclaimed loudly. This time a waitress approached and asked if there was a problem. I explained what I had seen and how privileged I felt. She said, "Oh, that's nothing to get excited about; we see that every day at this time of the year." We did not share the moment, yet I did not let go of the joy I experienced. I hypothesise she did not feel free to enter into the spirit of the moment. In any event, she may not have seen the breach that morning. Although we did not experience sharing the intimacy we could have, I remained free to decide not to let that dampen my spirits.

Different people will react differently to our spontaneous expression of pleasure. That is OK and they are OK. In this case, the wow moment was met with indifference. We may also find we are met with derision, scoffing or rudeness. However, when we feel OK about ourselves, we can accept all kinds of responses without feeling distressed. If the other gets it, or if they don't get it, we are free to remain OK about the moment, about ourselves and also about them.

Autonomy is the freedom to enjoy the moment, no matter what others think, and from this we have opportunities for spontaneity and intimacy. We also have opportunities to allow ourselves to feel good about being grounded, without needing to diminish others. This is about being the judge of our own behaviour rather than allowing ourselves to be judged. In my experience, life is full of wonderful moments, just experiencing the joy of being alive. These moments are deepened when we share them with our fellow men and women.

There will always be a risk in allowing oneself to be open in the sharing of intimate moments. The other person may not be so available for sharing, and may lack the emotional intelligence to drop their defences. They may also be concerned about your intentions. We cannot know what others' unconscious processes are telling them. We can accept we are all different and this is OK. In this case, the moment of wow can be met with derision, scoffing or indifference. When we are secure in ourselves and manage our interactions assertively from the win-win position, others' opinions need not bother us and we remain the judge of our own behaviour, thoughts and emotions. However, we can also experience discomfort when the offer is not accepted. At such times, it is important not to allow ourselves to think in terms of rejection, but to just experience the sadness of the lost opportunity. We do not need to blame or attack the other, nor does it help to see ourselves as the victim.

Prior to my training as a therapist, which also involved me having therapy myself, I was often concerned about how others saw me. I tried to second guess what they wanted from me and to over-adapt to them. In therapy, I had a liberating insight. I had choices: I could do all in my power to impress people and make them like me, and some would like me, whilst some would not. I also had the option to be myself, let others see me for who I am, and not fear the consequences. Applying this, I quickly found that some people liked me, and some did not. It seemed obvious that over-adapting did not work, left me in relationships that were not built upon reality and were emotionally costly. When I was just being myself, I discovered the relationships I developed were more satisfying. Whilst they often involved sharing strong emotions, they were emotionally satisfying.

During that mountain scene experience in Geneva, I was experiencing the warmth of an emotional high when I arrived at the seminar. The seminar was a stress management event for a multinational computer, printer, and test equipment company and the delegates were all senior sales engineering managers. In our opening and icebreakers, I shared my experience with the group. One man said, "How interesting. I see this sunrise quite often and over time I had forgotten how amazing it is. I will look again the next time. You are right. I forgot how good I feel when I stop and take it in." Others followed suit, and it opened a discussion of how good we feel, and how de-stressing it is to simply enjoy some of the simple things in life. Many were also able to identify how their pleasure was heightened when they shared it with others.

I achieved a similar ending with the waitress in Maui when I continued the conversation about how the event had moved me. She began to tell me she could see how impacted I was and she had forgotten how lucky she was to have such a great environment to work in. She provided me with information about the boats that went out to watch the whales and how I could book a trip. After that, we greeted each other warmly each day and chatted a little. What could have led to me feeling low and discouraged eventually developed into something much more pleasant. I love it when I experience these chance moments with strangers. By being friendly, we allow our body to feel the benefit of being flooded with feel good neuropeptides.[11]

I have discovered that many of the simple pleasures of life, like visiting an art gallery, going to the opera or a rock concert, going to the theatre or a film, are more pleasurable when shared with a close friend or loved one. It is a real-life example of synergy.[12] In relationship we can enhance our pleasure and joy. Equally, the opposite is true. When we are not authentic with each other, we can seriously diminish our joy and pleasure. Relationships are like emotional amplifiers; it is up to us to select the win-win option as a relationship model. This means going for bonding, attachment and cooperation as opposed to the spiral into disruption and dysfunctionality wherein is distress that compounds our defective learning from childhood.

The potential for each of us to block the opportunity to share a moment of intimacy is numerous. Sadly, avoiding intimacy is more common than allowing ourselves to take the risk of being real with people. I have often heard how people avoid discomfort by hiding behind politeness. We use beliefs, largely untried and therefore hypothetical, to restrain ourselves from imaginary hurts. This is a similar process to early maps where unexplored lands had written on them, "Here there be dragons." Many explorers would avoid going where there could be dragons, and the new lands remain unexplored.

---

11. Neuropeptides are molecules our bodies use to communicate emotions between each cell and the brain and vice versa. I recommend you read Candace Pert. *Molecules of Emotion*. ISBN-13:978-0-6710-3397-2. New York: Touchstone, 1999.
12. Synergy can be defined as: the increased effectiveness that results when two or more people or groups work together. Broadly, it is when the total output is greater than the sum of the input. It is about efficiency.

Dr Stephen Karpman[13] identified mechanisms we may use to block or shield ourselves from intimacy. His book, *A Game Free Life*, is packed with information about how to avoid the negative and find the positive in connecting. He identifies how we shield ourselves from intimacy. He speaks of four signals we send to avoid intimacy using the negative C.A. S. E. shield behaviours of being condescending, abrupt, secretive and evasive. He suggests we can seek intimacy by using the positive C.A. S. E. behaviours as an antidote, which are: caring, approachable, supportive and engaged. We will return to Dr Karpman's work later when we describe the Drama Triangle.

One of my therapy clients, who had the drive to please people, once told me this story:

For many years, it has been our family's tradition for everyone to come to my house for Christmas lunch. Every year, I set the table the way I wanted with the colour scheme I preferred. Every Christmas my mother brought a poinsettia as the table centrepiece. I hate poinsettias and always hoped she would not bring one. Nonetheless, each year I smiled and showed gratitude and pleasure, so next year mother did it again. I have just realised; I could thank her for her thoughtfulness and tell her the truth; I don't like poinsettias. Or would you be willing to bring some holly this year? I could admit to her I did not want to behave in a hurtful way and now understand I had been denying her the opportunity to give me something I really wanted.

In my life experience, there have been many times when I have taken the risk to offer openness, friendship and intimacy. Most of the occasions I have moved towards others, it has opened the door to a range of lovely experiences. Naturally, I have also had occasions when others were not ready for this and they reacted negatively. However, when I understood that however I behaved, I could not control what people thought of me, or how they felt, I

---

13. Dr S B Karpman MD, *A Game Free Life*: San Francisco, California: Drama Triangle Productions, 2014 (SBN 13: 9780990586708).

was liberated. It was my choice of which path to take. I have chosen to be me, as much as I can, and accept the consequences. This path leads to knowing who my true friends are and who are not.

Another example of warmth and affection goes back to a holiday in the south of France. My partner and I had taken our children on a day trip from Cannes to the Ile Saint-Honorat to visit the monastery where we could buy some *Lérina liquor,* a wonderful drink the monks make.

As we knew there were little or no facilities on the island, we had taken a picnic hamper with plenty of soft drinks. On the island, we met a Moroccan family with three small children who were very thirsty and agitated. We gave the children some drinks and struck up a conversation with the parents. As a result, we established a friendship with the family that was very rewarding and we met several times back in Cannes, ate together, and took our children out with theirs. This relationship further developed as reciprocal sharing began. When it was time to drive north on our way home, they connected us to other members of their family across France. As we drove towards the ferry port, we stayed overnight with their family in Macon. They greeted us warmly on the strength of the relationship we had developed with their family in the south.

In Macon, we were taken to see one of their friends who owned a vineyard. He gave us a wonderful afternoon of wine tasting. We dined that evening in their home, with their extended family, tasting many different and exotic Moroccan dishes. We spent hours laughing, joking, talking about culture and cultural differences, philosophy, etc. We spoke well into the night before going to bed. Our children played with their children and we deepened our connection with this lovely family. This all came from just a chance encounter that went beyond fore-play, because both sides were open to each other.

Life is full of such opportunities, and we can either take the risk and develop more human contact, thus building connections and friendships. Alternatively, we can use our anxieties, social phobias, cultural rules, and traditions, etc., and block ourselves from experiencing the joy of intimacy. This is how we develop a pattern of missing out on opportunity. Imagine a world where humans actively sought friendship, cooperation, and collaboration. A world where resources were shared, difference was celebrated, and we all operated from a sense of fair-play that flowed from respectful fore-play. A world where foul-play was rare and actively confronted. This could all be real if we began by having an active willingness to being open and undefended. Emotionally Assertive people is the key, and for this we need to enhance our capacity for emotional intelligence. To achieve this, we should use our emotions authentically, be available to hear other people share their emotions and give them an honest response. By honest response, I mean being open, caring and non-competitive. People who will tell you their 'truth' and take joy in catching you out are not being respectful. This is often an act demonstrating their own insecurity, and it is generally about feeling OK when we have found and exposed the flaws in others. I categorise this relationship-damaging behaviour as repetitive acts of foul-play.

Sadly, however, we can block the potential for gaining a deeper awareness of others and remain sheltered and isolated. Naturally, when one makes a move to offer intimacy, we risk rejection. Some fear this because they are afraid it may lead to uncomfortable feelings, misunderstandings, conflict, and unpleasantness. However, I have discovered that the rewards of building friendships with others, especially people who are different from me, creates a wider understanding of others. I find this helps to build a broader and perhaps a healthier view of humanity. Forging bonds with strangers of all races, religions and persuasions is far more satisfying than remaining distant and anxious. If we could all do more of this, we would significantly reduce the violence and racial tension in our tortured world. Friendship is built upon mutual respect, which in turn can lead to developing goodwill towards each other and the ability and desire to look for ways to cooperate. This is not about avoiding conflict; rather, I believe that healthy relationships will inevitably have to deal with conflict. However, conflict can be either relationship building or relationship destroying. It can stimulate energy, creativity, drive and efficiency, or it can drain our batteries and lead to dysfunctionality.

The Real Self

I am convinced we all have a real self inside that is mostly in hiding, just waiting to get out. As a therapist, I have seen first-hand that all of us, including myself, have inhibitions and rules of engagement for living. The rules are a mix of sensible values and beliefs, gained by experience and misguided inhibition and repression, that lead us to miss opportunities to connect with others. Imagine how different the world would be if we were more open and friendly towards each other. How might our world be if we used our emotions more sensitively to build relationships rather than destroy or avoid them? It is exciting for me each time I am presented with an opportunity to make friends with a stranger. Naturally, I experience people who look at me as if I am a dangerous person, possibly with some mental illness or hidden motives. I certainly do not conform to the usual UK cultural norms. On the other hand, there have been occasions when I have had a wonderful shared journey facilitated via deep conversation with people I may never meet again, but whose warmth and openness revive my faith in humanity.

Our success in forming and maintaining healthy human relationships is directly proportional to our capacity to establish bonds and make attachments. This capacity varies because of childhood development processes which were largely influenced by the style of parenting our caretakers used in attempting to meet our needs in a good enough way. Thankfully, where parenting is concerned, good enough really is good enough. Parents do not have to be perfect, Indeed, it would be close to impossible for any human to be the prefect parent. Our parent's capacity to be good enough was in turn influenced by how their parents parented them. Philip Larkin's poem, *This Be the Verse*, offers an interesting insight into the nature of familial parenting mistakes handed down across generations.

This Be The Verse
By Philip Larkin

They fuck you up, your mum and dad.
They may not mean to, but they do.
They fill you with the faults they had
And add some extra, just for you.

But they were fucked up in their turn
By fools in old-style hats and coats,
Who half the time were soppy-stern
And half at one another's throats.

Man hands on misery to man.
It deepens like a coastal shelf.
Get out as early as you can,
And don't have any kids yourself.

Larkin shows in three verses each of four lines just how damaging parenting errors can be. In his first verse, he says how he believes parents mess up their children. In the second verse, he shares his insight that probably they do not do this out of spite, but because of the inadequate model they received from their parents. For me, the third verse is the most poignant. Rather than saying his parents did the best they could with what they had, and we need to forgive them and get on with life, he says the best thing to do is to "get out *(of life)* as early as you can, and don't have any kids yourself." In a few words, Larkin elegantly describes how we learn not to make bonds and describes the potential harmful outcomes that can lead to us adapting the defective messages we learned in childhood.

Larkin died age sixty-three with no children, and his poem seems prophetic. What is clear is that much of the unconscious defence mechanisms we employ to help us get through life can actually impede our capacity for intimacy. These defence mechanisms were learned in our formative years, but we are not condemned to suffer their consequences as change is possible.

CHAPTER 4

Authentic Emotions and Cover-up Emotions

Words like intimacy, attachment, commitment, spontaneity and authenticity all sound attractive in terms of a good relationship. However, these ideals are not so easy to attain and most of us experience relationships as requiring work, compromise, adjustment, patience, persistence and forbearance. In addition, attachment has an attendant risk; once we experience the joy of attachment, we are exposed to the risk of the loss of attachment. Losing a loved one is painful, be it through separation or death. Whether or not we are aware of it, relationships require management; both self-management and management of the relationship itself. How we manage ourselves and our interpersonal relationships as an adult has its template in childhood learning.

Using the concepts of emotional attachment and bonding in relationship to adult interactions, I will look at some ideas drawn from Bowlby. He hypothesised that both infants and mothers have evolved a biological need to stay in contact with each other. The interruption of this process leads to emotional issues that permeate throughout the person's life and are particularly observable in their relationships with others.

His observations were of the behaviours of primary carers towards the infant, and how the child may form a working model of itself in the context of a relationship in terms of:

- Is this a positive relationship? Conclusion: I am loved and accepted.
- Is my experience negative? Conclusion: I am unloved and rejected.
- Is my experience unreliable? Conclusion: I am angry and confused.

The three behavioural manifestations of these responses are shown in secure attachment behaviours, avoidant behaviours, or resistant behaviours. The kind of parenting that leads to secure attachment is that which shows consistent reliability and sensitivity to the child's needs. It is not about which figure spends the most time with the child, but which caretakers are best at interpreting the child's needs and show care. Whilst one may think that a lack of care is the most damaging parental behaviour, it is not necessarily the case. More often, inconsistent and confusing parental responses and behaviours are most likely to lead to serious disruption to the attachment process.

More simply, children either developed secure attachment or insecure attachment and this is observable in behaviour patterns not only in children but also later in life through our adult relationship patterns. If our experience of attachment in childhood was mostly healthy, this will lead to us developing healthy attachments in our relationships. At the root of healthy attachment is the sense of trust we built in our relationships with our caretakers. Having healthy patterns of attachment means we can open ourselves to experiencing intimacy with others. On the other hand, where our basic needs were not adequately met in childhood, we will not have developed trust, and this can lead to developing unhealthy patterns of relationship.

It is very unlikely our parents never made mistakes, were never tired or stressed, and never displayed unhealthy parenting behaviour. However, for many of us, our parents were good enough, and we grew up with relatively few disruptions in our attachment behaviours. However, when our parents got it wrong, we will have learned to cope through establishing patterns of behaviour that evolve into complex defence mechanisms.[14] This is because these behaviours acted as primitive defences against perceived distress or potential emotional trauma in those formative years. As we saw in the previous chapter, it is as if we have a core self who wants to have direct, intimate, and authentic contact with others, but

---

14. A defence mechanism is a psychoanalytic term used to describe ways we unconsciously protect ourselves from unwanted emotional experiences. They are often triggered by unconscious internal conflicts.

we have learned this is not always safe. We therefore established, through trial and error, how much of this real self we show the world. These primitive childhood defences become unconsciously held beliefs. In adult life, these beliefs restrict how much open and authentic contact we permit ourselves to have with others. The beliefs are not based upon reality, but upon the memories and patterns we built up from how we related to others during these formative years. In other words, how we relate to people today is patterned upon our early relationships.

Unconsciously, we follow destructive patterns from beliefs just outside of our awareness. This process tends to reinforce the destructive beliefs. Because the distortions in our belief systems are usually well outside our awareness, we find ourselves seemingly stuck in the same self-defeating behaviour. Remember that as children, we were not playing with the full deck of cards. How come? Because we did not have all the available information about life and how people relate to each other, and why they do those things. We did not know, for instance, that when our caretaker lacked sensitivity to our needs, it was because they were tired or distressed. Instead, we might have concluded, "I am not loved, or I am a nuisance, or I can't trust people." Hence, we made mistakes as we attempted to make sense of our human relationship environment, and these mistakes formed deep-seated beliefs and distortions of reality.

Because we had a limited understanding of human relationships through our formative years, many of the patterns we thought we recognised were not actually patterns at all. Rather, they were our primitive attempts to understand a world full of people whose behaviours were difficult to understand. We had insufficient information upon which to construct an accurate assessment of reality. As Eric Berne said, we were rather like little Martians, come to this planet full of alien creatures, i.e., the grownups. As adults, we all hold in our subconscious, which is akin to our computer operating system, the information about how to be us in this world full of others we must get along with. Much of what we programmed ourselves with works on a day-to-day basis. However, unfortunately, we also programmed in many error messages, and it is these error messages that affect our ability to relate to others on healthy and open terms. As we wake in the morning, it is as if our computer boots up the operating system to drive us with all its flaws and programme errors.

Once this programme is loaded, we interact with each other based upon myths and misunderstanding. The exchanges between us, when these false beliefs are activated, lead us to exchange invitations to feel uncomfortable but familiar feelings. These familiar bad feelings, in turn, reinforce the negative belief. It is a negative spiral that serves to maintain the defective beliefs and associated patterns of behaviour. We sometimes realise something is wrong when we ask ourselves, "Why does this keep happening to me?" Sadly, it is because we lack the awareness we are forcing negative patterns of behaviour into our interpersonal relationships by inviting others to relate to us how we believe they will, rather than how they may want to. The result is that the false beliefs lead us to reinforce the very same false and negative beliefs. They are self-fulfilling prophecies.

Sadly, this situation can be worsened because it can be a two-way process. We each invite the other to play the game and it is incredibly difficult to resist the urge to join in. Therefore, day by day, we can go through life missing wonderful opportunities to be more friendly and intimate with others. Why? Because we simply follow well-tried, defective patterns of behaviour that are ineffective and frequently lead to distance rather than friendship.

Why do we do this? Because we are accustomed to life this way and there is a strange comfort in knowing what to do next. Without this degree of predictability, we will have to decide moment by moment how we will react in each new situation. Having an unconscious script to read from, or a plan of interaction, seems safer. Therefore, outside of our awareness, we frequently miss opportunities to make new friends and allies, and to find warm, loving and committed relationships. The Transactional Analysis modality of psychotherapy uses the concept of life scripts to analyse how the defective error messages came to be recorded. It also looks for ways to reprogram our internal computer operating system with new and liberating messages.

The concept of each of us acting out the scripts for our lives is not new. William Shakespeare wrote:

All the world's a stage,
And all the men and women merely players;
They have their exits and their entrances,
And one man in his time plays many parts,
His acts being seven ages.
("As You Like it" Act II, Scene VII).[15]

For us to follow our life script, inevitably we must forsake our authentic emotions in favour of cover-up emotions. In the process, we also abandon the opportunity to find creative and healthy solutions to our relationship difficulties. The long-term consequences often lead to us terminating relationships, again serving an unconscious drive to reaffirm our hidden defective beliefs. Our need for maintaining the false security of patterns is very powerful, even though it is mostly hidden from our awareness. Relationships with this form of destructive behaviour frequently begin with us unconsciously detecting in others their capacity to provide the complimentary forms of feedback to validate our mistaken beliefs. It is as if we need to achieve the painful outcomes called for in the script. However, it is often an unconscious drive to find a better ending that provides the hook into the self-defeating behaviours. We somehow find ourselves attracted to something familiar about this new person. Often, this can be that they remind us of someone from our past, though again, we are seldom fully aware of this. It is as if we are trying to get from this new person what we did not get from the archaic figure. Unfortunately, playing out the hidden agenda leads to the reinforcing feedback.

Does it sound as if we are all doomed? Fortunately, it is not as depressing as it sounds. Not all scripts are dangerously negative and lead to bad outcomes. However, any form of human interaction based upon pre-ordained behaviours come from unconscious

---

15. As you like it, was written C. 1598. Possibly first performed at the opening of Globe Theatre in 1599 and registered with the Lord Chamberlains office 1599. First known copy published in 1623 in a folio of his work.

defective beliefs that limit spontaneity. The capacity for being spontaneous is an essential ingredient for us to be truly open with others. The capacity for spontaneity and openness is an indicator of emotional intelligence. Let us examine some differences between relating with others spontaneously, from a position of vulnerability and openness, and responding through the filter of the defensive belief systems held in our script.

Differences

Table 1: Authentic vs defensive emotional expression

Emotion	Authentic Spontaneous Expression	Defensive Non-Authentic Expression
Happy	**Words:** happy, glad, excited etc. **Tone of voice:** warm, playful, caring and friendly. **Facial expression:** smile with eyes and mouth. **Gestures and posture:** open, inviting, open-handed.	**Words:** are flowery and/or cheesy. **Tone of voice:** can sound like there is some anxiety or be too much. **Facial expression:** smile with mouth but eyes do not match. A grin becomes a grimace. **Gestures and posture:** looks false or sycophantic.
Angry	**Words:** angry, annoyed, troubled (wide range of words depicting differing levels of anger). **Tone of voice:** non-threatening, firm yet without aggression. **Facial expression:** little or no expression. **Gestures and posture:** erect whilst relaxed.	**Words:** angry, furious, wide range depicting blame or attack. **Tone of voice:** aggressive and often loud. **Facial expression:** piercing eyes, accusative look. **Gestures and posture:** haughty, superior, imposing or intimidating.

Emotion	Authentic Spontaneous Expression	Defensive Non-Authentic Expression
Sad	**Words:** sad, down, low, etc. **Tone of voice:** low register, quiet and shaky. **Facial expression:** looks genuinely sad with eyes and mouth drooping, sometimes with tears. **Gestures and posture:** head and shoulders drooping.	**Words:** I'm OK, it's nothing, leave me alone. **Tone of voice:** annoyed, hurt or angry, maybe tinged with sadness. **Facial expression:** may look angry, sullen or sad or have no expression. **Gestures and posture:** sending mixed messages.
Scared	**Words:** scared, afraid, worried, anxious. **Tone of voice:** slight quaver in the voice at times, slightly low on energy. **Facial expression:** looks fearful, or suspicious. **Gestures and posture:** may tremble, or simply look listless.	**Words:** says nothing, or uses aggressive words but unconvincingly. **Tone of voice:** sounds angry, yet conflicted. Or may sound excessively anxious. **Facial expression:** little or no expression. Or may look paralysed by fear. **Gestures and posture:** may look withdrawn (avoiding eye contact) or contorted in excessive anxiety.

Table 1 is not intended to be exhaustive, but to provide some clues to help us differentiate between healthy, authentic expressions of emotion and some of our familiar bad feelings. Generally, when someone is showing a cover-up emotion rather than expressing an authentic emotion, we unconsciously sense it. Our capacity for intuition is built upon us noticing subtle changes conveyed through words, tones, gestures, posture and facial expressions. This is because when we use non-authentic emotions, or cover-up emotions, our words, tones, gestures, postures and facial expressions leak evidence of the underlying authentic emotion. The untrained observer may not be able to tag what is wrong, but unconsciously picks up discrepancies and intuitively experiences discomfort. We will delve into this a little deeper when we look at Paul Ekman's work.

Cover-up Emotions

In the Transactional Analysis Model,[16] cover-up emotions are called Racket[17] Emotions. This is a reference to the North American concept of a racket as a deceitful means to fraudulently extract payments from someone; a racket is dishonest manipulation for personal gain. An example of the model can be explained in the way children learn that some emotions are not acceptable in their family or culture. Whenever they express an authentic emotion the family did not like to experience, they were put under pressure to hide that emotion and to cover it up with another.

Most emotions are triggered by external stressors, or problems, and are indicators of the nature of the problem with a lead to finding a solution. Therefore, expressing the authentic emotion is directly associated with problem solving, particularly within interpersonal relationships. Covering the authentic emotion and expressing the replacement emotion instead does not lead to healthy problem solving. It also prevents the initial stressor from being dealt with directly. Because the authentic emotion remains unaddressed, the problem is much less likely to be solved, and the cover-up emotion will therefore be displayed with inappropriate levels of energy. For example, the expressed emotion will be too large or small, or the emotion lasts longer than one would expect.

16. Transactional Analysis is a theory and method of psychotherapy. It is the brainchild of Dr Eric Berne, though much of the model also contains contributions from others who were Berne's colleagues, friends and disciples.
17. The term racket is intended to convey the inherent dishonesty or manipulation of the process. It comes from the term used to describe protection rackets where one pays the person not to attack you.

Cover-up or racket emotions can even be generated without the presence of any obvious stressor. It can be pulled forward from the future, i.e. I can begin feeling anxious about an exam weeks before the event, making revision and study more difficult. It can also last longer than appropriate. For example, I can make my irritation towards my partner last for several days, rather than dealing with it straight away. It can be simulated through after-burn, i.e., looking back and recalling bad times. In these ways, I can make the exam anxiety last for many weeks. Pulling the anxiety forward, I don't prepare well, so am anxious during the exam. In the exam, I can't concentrate. After the exam, I keep recalling how awful the exam was until I get the results. Then I beat myself up for doing badly. When we enter a racket feeling, we frequently end up saving bad feelings, like people once saved stamps when buying petrol from a filling station. When they had collected sufficient stamps, or even books full of stamps, they could cash them in for a prize. In the same way, stamps collected from racketeering can be collected and cashed in later for some guilt free behaviour such as hitting someone, getting a divorce or an alcoholic giving themselves permission to take a drink as a prize for being good for a month.

The cover-up or racket is used as a complete system of thinking, feeling and behaviour, all designed to prove that negative views of self, other and life are true. It can also be used when examining a relationship and how communication may become confused when both parties' rackets are complimentary. In such cases, we can say the racket systems are interlocking. When we experience this, both people are unconsciously exchanging uncomfortable emotions that serve as negative tokens that prove their individual negative view of reality is the truth.

The Racket System: Its Origins and Self-Destructive Outcomes

In one family, children learn to cover their authentic anger by looking hurt and feeling depressed. In another family, sadness may not be allowed whilst anger is accepted, so here children may learn an anger racket to avoid feeling sad. In other words, they learn to cover their sadness with anger—anger is their racket feeling. In

Transactional Analysis, there is a tool for assessing our rackets called the racket system.[18] (See the drawing below.) Any authentic emotion can be covered with an unauthentic or racket emotion. It depends upon what messages you received in childhood and how you understood them.

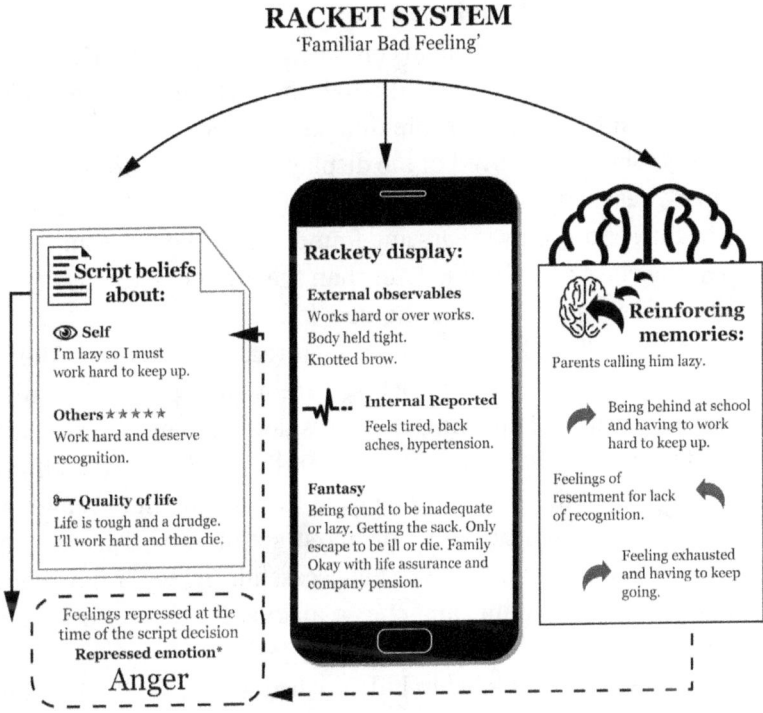

RACKET SYSTEM
'Familiar Bad Feeling'

Script beliefs about:

Self
I'm lazy so I must work hard to keep up.

Others ★ ★ ★ ★ ★
Work hard and deserve recognition.

Quality of life
Life is tough and a drudge. I'll work hard and then die.

Feelings repressed at the time of the script decision
Repressed emotion*
Anger

Rackety display:

External observables
Works hard or over works. Body held tight. Knotted brow.

Internal Reported
Feels tired, back aches, hypertension.

Fantasy
Being found to be inadequate or lazy. Getting the sack. Only escape to be ill or die. Family Okay with life assurance and company pension.

Reinforcing memories:
Parents calling him lazy.

Being behind at school and having to work hard to keep up.

Feelings of resentment for lack of recognition.

Feeling exhausted and having to keep going.

* In this instance the repressed feeling is anger. However, all emotions can be repressed in individual racket systems.

Figure 7: The Racket System from Erskine and Zalcman

Some people call the racket feeling, their familiar bad feeling (FBF), i.e., the uncomfortable feeling they regularly have. The racket system, as shown in figure 7, helps the therapist to gather

18. This term was devised by Richard Erskine and Marilyn Zalcman. The system looks at three components and how they interlink to form a self-locking and reinforcing loop of thinking, feeling and behavioural cues.

information about the person's beliefs, behavioural manifestations of when the beliefs are operating and the memories they call up to reinforce the belief system. It also shows the authentic emotion that was suppressed when the negative beliefs kicked in.

Personal example of a Racket emotion and how it fits into my belief system

As a child, I was rather small in comparison to my peers. My maternal grandmother raised me and taught me to turn the other cheek if someone hit me. At the same time, my mother told me big boys don't cry. She disapproved of me displaying fear and preferred me not to express sadness, either. No show of weakness was permitted.

I began school at five years and found it a hostile environment. I joined the class a week or so later than the other children, as I had been ill with measles. I was the new kid, and small, so I became a target for bullies. I came to hate each recess as this was when I would be jumped. I had conflicting parental messages of turning the other cheek, not showing weakness, and looking out for yourself. I told my mother of the bullying and she said, "Don't tell me, just take care of it." I had no idea what that meant and I remained afraid but could tell no one. For about six months, I tried to be invisible during recess and was unsuccessful. Indeed, I now know that acting as the victim can act as a magnet for those who like to bully.

Over the months, I tried to hide my fear and brave it out. Then, one day, I had had enough. When I was picked upon, all my pent-up anger exploded. Although the other boy involved was much bigger than me, I pushed him to the ground, knelt upon his chest and beat his head into the ground. I had just seen red. The stored-up anger gave me lots of adrenaline, and I dumped months of anger on him. Two teachers pulled me off him but, still enraged, I began trying to kick them, so I could get back to dealing with the boy. A large group of other children had been watching this, all shouting, "Fight! Fight!" My unexpected response was duly noted by the other children, and by the next recess, no one attempted to bully me. This was confusing at first. After a few days of peace, I figured out why the bullying had stopped and thought, "Ah, that is what she meant by 'just take care of it.' Why didn't she just tell me to hit them back? I can do that."

From then on, I wasn't bullied anymore. I had made the decision, "If someone wants to scare me, they had better watch out, because I can be angrier and scarier than them." I did not become a bully, and I never began a fight. However, I often got involved in protecting others who were being bullied. Also, each morning, a small group of children would come to my home to be escorted to school because they felt safe when they were with me.

I do not recall feeling fear from then on, but was angry a lot, frequently angrier than necessary. It was not until I was much older and in therapy as a part of my training to become a therapist that I discovered and changed this racket behaviour. I no longer go from zero to one hundred in one split second, switching from fear to anger. Now I can experience my fear and do something healthy with it. I also manage my anger by being able to express it authentically in a win-win way, rather than looking for the win-lose outcome I had previously become accustomed to.

In this racket, fear was my authentic emotion, and I covered it up with anger. In my subconscious, I believed I was only safe when I could show more anger than the other person. Then they would feel afraid, and I would not have to. My external visible message was to look unafraid, and to never be a willing victim. I had memories of how it was to be afraid and not fight, and how good I felt when I stood up for myself. This all proved my belief I was on my own and had to stand my ground. This all fed into a larger picture where I would be the protector of those being victimised. I can now differentiate between people who really are being victimised and need help and protection, and those who could learn how to take care of themselves. I am grateful for my journey as a psychotherapist, as it was this that facilitated that important personal development. It is also interesting that I chose to be a therapist, a positive life decision probably influenced by my early life experiences and decisions.

Difference between Authentic Emotions and Cover-up (Racket) Emotions

Authentic emotions are intricately linked to problem solving.

These emotions direct us towards the action required to solve the problem. When these feelings are accounted for and acted upon, appropriate problem solving takes place. When the stimulus that provided the trigger for the emotion is addressed, the problem will be solved. When the problem is solved, the resultant emotion dissipates. Racket feelings, however, do not tend to lead towards finding the solution to our problems. Instead, they reinforce our defective beliefs and worst fears.

As suggested earlier, racket feelings are often connected with collecting emotional stamps.[19] When we go into our racket, we may hang on to our unexpressed emotions until we are ready to use them. You may recall how I saved up my anger until I had enough to act. The delay can be days, weeks, months, or years later. Often we collect the emotions in our muscles, skeleton and organs. When we do, we may be aware of tension in some part of our body. In my case, I feel tension in my shoulders and neck. Sometimes, these areas were so tight I had to have a massage to release them. If we store up our emotions, we are likely to attempt to cash in on the emotional trading stamp collection. At some future date, someone may behave in a mildly irritating way, but rather than showing annoyance, we go off like a firework. Often at the time of cashing in, we may exclaim, "I have had enough!" or "That's it!" These expressions flag we now have enough feelings stored to justify some action to help prove a negative belief. Some collect enough emotional energy to justify handing in their notice, others collect enough to take time off sick or to have a coronary, whilst some display very high levels of aggression.

The result of us recording the decisions we made in childhood that helped us to fit into the weird world of the grownups is the build-up of these defensive emotional manoeuvres into the unconsciously held life script; the scenario of how to live our lives and manage potentially emotionally painful human interactions. This

---

19. The term stamp collecting relates to a process whereby we save up uncomfortable feelings to be cashed in later, usually to prove a negative belief. The point of cashing in is often accompanied by an expression such as, "Well, that is the straw that broke the camel's back", or, "I have had as much as I can take," or, "That's enough," etc.

unconscious programme effectively boots up each morning as we awaken and runs in the background, guiding us through the intricacies of human interaction. It has far-reaching consequences and interferes with our capacity to be open and authentic with others. It is full of messages we thought made sense when we learned them. It is important not to blame yourself or others for this. At the time we made the decision, we were doing the best we could, and really thought it was helpful. However, in our adult world, these error messages regularly act like trip wires that lead to misunderstandings and failures in how we relate to others. The messages are derived from our family history and the culture we grew up in. Some messages were learned from school friends and schoolteachers or found reinforcement there. Some were helpful, but others were debilitating in terms of our ability to connect and stay connected to others. As we saw previously, this leads to at least two different versions of the self, the real self, based upon our needs, drives and spontaneous reactions to others in our environment, and the false self, drawn from the jumbled unhelpful messages we laid down in our personal programme for life.

CHAPTER 5

Paul Ekman and Darwin: The Universality of Emotion

"Descartes would have been more nearly
right in saying, I feel, therefore I am."
Ralph W. Gerard (1941-1974)

In this chapter, we will examine the work of Charles Darwin and Paul Ekman. Darwin noticed the expression of emotion appears to be universal across humanity. He was amongst the first to suggest emotions had a primitive survival function. However, apart from Darwin's hypothesis (1872),[20] little focused research was conducted until the 1970s. There were ideas and intuition; some are accurate, others are less so. However, in more recent decades, the research has been taken more seriously.

Questions began to be raised in earnest at this time, such as: "What are emotions? Where do they originate? How are they expressed? What is their purpose?" Prior to this, such research was mostly observational, based upon a subjective interpretation of data relating to behavioural manifestations of emotion. The early researchers had recognised the evolutionary value of emotions; for example, Darwin remarked upon their value in communication back in 1872: "an important function of emotional expressions is communication between individuals - they show others what particular emotional state one is in." He saw emotions as signs of aggression to dissuade an enemy from attacking, signals of sexual receptiveness to establish reproductive encounters, signals of friendship and kinship, or signals of impending threat from other predators. He understood all these functions had a direct link to survival. However, probably his most remarkable intuition was

20. Charles Darwin, *The Expression of the Emotions in Man and Animals*, 1872.

that the facial expression of emotion is universal in all humans. You will probably be aware you can make a very close estimate of someone's emotional state just by looking at their faces.

In a previous chapter, I said attachment and bonding were closely linked to emotionality, and we see the facial evidence of this when we observe parents with their children. In paintings, such as renaissance, religious portrayals of Mary and Jesus, we can observe nurture, comfort and adoration on the face of the mother and signals of attachment on the face of the baby Jesus. Love and adoration towards our children is shown in our facial expressions. Similarly, such expressions can be observed between lovers and people in close relationship. We show the depth of our attachments, and the sincerity of feelings of care and concern for people in our facial expression, posture, gestures and tone of words, much more than with the words we use. Emotional expression in humans is communicated over these several systems. If we accept Darwin's theory of evolution, I believe we can also accept that during the evolutionary process, those who made more effective attachments have a better chance of survival. Darwin's observations and conclusions suggest emotions and the quality of our relationships are fundamental to human survival. Research has proven his hypothesis about the universality of the expression of human emotion, particularly the ground-breaking work of Paul Ekman. We will delve into Ekman's work later in this chapter.

Darwin drew distinctions between expressions he saw as instinctual, for example, the involuntary startle response, producing sudden movement away from danger; as opposed to a warm smile of recognition, when suddenly meeting an old friend. The first is driven primarily by the fight-or-flight response and involves no cognitive processing, but the smile of recognition and greeting relates to activity at the cognitive and emotional level. Both are driven by the limbic system, although they are processed using different neural paths in the brain. We will discuss the limbic system and brain activity later.

He also spoke of the involuntary nature of the instinctive reaction, illustrating his point with his experiment to resist reacting to a venomous, striking snake. His experiment consisted of him approaching a venomous snake in a glass box. Although he knew the snake could not bite him, protected as he was by a glass barrier, Darwin could not resist leaping away from the snake as it struck at him. He repeated this experiment with other people, and they too could not resist the reflex of jumping away from the attack. Such rapid and automatic responses are essential for survival and are driven by the fight-or-flight mechanism in the primitive brain that will be described in more depth later. I think that the startle response is not an emotion, rather it is a reflex, requiring no cognitive processing. Naturally, there will be emotions connected to this reflex reaction, though these serve as refining information, assisting us to add cognition to the defensive action. Now we can not only remove ourselves from imminent danger, but can also understand what the danger is. We can use our thinking to process the emotional content, in the case of the threat or fear, and learn how to deal with it more successfully. We will re-examine this as we delve deeper into emotions in later chapters.

In the same way that bodily changes through pain, hunger, fear and rage serve the function of increasing efficiency in physical struggles, so do emotions. All these roads link back to the fight-or-flight response and therefore survival. Each time we enter the fight-or-flight response, we will have associated emotions that will help us understand, select appropriate responses and incorporate our experience as learning for the future. These emotions are about our person and learning, and interpersonal relationships and communication. Survival and natural selection are central to our emotional life. Understanding these mechanisms helps us to better grasp our own emotions and use them in managing our connections to others. Both authentic and useful emotions, as well as unhealthy and destructive expressions of emotion, have links to survival adaptations. However, it is the healthy, authentic expression of emotion that serves us best in our need to form and maintain relationships. The unhealthy expressions stem from less healthy patterns of relating we learned whilst developing.

One of Darwin's observations was that the expression of emotion, especially as seen in facial expression and body language, is common across all human groups and across other species.

For example, the growl and snarl of a dog can also be observed in modified forms in felines, apes, monkeys and human beings. Darwin observed facial expressions of fear, anger, sadness and joy were common across all human races. These non-verbal clues were observable even on the faces of those born blind and who had therefore no possibility to learn the expressions from others. In other words, the facial expression of emotion is hard-wired. He concluded, therefore, that emotions serve a primary, evolutionary function. This early commentary on facial recognition of emotion has been researched by Paul Ekman, professor of psychology at the University of California San Francisco Medical School, and we will briefly discuss Ekman's work later in this chapter.

Back in the early 1990s, I conducted an experiment to test recognition of emotion. I asked trainees in workshops and seminars to identify four basic emotions from line drawings.

Happy

Angry

Sad

Fear

Figure 8: Simple line drawings of emotions

These seminars were run all over the world, though mostly in Europe. The results showed that the smiley face is one hundred per cent identified as happy; the angry face is also consistently recognised. Whilst emotions can be approximated with a minimum of drawing ability, the happy and angry faces were the most consistently recognised, whilst there was slightly less consistency with the sad and scared faces, though the mistakes were insignificant statistically. This may be a function of my limited drawing ability, but when I asked others to draw the faces, they too had more difficulty in depicting the sad and scared faces. I believe this to be because happiness and anger are the two principal emotions, and sadness and fear have a secondary role in refining and identifying needs. In my observations of babies of less than six to nine months old, they only seem to show happiness and anger.

I think it is interesting that in modern written communication such as emails, text messages and chat rooms, emoticons are used to add an emotional content to what would otherwise simply be words. This strongly suggests to me that, when communicating, humans have a need for more connectivity. Emotionality is the tool for that connectivity. Emotional content adds flavour to the message we are conveying and can lend either credibility or, if discordant, can detract from the message. Using only the written word, we miss important additional bandwidth[21] of visual recognition and tonal quality that conveys the emotional content. We know that face-to-face communication involves not only words but also tone, gestures, posture, and facial expressions. We also have reliable research about how little value words hold compared to the other components. This is not to deny the importance of what we say, but to emphasise that the meaning of what we say is communicated also by how we say those words. Emotional Assertiveness is, in essence, ensuring we say what we want with the highest fidelity of transmission, so our message is heard. For this, we need to be self-aware, capable of self-management, aware of others and take our responsibility for managing our side of relationships.

---

21. The term bandwidth is intended to indicate the fidelity of the transmission of the message. In electronics, the broader the bandwidth, the more information can be transmitted whilst reducing distortion.

Whilst these rather crude drawings provide enough basic information for detecting emotion on the face, for accurate assessment, it is more reliable to observe the whole face. There are forty-three muscles in the face and there are more than 10,000 distinct facial expressions. However, the good news is it is unnecessary to have the capacity to notice them all. In the expression of authentic emotion, we spontaneously move the muscles needed to show the emotion on the face. It is also very difficult to put a convincing false expression on the face. For example, it is quite hard to fake a smile. Whilst we can make the mouth take the correct shape, making the eyes join in the display is much more difficult. It is possible to produce a smiling mouth even when feeling unhappy, though the eyes will usually be a giveaway to even the most casual observer. Authentic emotions are expressed spontaneously; we just do it and we do not think about it. On the other hand, faking an emotional expression is difficult because it requires us to activate the correct facial muscles, and this is not so easy to achieve deliberately. Although some can learn to do this quite well, for most of us, it is challenging and requires practice. There is really no need to fake emotions in any event, as being authentic is the key to communication and relating. Detecting emotion is done outside of awareness. Sowing emotion is a spontaneous reaction. Our facial expressions of emotion are detected by others preconsciously. This phenomenon is a part of what creates intuition. Learning to gain awareness of what we are noticing is a useful skill to develop.

We can learn how to be more aware of changes in emotions on people's faces, it simply takes knowledge and application. The more we take the time to notice what is there and bring it into awareness, the better we become. Practice listening! As you listen, watch the face of the other, notice the tone of voice and posture. Notice your own feelings. Are you comfortable? Are you uncomfortable? Ask yourself, why am I feeling this? When you have an answer, take time to check reality with the other person, as our intuitions are sometimes wrong.

The important facial areas for accurate detection of emotion are the eyes, eyebrows, areas around and under the eyes, together with the mouth; careful observation of the muscles reveals a lot about the person's emotional state. In one research paper at an American Academy of Neurology meeting, it was suggested that most people look only at the lower part of the face to assess someone else's feelings. The paper claimed this is consistent in both men and women. However, Paul Ekman is reported as commenting on this paper that, whilst there are extremely reliable signs of fear, anger, sadness and disgust on the lips, that research, which was conducted using line drawings, may be misleading. He believes the drawings may have biased the research by creating an unnatural situation. Ekman says, "In life, the eyes are much more noticeable and important."[22] However, Ekman and other researchers agree there is consistency in the facial recognition of emotions and the accuracy of recognition increases with the available evidence. In other words, emotions are clearly expressed in changes of facial muscle tone and the more you scan the face for information, the more accurate your analysis will be. I would add that this accuracy level further increases when we include tone of voice and other body language.

Our Need to Add Emotional Content in Written Communication

I previously mentioned my observations about our human need to look for emotional content in communications as revealed using emojis and emoticons in written exchanges. These add an emotional content to what would otherwise simply be words and help us to convey our intent with reduced room for confusion. This suggests that when communicating, we humans have a need for more connectivity between us than can be conveyed by words alone. Using only the written word, we reduce the communication bandwidth and increase the potential for the other to read between the lines. This, in turn, can lead to needless conflict, especially when the interpretation the other put on the received message is incorrect. Such mistakes can, if left unchecked, lead to communication spiralling into the ground. So, by adding the emoticon, we add an element of visual recognition of the emotional meaning

22. Reporting from the American Academy of Neurology meeting in San Diego by Michael James, ABC News, 2000.

in the message. Take the following sentence: "When will you be home?" This is a simple question. However, if, when I receive the message, I am feeling anxious because I am late once again, I can imagine an angry tone in this sentence that was not implied nor intended. Then, I may respond, "I have had a hard day, and I have had enough!" Here, the words convey anger, frustration and defensiveness. The sentence structure has an edge to it. If I add the emoticon 😖 or 😊, I change the meaning entirely. The first shows some annoyance and frustration, but not directed at the other. Whilst the second shows a clear message that they are looking forward to being with you.

In response to a picture my wife proudly sends me of her new shoes, I could write, "Another pair of shoes? 😎" By adding 😎, I am saying it's cool as opposed to being critical, which it could sound without the emoticon. Due to the risk of misunderstandings, when I need to discuss or negotiate a tricky issue, I prefer to speak face to face or use Zoom at a minimum or some other internet conference facility. Even the telephone lacks the useful information we exchange through the visual channel. The telephone also lacks audio bandwidth so the tone can be distorted.

As we know, face-to-face communication involves not only words but also tone, gestures, posture and facial expressions. We have reliable research on the actual value of the words compared to the other components. One of the most quoted research projects is that of Albert Mehrabian and Susan Ferris.[23] They conducted research on verbal communication that investigated the interplay between words, tone, gesture, posture and facial expression. They said words carry about seven per cent of the communication, tone thirty-eight per cent and posture fifty-five per cent. These ratios are often quoted as hard facts but are over simplified. Their basic findings are illustrated in figure 9:

23. Mehrabian, A., & Ferris, S. R. (1967). "Inference of Attitudes from Nonverbal Communication in two Channels." *Journal of Consulting Psychology*, 31(3), 248–252.

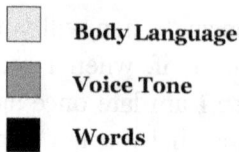

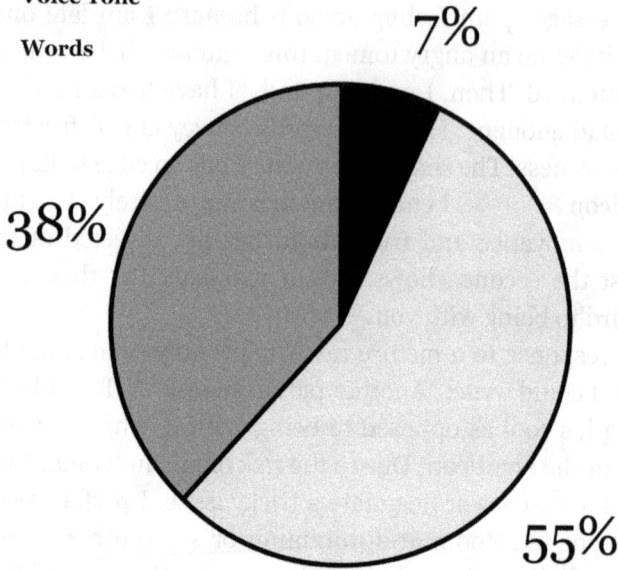

Figure 9: Data from Mehrabian and Ferris, "Inference of
Attitudes from Non Verbal Communication in Two Channels."
Journal of Consulting Psychology, Vol 31 1967

What we can conclude about face-to-face communication is:

- Communication is not a matter of just words. Most of it comes through non-verbal channels.
- Without seeing and hearing the non-verbal components, it is more likely we will misinterpret the meaning in the words.
- When we are unsure about what the words mean, we pay more attention to the non-verbal message.
- We tend to add emotional content in the absence of hard information and are often mistaken.
- Miscommunication is very common.
- When we miscommunicate, it is frequently unintentional and due to one or the other or both parties not being clear.
- With goodwill, and emotional assertiveness, miscommunication can be ironed out and normal services resumed. ☺

Consider simple communication using just two words, like "Good dog" to a pet. If I say this with a gentle voice, bending down to pet the animal whilst smiling and holding my hand out, the dog will wag its tail and come for a stroke. However, saying the same two words whilst standing erect, face looking stern, in a sharp and firm tone of voice, the dog is likely to adopt a submissive posture.

Perhaps you would like to experiment with a friend or a family member to see how many meanings you can give the word "no," by altering your tone of voice, posture, gesture and facial expression. You might then want to trade places and the other person does the same with the word "yes." If you want to experiment further, you may agree to share with each other your range of emotional responses to each variation in the meaning of the word.

This experiment offers a lovely example of how much importance we place on emotion in our relationships. Relationships depend upon communication to thrive and grow. You can extend the experiment by using other words. Almost any word can be given a spin depending on the tone, posture, gesture and facial expression used.

After the experiment, take a few moments to clarify with each other that this was just an experiment and there was no intent to communicate anything of any meaning.

Note of caution: Do not conduct this experiment if you and the other person are currently involved in a conflict or have recently had an argument.

Paul Ekman's Research on Emotions
Across Cultural Barriers

Paul Ekman is best known for his work with micro expressions. He teaches that micro expressions are very brief facial expressions, lasting only a fraction of a second. They occur when a person either deliberately or unconsciously conceals a feeling. Seven emotions have universal signals: anger, fear, sadness, disgust, contempt, surprise, and happiness. You can learn to spot them. Ekman runs seminars and webinars to teach his methodology. He helps people to develop the ability to recognise and respond effectively to emotions. This is an invaluable skill central to a healthy emotional life. Ekman's corporation has offices all over the world and I highly recommend them to people with an interest in Ekman's work.

Two theorists, Haggard and Isaacs, were the first to describe micro expressions around 1966. They conducted a study of videos of psychotherapy interviews and noticed brief transitory facial expressions, lasting less than a quarter of a second, they called "micro momentary expressions." They thought the appearance of micro momentary expressions was the result of repression, i.e., the client was unconsciously hiding an emotion even from themselves. However, they thought these fleeting expressions could not be recognised in real time. On the other hand, Ekman and his colleagues demonstrated that, with training, anyone could learn to see micros when they were present. Ekman offered a more elaborate explanation of why micro expressions occur, explaining that micro expressions happen when people have hidden their feelings from themselves 'repression' or when they deliberately try to conceal their feelings from others 'suppression'. Importantly, Ekman notes that both instances look the same; you cannot tell from the expression itself whether it is the product of suppression, i.e., deliberate concealment, or repression, unconscious concealment.

In his ground-breaking work, Ekman differentiated between four forms of emotional expressions:

Macro: are normal expressions usually lasting between a half of a second and four seconds. They often repeat, and there is a fit with what is being said and the tonal quality and modulation of the person's voice. In other words, as all the cues are syntonic, there is no confusion or ambiguity.

Micro: These are very brief, usually lasting between one-fifteenth and one-twenty-fifth of a second. They often display a concealed emotion and are the result of suppression or repression. However, without investigation, we can't know the cause. Because of this, it is best not to make assumptions, and it is always important to ask questions to clarify what you have seen.

False: A deliberate manufacturing or simulation of an emotion that is not actually being felt. This may last more than four seconds. Once again, without clarification, we cannot know what the other person is feeling or thinking, nor why they are attempting to display a false emotion. However, when we observe this, we are likely to experience some discomfort, uncertainty, and/or mistrust.

Masked: A false expression made to cover a macro expression. This may last more than four seconds. Yet again, it is important not to make assumptions about what this means, although when one observes this phenomenon, it will often leave you with questions about sincerity, motive, and trustworthiness.

Naming Emotions

Many of the early researchers into emotionality, including Ekman, compiled lists of recognisable emotions; for example, one proposed eight basic emotions: surprise, interest, joy, rage, fear, disgust, shame, and anguish. These were thought to represent innate, patterned responses that are controlled by hard-wired brain systems.

Paul Ekman's early research on this theory had him visit remote cultures, e.g., Papua New Guinea, to show them pictures of faces of people from a culture they did not know (New York). He asked them to identify the emotions on the New Yorkers' faces. He then reversed the process, taking pictures of indigenous peoples from Papua New Guinea and showing them to people in New York. Both sets of subjects were consistently able to accurately identify emotions, illustrating that facial recognition of emotion was consistent across cultures.

On the following pages are examples of faces like those used by Ekman in his research.

Facial expression - **Happy**

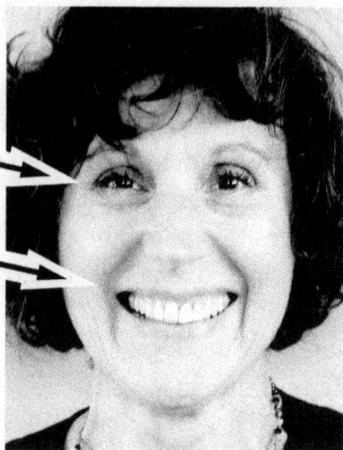

Creases at edges of eyes* 'Crows Feet'

Creases of lips pulled upwards

* Reliable muscles

Figure 10: Happy

Facial expression - **Anger**

Eyebrows pulled down

Upper eyelids pulled up

Lower eyelids pulled up

Edges of lips rolled inwards*

Lips sometimes tight

Chin raised or thrust forward

* Reliable muscles

Figure 11: Anger

Facial expression - **Sad**

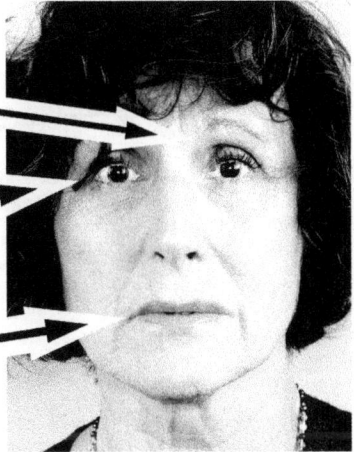

Eyebrows pulled together and raised*

Eyelids loose

Corners of lips pulled down*

* Reliable muscles

Figure 12: Sad

Facial expression - **Fear**

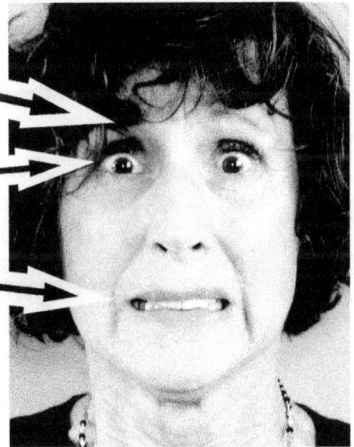

Raised eyebrows*

Top part of eyelid raised

Mouth stretched laterally

* Reliable muscles

Figure 13: Fear

Facial expression - **Contempt**

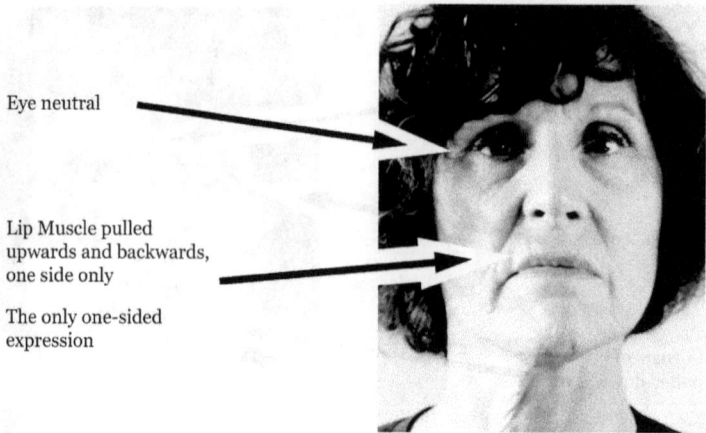

Eye neutral

Lip Muscle pulled
upwards and backwards,
one side only

The only one-sided
expression

Figure 14: Contempt

Facial expression - **Disgust**

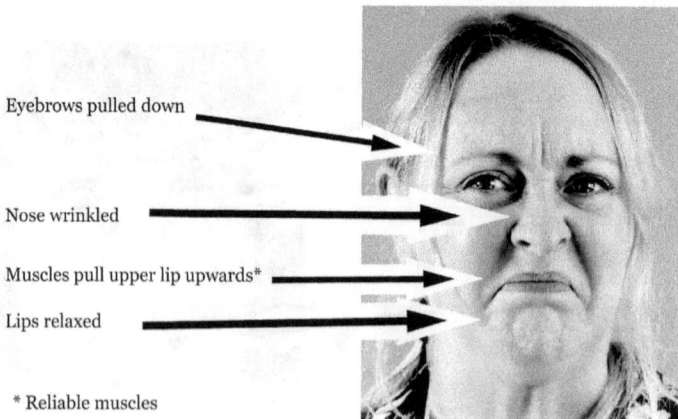

Eyebrows pulled down

Nose wrinkled

Muscles pull upper lip upwards*

Lips relaxed

* Reliable muscles

Figure 15: Disgust

Other researchers have compiled lists of emotions numbering
from twenty-five in one study to 34,000 in another. Other theorists think of emotions as drives. Jaak Panksepp identified seven
primary-process emotional systems associated with specific brain
networks. They are seeking, rage, fear, lust, care, panic/grief and

play. Interestingly, using these seven systems, there is evidence to support the probability of evolutionarily shared experiences, equivalent across different species of mammals. See table 2 for Panksepp's work:

Table 2: Primal emotions and respective affective feelings

Primal Emotions	Affective Feelings
Seeking	Enthusiasm
Rage	Very Angry
Fear	Anxious
Lust	Sexually Interested
Care	Tender and Loving
Panic (separation anxiety)	Lonely and Sad
Play	Joyous

I have grouped these drives in table 2 to match four emotions: happy (white background), angry (dotted background), sadness (dark grey background) and fear (diagonal line background). I will explain my reasoning when I outline my model.

In the 1960s, research drew attention to the physiological state of arousal, i.e., sweaty palms, rapid heartbeat, muscle tension, etc., and suggested these physiological responses in emotion inform our brain that a state of heightened arousal exists.

However, since these responses are similar in many emotions, they did not identify what kind of aroused state we are in. They suggest, therefore, that we tend to label the aroused state as fear or love or sadness or anger or joy, according to our interpretation of the situation in which we experience the so-called arousal attributions. In other words, emotions are subjective and open to interpretation. I do not go with this assumption, but think of emotions as discrete bits of data that are useful to inform our problem-solving capacity.

I focus your attention upon the four basic emotions of happiness, anger, sadness and fear, because I am convinced these four emotions form the bedrock upon which all our emotional experiences are based. Other emotions listed represent a compound mix of the primary emotions. I see this much like a colour chart where the red, blue and yellow can be mixed to produce the whole range of secondary colours and shades. White light contains all the colours in the rainbow and to see the full spectrum of light, we split it using a prism. Various materials respond to white light by reflection and absorption, giving rise to the colour they display. If we inadvertently add filters as we view light, what we see is contaminated by the filter. For example, when wearing sunglasses, we do not see what is in the environment, but a light contaminated view of reality. Taking this metaphor and applying it to emotions, the primary emotional colours are anger, sadness, fear and happiness. The colour of the emotion we show will depend upon how we apply our internal emotional filters. Similarly, how we see and experience the emotions others display will also depend upon if we are seeing what is there or we are unconsciously applying filters. It is essential to emotional assertiveness to have an awareness of our own emotional processing and be mindful those we relate to will also have their own capacity for processing emotional content without internal filters, or unconsciously confusing emotional content with their filters.

We all have emotions; emotions are essential to our survival as individuals and as a species, and managing emotionality is an art that can be learned. Emotions, when expressed in a healthy way, assist us in building healthy, cooperative relationships and groups. They are not a curse, but a blessing, although when we fail to learn how to express them in healthy and authentic ways, they can lead us to disruption in our relationships. Therefore, teaching our children how to express their emotions in a positive and healthy way is an essential part of parenting. Sadly, as most of us were taught how *not* to express our emotions authentically, we would all benefit by learning how to be emotionally intelligent and to gain the skill of emotional assertiveness.

CHAPTER 6

Emotions: Our Brain and Our Body

The Triune Brain

In this chapter, we will take a snapshot of the brain and how it operates emotionally. This is not intended as an introduction to neuroscience, but rather as a simplified block diagram of the brain and how it functions regarding emotions. A simplified view of the brain has been proposed based on its evolutionary development. This model suggests the brain can be loosely divided into three separate sections. Each section reflects an evolutionary step. Basically, our brain echoes our evolutionary development from reptiles (hind brain) through mammals (mid brain) to humans (fore brain). As the brain develops, so do the three parts mentioned above.

The hind brain or reptilian brain will control life support systems such as breathing and heart rate, etc. It also contains our primitive alarm system, responding to stimuli by entering fight or flight. This system is activated any time we experience changes in the environment. For example, if a car horn sounds, we become aroused and prepared for action. We will either run faster or jump back to the pavement quickly. We do not have to think about it, we just react. The response is rapid. This fight-or-flight mechanism is at the core of our emotions, and any stimulus will cause us to have an emotional reaction before we have had time to assess what the stimulus means. In emotions, the reptile brain is connected to the mammalian brain, and the system is called the limbic system, [24]taking this name from the fact that it looks rather like a border around the parts of the brain used in processing emotion and the fight-or-flight response. By the time a baby is born, their brain has the three well-developed parts, although development of the cortex

24. For a two-minute description of the limbic system, go to https://www.simplypsychology.org/limbic-system.html

continues for about twenty years after birth, and a baby has very little cortex at birth.

When our sensory organs detect something, that sensory information goes to the thalamus,[25] which is rather like a main switchboard for the brain. The thalamus relays the information to the forebrain (neocortex). In the neocortex we sample the signal, decide what it means and send a message to the amygdala that "this is not dangerous", or "let's have more adrenaline, we need to act immediately".

However, the thalamus sends sensory information to both the amygdala and the neocortex (our human or thinking brain). The path to the amygdala is shorter than the path to the neocortex and back to the amygdala, and this time lapse can sometimes be problematic. If the amygdala senses danger, it makes a split-second decision to initiate the fight-or-flight response before the neocortex has time to over-rule it. This triggers the release of stress hormones, one of which, epinephrine or adrenaline, triggers bodily sensations and other physiological reactions. These networks operate to produce an emotional response before we have had time to think clearly about what is going on and what we need to do about it. This is because when there is imminent danger, taking time to think could cause a slow reaction time. When faced with danger, we must do whatever is necessary to survive. Daniel Goleman called this a "limbic hijack," a term that describes the process very well. It is a very reliable system for survival in the days of our primitive ancestors who needed to know if this was something I get to eat, or that gets to eat me. However, it is rather too binary for us living in the modern world, where generally going to hunt in the local supermarket is seldom accompanied by the need to watch out for tigers. Nowadays, we need to create space to process our emotions, decide what they mean and then use that information in problem-solving. When we look at my model, we will see how we can achieve this. The problem is that humans have developed faster socially than our bodies can evolve to keep up with the change. Also, though our

---

25. The sense of smell bypasses the thalamus and goes directly to the amygdala, suggesting that in our ancestors, smell was more developed and more important than it is to us today.

world is less fraught with primitive dangers, there is still a need for the fight-or-flight system—we are unlikely to lose this as it can keep us safe.

But why do we lose our most human capacity, that of thinking and problem solving, at a time we may need them the most? To answer this question, I invite you to imagine being in the wild, hunting for a rabbit. You carry only a long stick with a point at the end. Suddenly, you are confronted with a tiger, who obviously sees you in much the same way you see the rabbit. What good will your negotiation skills do you? None; you cannot get away with offering the tiger to share your catch of the day. You cannot run away, as tigers run faster than you. Your only chance to survive is to take your stick and poke it in the tiger's eye, or down its throat. If you stop and think about this action, logic tells you, "Do not do that, it will not like it and may make matters worse." Your hesitation may cost you your life. So, the body decides it's time to cut this thinking out. It diverts oxygen away from the neocortex, so we cannot think clearly. It diverts blood enriched by adrenaline to the muscles, so we have more energy and strength to fight. Soon, we have tunnel vision.

Now, bring this scenario into the present day when we are in conflict with our partner. All the fight-or-flight machinery goes into action. At the time when we need to be clear thinking and rational, these facilities seem to slip from our grasp. We act as if we are facing a mortal enemy and enter tunnel vision and well-tried behaviours we know will not work. What can we do? We need blood and oxygen back in the neocortex. We need to create space to do this. Take time to think, and breathe deeply to enrich the blood with oxygen to kick start our logical brain. My grandmother used to tell me to count to ten before I expressed anger. Great, but only partial advice. Count to ten, take ten deep breaths, and ask yourself, "What am I feeling, and what do I need?" Also, more importantly, "How can I negotiate respectfully, accounting both for myself and the other?" The more we practice this, the more we find ourselves capable of making it a habit. You are unlikely to achieve this all the time, so take time out when you find yourself dancing to the tune of the primitive instinct. I say to myself in these moments, "I am aware I am angrier than I need to be. I need to take time out to cool down. Let us stop for ten to fifteen minutes, then come back and finish the discussion." I use the cool-down period to consider why I am so angry and what I really need. I do not need to resume the discussion until I know I am thinking clearly.

Whilst many believe emotions are not very important and impede thinking clearly and having good relationships, nothing could be further from reality. In fact, as we see, the brain is hard wired to be emotional for very good reasons.

Emotions are linked to changes in the limbic system, essentially the fight-or-flight mechanism. The limbic system has two states, relaxed and aroused. While the environment remains stable and safe, as we expect it to be, we are relaxed. As we receive sensory stimuli, we shift into a state of arousal. Arousal occurs whatever the nature of the stimulus, welcome and positive, or unwelcome and negative. Arousal causes a change in the flow of blood to the muscles, preparing us for fight or flight. It also causes brain chemicals, called neuropeptides,[26] to be released into the system communicating with the whole body. The fight-or-flight mechanism is managed by the more primitive areas of the brain such as the thalamus, amygdala, hypothalamus and hippocampus, as well as some of the more recently developed parts of the brain, i.e., the various sensory perception areas of the visual cortex and the auditory cortex.

In basic terms, the thalamus acts as a central switchboard, taking incoming stimuli and splitting it to be sent to different parts of the brain for sampling. A very short neural pathway exists between the thalamus and the amygdala, whose task is to act as an alarm system. Therefore, any change in the environment will almost immediately be detected as a potential threat. The amygdala has a very limited ability to learn and cannot be subdued, except through some very deep yoga and meditation exercises. The alarm causes a release of adrenaline into the system, a powerful stimulant, and the body is prepared to either fight or run away with vigour. At the same time, the incoming signal is also sent, via a much longer

---

26. For more information on neuropeptides, you may enjoy "Molecules of Emotion" by Candace Pert, PhD.

bundle of neurons to the sensory areas of the cortex (e.g., the visual or auditory cortex) for processing: "Have I heard this sound before? Is it safe, dangerous, or unknown?" Once the meaning of the stimulus has been determined, the cortex will relay a signal to the amygdala to remove the alarm call if it is recognised as safe or, if there is some form of danger, the alarm is fully activated. The time delay between these two activities is between twelve and fifteen milliseconds. This is long enough for the reflex reaction of fight-or-flight to have been triggered, even if there is no danger. In other words, there will always be a reaction, irrespective of the nature of the incoming stimuli. We experience this reaction as an emotion and we can therefore see that to every change in the environment, including events triggered by our imagination, we respond automatically with an emotion linked to arousal.

Over the years, I have observed that the initial stage of arousal in response to incoming stimuli causes physiological changes rather like those observed in anger. Therefore, I define this stage of arousal as a form of low-level anger. However, we generally fail to notice this emotional response and would not normally identify the associated bodily changes as anger, if we even notice them at all. However, under test conditions, I have found that most people will notice physical reactions to a sudden sound and report similar bodily sensations.

The level of arousal will be proportional to the degree of the initial stimuli; for example, sudden loud noises cause higher levels of arousal than low-level sound; equally, people with strong fears or phobias can imagine the feared object and react with fear, although they know that the cause of their fear is in their imagination. I view arousal as a means of providing motivation to act, low levels being about increased awareness and higher levels of increased energy to move towards or away from the source. The range of emotion we currently call anger is due to increased levels of arousal brought about by something that disturbed the conditions we need for happiness. Not only negative influences cause this; even positive change is at first experienced this way before we have taken the fifteen milliseconds to recognise the opportunity.

Dr Candace Pert, author of *The Molecules of Emotion,* has

demonstrated, in many laboratory experiments, the role of neuropeptides (brain chemicals) in communicating emotional data around the body. She tells us that with modern research into how the brain hormones operate in the body, we can no longer maintain a view of the body and the brain as working separately from each other, but rather that the brain and the body are one inter-related and interconnected system. She shows that neuropeptides have receptors in all our body cells, including even our blood cells. Wherever there are receptor sites, the cells are also able to release neuropeptides, and through this mechanism, the body communicates with the brain and the brain with the body. Our ability to differentiate emotions lies not just in simply asking, "What emotion am I experiencing?" It also depends upon our ability to be aware of the whole bodily reaction. "What is happening in my body? How do my intestines feel? What is happening on my skin surface? How am I breathing? How are my limbs?" And so on. Bodily sensations are strong and clear indicators of emotion and I suspect this is the reason we use the terms emotions and feelings interchangeably. When we have an emotion, we feel it in our body.

As a psychotherapist, I utilised this in my work with my clients. I would closely observe how their bodies communicated their emotions to me and often spotted even the most rapid and transitory emotions they experienced, sometimes before they themselves were aware of having had an emotional response. By spotting this and drawing their attention to their reactions, they could discover emotions they had denied having for years, for example, anger at a parent for something they had said or done in the past. Using this information and using their bodily experience, it was often possible to aid strong memory recall and the recovery of authentic but unexpressed emotions, discuss and express them, enabling them to move on past archaic periods of arrested emotional development.

I also became more aware of my own bodily reactions and gained a deeper understanding of my own emotions by noticing what my body was telling me. This, in turn, led to a heightened capacity for communicating my emotional reactions to others. I found that the more aware I allowed myself to become, the more I could use myself as a tool for understanding my clients and communicating

PART II

Emotional Assertiveness: The Model

Chapter 7

The Four Primary Emotions

"Tapestry" by Carole King
written by Carole King

Feeling Cycles: A model for the expression of emotions

I developed this model because I found the books on emotional intelligence provided no guidance about how to develop skills for application in real life. The roots of this model lie in the therapeutic methods I developed to help my clients connect their thinking with their emotions and to problem solve. Our emotions provide us with rich information about the state of our relationships, especially about what we need. When we understand our emotions and combine them with clear thinking, it becomes easier to communicate our needs without blame, attack, or assuming the victim position. We can also maintain a higher degree of control over our limbic system and avoid assuming the fight-or-flight response. This frees our human brain to think clearly, both about our own thoughts, emotions, and needs, as well as listening non-judgementally to the thoughts emotions and needs of others. It is the route to forging win-win, cooperative relationships.

Naturally, it takes practice to acquire and polish these skills, although the rewards we reap for doing so are well worth the effort. There are rules of etiquette, both cultural and religious, that get in the way of us being assertive, especially emotionally assertive. However, these are not insurmountable; we simply must notice them, make assessments about how valid they are for us today and then give ourselves permission to break the rules. Most of the rules relate to how we socially engage with others and, at their root, is the notion that it is bad to disturb others. What does this mean? The problem is, we all have our own unique answer to this question. It may mean we have to put our needs below those of others. It is rude to want to raise a new topic of conversation, or we are somehow responsible for how other people feel or for what they think. The list could be very long, as we will all have learned our own set of injunctions to being assertive, depending upon the generally agreed rules in our family of origin, along with the many other rules and values gained through school and so on. Collectively, we will have some shared unwritten rules and we will also have our own unique rules, not known to others. When we are stressed due to some conflict, especially with those close to us, we run the risk of following these rules because they influence us at the unconscious level. However, by following some simple guidelines, we can begin to understand our own inhibitions that we use to restrict our availability for intimacy, and then remove these unconscious road blocks.

As a parent, I learned it was not my job to teach my children how to avoid disturbing others by expressing their emotional needs. Rather, I was supposed to teach them how to disturb others in appropriate ways. When I am in a relationship with someone, I want them to disturb me when they have an emotional need. This is how we build relationship and trust. By making ourselves available to our loved ones, friends and colleagues, we say, "our relationship is important to me". If you noticed the behaviours of very small children, you will have seen them do this naturally. Our children often spontaneously connect with us many times a day. In this they are showing their love, and their attachment to us as well as their need to know they are welcome. When we respond with reciprocity, we exchange psychological energy that is health giving. This energy from healthy human contact acts like emotional fuel that powers us through the day. Sadly, sometimes we tend to teach them it is not acceptable to be open with us, and by implication, with others either. We parents do this because we believe we can get some peace and quiet and not be disturbed. Oddly, we seem not to notice our children resist these messages and find all kinds of creative ways to disturb us. Parents do the best they can because that is how they were taught. However, as we have seen previously, parenting mistakes lead our children to be less assertive and to unconsciously avoid full on healthy relationships.

An analytical tool connecting thoughts, emotions and behaviours

The purpose of the model is to facilitate a structure for analysis of our emotions, so we can think about them clearly and make rational decisions about how we communicate and behave. In the interest of simplifying the model, I begin by describing emotions as if we experience them one at a time. However, this is seldom the case and I will therefore discuss more complex emotions in later chapters. Emotions can combine to form dyads and triads, much in the same way primary colours can be used to create millions of colours, tones, shades and intensities.

I have never met anyone who manages their emotions healthily all the time. However, the model will help you gain insights and new directions for emotional expression and building healthy relationships. Relationship is a dance of two or more people; in the dance, we use emotions to guide our steps. They are rather like the melody and rhythm of our moving towards and away from each other, and it is most satisfying and enjoyable when all involved listen to the same tune.

Alternatively, we could use the metaphor of an orchestra, where all the musicians are reading from the same score, but they play best together when there is a skilled conductor. Using that metaphor, we see how a trained therapist or mediator can act to bring both parties to understand the music and play in harmony. Even without the aid of a therapist, we have an analytical tool to help us better understand our emotional environment.

Emotional assertiveness enables us to pick up the rhythm of others and to share our own rhythm openly. It involves hearing what our emotions have to say, thinking about healthy ways to negotiate, and behave with authenticity. When we achieve this, we forge alliances by sharing the responsibility to maintain relationship and looking for win-win solutions in conflict resolution. We cannot make other people think or feel, and therefore cannot ensure our best intentions and plans will always lead to positive outcomes. We can ensure that however things proceed, we will have ways to manage our own emotions, retain our equilibrium and regain it should we lose the beat.

Definitions

Assertiveness is the act of calmly saying what one wants and being willing to repeat it whilst remaining calm and respectful. This process encourages others to hear how important an issue is to you. It is about maintaining a win-win attitude whilst standing one's ground.

Assertiveness is about persistence, calmness, standing firm, being confident and seeking cooperative outcomes. It is often thought of as aggression, however, this is a misconception. Aggression is far from assertive. Rather, it is at the core of manipulation. Unprovoked aggression seeks to find the I win, you lose outcome and is disrespectful.

Emotional assertiveness is the act of assertively expressing one's authentic emotions with the clear objective to strengthen and deepen friendship and cooperation. As such, it is an essential building block of healthy families, teams and organisations.

Emotional assertiveness is the skill of inviting healthy cooperation, looking for the win-win outcomes and building healthy and effective relationships. It is a rejection of aggression, vindictiveness, vengeance and playing the victim to invite petty or rescuing attention.

Frequently, at the unconscious or preconscious levels, how we manage emotions and interpersonal relationships is driven by unwritten culturally programmed rules. In the UK, we are known for taking a very long time to get to know strangers. So perhaps, after three to five years of pleasantries, we might consider inviting them to dinner. In comparison, my wife, who is from a Latin-based culture, is used to getting to know her neighbours very quickly and sharing quite intimate personal information with them. She was shocked when we came to live in the UK, and after several years, still only had a passing connection to the neighbours. "It looks a bit like rain today" over the fence, is standard operating procedure here.

We British do not readily express emotions publicly and tend to be rather private. I believe that there may be many reasons for this, including the numerous invasions our ancestors experienced through history. The Roman conquest of Britain used divide-and-conquer strategies with the Celtic tribes to maintain Roman dominance. Even when locals lived side by side with the invaders, there were tensions between them. For example, the Saxons and the Vikings shared

England, but there were many skirmishes between them. Alfred the Great was instrumental in unifying these two groups, but it took a long time for this new, more peaceful paradigm to be established. After Alfred we had the Norman invasion, which once again resulted in violence and change. The people of these islands therefore have had an innate sense of the need to be guarded.

We display our need to take time to get to know others through our well-prescribed fore-play conversations. For example, we talk about the weather, what roads we used to get to the pub, what we do for a living and wasn't that a smashing deal Ryanair offered to Tenerife? We ask people, "How are you?" when we greet them, and we usually do not want to know the true answer. Instead, we hope for a superficial response: "I'm as well as could be expected" or "I'm fine and how about you?" However, even the English have emotions, we just suppress them more than other cultures. In my travels, I have visited other cultures even more repressed than we are. Emotional Assertiveness will train us to discern our genuine emotions, overcome our inhibitions and express our emotional needs, whilst conforming as much as possible to our cultural norms. We do not ask you to break all the rules or throw them away, but to apply them with clarity of thought so they become guidelines and not straightjackets.

The Primary and Compound Emotions

There are four emotions that I define as the primary emotions. These are happiness, anger, sadness and fear. I see them in much the same way as I understand the three primary colours, i.e., they are the building blocks of all other emotions. I also view them as the key information components of our emotional lives. If we are to use our emotions as keys to relationship problem-solving, we need to find a method to clarify which of the primary emotions are involved in any situation and then organise or problem-solve to meet interpersonal needs. I need to remember that both my needs and the needs of others are equally important and therefore must become self-aware, show self-management, be aware of the emotional states of others and take fifty per cent of the responsibility for managing and maintaining my interpersonal relationships.

In Chapter 8 about the Feelings Wheel, we have a diagnostic tool for analysing our emotions and deciding how best to express them. This shows us how to be Emotionally Assertive and respectful of self and others. When looking at compound emotions, we need to consider that the parties involved may construct their compound emotions differently from us. We are responsible for understanding and decoding our own complex emotions and it is wise to ask for clarification of the needs of others, because when they express a compound emotion, we can only guess the mix of primary emotions. Below are suggestions, rather than rules, about some of the more common compound emotions:

- Many compound emotions present as unhealthy emotions. However, once we refine them back to primary emotions, we can often find healthy motives underpinning them. For example, the jealous person demonstrates the other is important to them, whilst they themselves struggle with fear of loss of attachment.
- All the compounds below are primary emotions in varying percentages. I ask the reader to determine how they mix their compound emotions. Hence, some compound emotions have a mix of anger, sadness and fear, but in varying degrees.

Table 3: Primary emotions and their compound or secondary emotions

Primary emotions	Compound or secondary emotions
Anger, fear and sadness	= Jealousy
Anger, sadness and occasionally fear	= Envy
Sadness and anger	= Sullenness
Happiness and fear (excitement)	= Delight
Anger, fear and sadness	= Disgust
Anger and fear	= Surprise

Chapter 8

The Feelings Wheel of Healthy Emotional Flow

"Windmills of Your Mind" by Noel Harrison
Written by Marilyn Bergman, Michel
Legrand and Alan Bergman

The Flow of Emotions

As we have seen, the body uses an electrochemical communication system, and emotions are experienced when chemicals build up and are then reabsorbed again. This process is not binary, i.e., on and off, but is analogue, taking time to grow and dissipate. When our calm is disturbed, we become aroused and the electrochemical process begins. If we recognise the associated bodily sensations and identify the emotion, we can use this as information relating to a change in the environment. This means we are being alerted to focus upon a potential problem or opportunity that requires our attention. The attendant emotional charge provides motivation to solve the problem or seize the opportunity. When the situation is attended to, the process will be reversed, and the chemicals reabsorbed. Hence, emotions are transitory events directing our being towards healthy survival.

Depending upon our perception of the magnitude of the problem and the time taken to solve it, these chemical reactions ebb and flow to greater or lesser degrees and time periods. Therefore, I see emotions being experienced in waves and not as pulses. In the diagram of the model, I propose this as a circular movement starting from our homoeostatic position of happiness, flowing through arousal and growing awareness of the disturbance to recognition of the problem, engagement within the relationship, and ending with the resolution of the problem, at which time the emotional charge ebbs and we return to homeostasis. (See the diagram of

Healthy Cycles.) Hence, the cycle is calm, arousal, recognition, engagement, resolution and return to calm.

The model states our healthy emotional position as calm, relaxed, and content. This is also our homeostatic state, which I label our baseline happiness. We are designed to be happy, but not joyous, just operating at the calm and unstressed level. Our emotional brain is relaxed, and we feel OK. When any change occurs, either externally stimulated through our sensory organs, or internally stimulated by our thought processes, our primitive brain notices the change, and the alarm system is set off. Adrenaline is released to prepare us for entering fight or flight. At this time, we do not know what change triggered the system. We are just ready to act to defend ourselves, or act to seize the opportunity. Microseconds later, our cortex has assessed the available information and by now we will be aware of the emotional charge. What we do next is a matter of learning. Did we learn how to manage this emotion appropriately and express it authentically, or did we internalise an error message, leading to misinterpretation of the most helpful expression?

Table 4 provides a list of primary emotions:

Table 4: Primay emotions and their functions

Emotion	Purpose
Happiness	Tells us all is well. Is health inducing both mentally and physically. Covers a wide range of intensity from calm and relaxed to joyous and euphoric.
Anger	Alerts us to a change in the environment that may need urgent attention. Provides motivation and energy to problem solve. It is a healthy drive towards the other to build cooperation, or in the case of self-preservation when in danger, to energise our defences.

Emotion	Purpose
Sadness	Alerts us to the loss of attachment. Prepares us for managing our distress. Draws us to a position of acceptance and celebration in preparation for carrying on with life.
Fear	Alerts us to threats and danger. Points us towards finding protection, either by use of personal resources or through forging alliances with others.

Table 5 details how the four emotions have a direct relationship to time:

Table 5: Primary emotions and their relationship to time

Emotion	Relationship to time
Happiness	Spans all time frames, present, past and future. I can be authentically happy about the present where my life is at this moment. I can be authentically happy recalling the past. I can be authentically happy contemplating the future. Authentic happiness promotes a healthy mind and body.
Anger	Is principally an emotion of the present. When something disrupts the conditions for me remaining happy, I experience arousal in my limbic system, a release of adrenaline, and a charge of energy to focus on looking for a solution. This, in turn, helps me regain my calm or happiness.
Sadness	Is an emotion directly related to loss and is therefore about the past. It focuses attention on acceptance of the loss, 'letting go,' moving on and returning to a state of happiness.

Emotion	Relationship to time
Fear	Is the emotion of the future. It is directly related to a potential threat and provides the impetus to find safety. Once we experience safety, we no longer need to feel afraid and can return to calm and happiness.

Regarding emotions and time, an ancient philosopher said:

If you are depressed, you are living in the past.
If you are anxious, you are living in the future.
If you are at peace, you are living in the present.
Of unknown origins. Often incorrectly attributed to Lao Tzu.

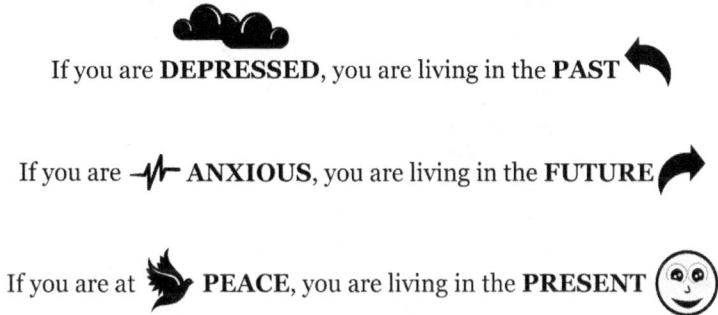

If you are **DEPRESSED**, you are living in the **PAST**

If you are **ANXIOUS**, you are living in the **FUTURE**

If you are at **PEACE**, you are living in the **PRESENT**

Figure 16: Of unknown origins. Often incorrectly attributed to Lao Tzu.

My discoveries are parallel discoveries, as is often the case; for example, penicillin, insulin and DNA were all simultaneously discovered, and the person named for the discovery was first to publish. The first diagram of the model in figure 17 is drawn for healthy emotions.

The following assumptions apply:

1. The circle represents the span of our four emotions, divided to show our homeostatic position of happiness in the centre, with the emotional nervous system arranged around the core.

They operate emotionally much in the same way our sensing organs detect and inform of environmental change.
2. The centre line represents the here and now. The left of the page represents the past, and the right represents the future.
3. The arrows indicate the ebb and flow of emotions. You will see all emotions start from happiness, flow through arousal and anger, and seek to return to being happy.

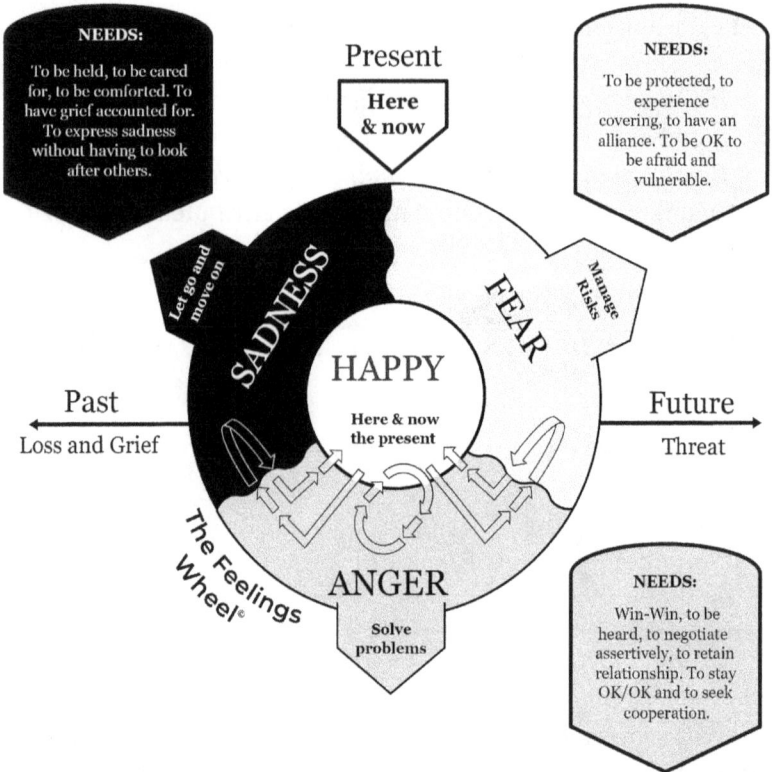

NEEDS:

To be held, to be cared for, to be comforted. To have grief accounted for. To express sadness without having to look after others.

Present

Here & now

NEEDS:

To be protected, to experience covering, to have an alliance. To be OK to be afraid and vulnerable.

Let go and move on

SADNESS

FEAR

Manage Risks

HAPPY

Here & now the present

Past

Loss and Grief

Future

Threat

The Feelings Wheel©

ANGER

Solve problems

NEEDS:

Win-Win, to be heard, to negotiate assertively, to retain relationship. To stay OK/OK and to seek cooperation.

Figure 17: Healthy cycle, © John Parr January 1997

Happiness is at the core of our being. It is the emotion the other three primary emotions are there to help us regain. It indicates all is well in our relationships, life and environment. When people relate to each other following the emotional energy flows indicated in the diagram, their relationship and depth of attachment has a fertile ground in which to develop. However, when there is a failure to relate authentically by completing the cycle, relationship and attachment may be disturbed. Because of the primitive origins of these emotional experiences, and the integration of unhelpful models of behaviour, it is sometimes difficult to manage our emotional reactions. Even when a problem has been solved, we may remain aware of the discomfort for some time afterward. This is because the chemistry of emotions cannot be turned off instantaneously, and takes time to decay. Where a perceived problem remains unresolved, the remnants of the recent emotional charges are still in our system and unhealthy emotional cycles can quickly be restimulated. This is rather like a fire that has died down with embers that are still hot, and it takes very little wind to reignite the fire.

Because of the problems caused within relationships due to this, some emotions have become labelled as negative. The so-called negative emotions are usually listed as anger, sadness and fear. Anger is especially labelled negative in many societies and by some religions, because of the damage we see done when anger is inappropriately expressed. I believe this is because cultural and family modelling sometimes does not teach us how to use emotions positively. Anger is often associated with violence and, as a result, becomes outlawed on the grounds that if we dispense with anger, we will do away with violence. If we teach our children how to express their anger in healthy ways, we can reduce the incidence of violence. Physical aggression is caused by a failure to express anger appropriately, or by the suppression of anger that eventually erupts into acts of violence. There are no inherently negative emotions because all emotions and their healthy expression are vital for peaceful and harmonious relationships.

Below I offer a schema for how to encourage helpful outcomes by expressing our emotions in a way that increases the likelihood we will be heard and understood. This is a method to invite cooperation between people, and how to deepen and strengthen connections and ties. First, we will examine the positive cycles where emotions are expressed using emotional assertiveness. Then, we will examine what goes wrong when we move away from authenticity to expressing emotions manipulatively. These will be accompanied by some suggestions regarding ways to use the model to achieve more compassionate relationships.

The Healthy Anger Cycle

Anger is our natural response to any change in the environment, and this low-level anger is called arousal. When the change is identified as unwanted, arousal turns into full-blown anger and the level of anger will match the degree of discomfort experienced. Where the discomfort is in the context of relationship, this emotion is designed to drive us towards the other, with an intent to find healthy conflict resolution. It is about mutual respect and a willingness to negotiate for a cooperative outcome.

In a conversation between the Dalai Lama and Paul Ekman, Ekman said:

> I maintain, though I don't have evidence for it, that what is built into the anger response is the impulse to remove the obstacle that is thwarting us. That does not necessarily require violence ... There isn't evidence, nor is there necessarily agreement among all Western scholars or scientists. I have listed here the most common events that precede anger: physical interference, frustration, someone trying to hurt us, another person's anger. One of the most dangerous things about anger is that it calls forth anger. It requires great effort to be able to not respond to anger with anger.

That anger begets anger is why we need to take time before we express our anger and to select respectful and appropriate ways to use the energy it provides in a healthy way. It is all about problem solving.

Like all emotion, anger has its roots in the fight-or-flight response, and it is therefore easy to move from the healthy expression to unhealthy expressions, i.e., move into fight. Thankfully, we can learn how to use the energy appropriately. Anger is the emotional consequence of arousal, so we must learn how to manage it or we lose a valuable tool for building relationship. Anger will be experienced through a wide range of intensity, from mild irritation to rage and fury. I believe appropriately expressed anger, that invites a cooperative response within relationship, is the key to maintaining relationship and regaining happiness.

The apostle Paul wrote, "Don't let the sun go down on your anger" (Ephesians 4:26, New Revised Standard Version NASB). This calls people to resolve conflict immediately and not leave it to fester. In Matthew 18:15, NASB, the author says, "If your brother sins against you, go to him and show him his fault. But do it privately, just between yourselves. If he listens to you, you have won your brother back."

I offer these quotes to show that the concept suggested in this model is not new or revolutionary; it has been around for thousands of years. Anger, appropriately expressed, is an act of love. We cannot have a fully committed relationship unless we learn how to express anger in respectful and safe ways. And unless we express anger authentically, we cannot be truly happy.

If we consistently behave this way, people with whom we are in close relationship, will know that when there is a problem, we will tell them directly and in a non-accusatory way, and they can trust us. Developing trust is a building block for relationship and so the process of healthy expression of anger benefits both parties and facilitates contentment (happiness).

However, anger inappropriately expressed is at the root of much of our interpersonal relationship tension and stress. Inappropriate expressions of anger are to be found in acts of aggression, passive aggression, vengefulness, vindictiveness or in forms of suppression as in excessive submissiveness, over pleasing, sulking, etc.

As the initial stimulus or stressor is processed and understood, we experience our anger, our libido or zest for life increases, and we move away from being happy and focus on problem solving. The purpose of anger is to provide us with energy to focus on problem solving, along with the motivation to stand our ground and to invite changes. As we express anger in a focused and appropriate form, we utilise this energy to solve the problem. In the model, I suggest that to be effective in the expression of anger, we need to communicate in a way that increases the chance we are heard. We need to behave assertively, be willing to negotiate and look for cooperative win-win outcomes like, "I'm OK-You're OK and therefore we can work this out." As we achieve the desired change, or agree on a workable compromise,[27] we regain our calm. The problem is solved!

On the other hand, if our negotiations do not lead to resolution, or the other does not respond with a healthy emotional expression, we will remain angry. This can then be focused on supplying increased resolve to solve the problem. Alternatively, we may decide that to remain angry is of no further benefit to us. In this case, we can focus our attention on letting go to return to happiness. This option is appropriate, for example, when no amount of anger or negotiation will result in us achieving the desired outcome, i.e., when change is outside our power or control. In this circumstance, deciding to respond differently to the stimulus is appropriate.

Relationship Needs When Angry

When we express anger, our most important need is for the other to hear us, account for us, accept us and our anger, and to maintain the relationship (I'm OK-You're OK cooperative behaviours). Where possible, we need to work together to achieve a negotiated change. If these conditions are met, we return to our state of satisfaction, contentment and happiness, in some cases even without achieving change. Being heard and accounted for is central to the healthy interpersonal management of anger and the maintenance of good relationships. By communicating using an information-sharing language and with goodwill towards each other, we can usually find resolution quickly and gracefully. Being open and freely sharing what we feel and want with the other, i.e., telling them things they can only know if we share the information, we invite collaboration. This is the opening most likely to enhance the likelihood of stimulating them to listen, and we increase the probability of being heard. (Note: Where anger involves the immediacy of loss, there may also be expressions of vulnerability and sadness.

---

27. Workable compromise is a term coined by Manuel J. Smith in his book about assertiveness, *When I Say No, I Feel Guilty*. New York: Bantam Books, Inc., 1981. A workable compromise is where both parties are OK with the outcome, and no one experiences a loss of self-esteem.

This is because, as well as anger, there will be sadness involved and sadness calls for a different style of relationship connectivity. (See the sadness cycle for more on this.) As Ekman points out, anger has the tendency to evoke anger in the recipient. As a result, they may not be receptive to hearing us, especially if they have a problem in dealing with anger, or your first expression of anger is not delivered with authenticity. In this case, our experience of communication around anger may be negative and we may shift into a negative cycle of expression.

Always remember that our route back to happiness is through the healthy expression of anger. I see anger suppression as a form of avoidance of intimacy and openness, as is anger expressed aggressively or violently. Some useful questions to help manage anger are as follows:

When someone is shouting at you, ask yourself, "Is this because I'm not listening?"

When you believe someone is not listening to you, ask yourself, "Is this because I'm shouting?" The adage "before expressing anger, count to ten" has some merit in learning how to manage anger and learn new means of its expression. Counting to ten whilst breathing deeply and slowly reduces our stress reactions, gets oxygen back to the neocortex or human brain so we can think more clearly, and provides time to think through our options. Shooting from the hip with anger is likely to come from an unhealthy position and will also invite a similar reaction from the other.

The Healthy Sadness Cycle

Sadness is about loss and is therefore a grief reaction associated with the past. However, if we learn about the loss in the present, it will trigger the fight-or-flight response and produce an experience of arousal or anger. As we accept the loss, anger gives way to sadness. Where the loss is significant, we may experience a period of denial before anger. This is the brain's way of creating time to process the event. This may redirect the energy of anger, causing us to dissociate from the trauma of the event, much in the same way as we sometimes automatically dissociate from extreme physical discomfort. The anger is the result of the disruption to our happiness. Sadness follows anger as we move through our anger into the recognition of the loss, and the degree of sadness will be proportional to the extent of the loss.

Author Elisabeth Kübler-Ross describes these processes in her book, *On Death and Dying*. She discusses the five stages people go through when grieving a loss as denial, anger, bargaining, depression and acceptance. She does not suggest all go through these stages and does not intend us to think depression is an inevitable part of grief. Rather, she says this stage is when the loss is particularly hard to deal with and where energy levels are lower. It is an attempt to avoid the discomfort of the loss. Sadness is a natural reaction to the disruption or loss of attachment. It is a healthy display of distress, which I view as a call for others in relationship with us, or sometimes even strangers who are attached by virtue of humanity, to show us care, kindness and nurture.

This sadness cycle is like the four tasks of mourning psychologist William Worden refers to. He suggests tasks, as opposed to stages, to imply the active involvement of the mourner. These are: 1. Accept the reality of loss, (involving anger), 2. Work through the pain and grief, 3. Adjust to an environment in which the deceased is missing, and 4. Emotionally relocate the deceased and move on with life.

Relationship Needs When Sad

In my model, when we feel sad, we need positive people to show us care and concern through talking, comforting, acceptance, love, sympathy, empathy and support. We require acceptance of the expression of our anger, and we need time to grieve within the context of a nurturing relationship. As we experience comfort and acceptance, we can fully enter the grieving process and eventually work through our sadness. We will then have the strength to let go of the object of loss and recover our libido (zest for life). I define the accompanying increase of energy as renewed arousal, providing energy now directed at getting on with the accepted new reality. Following the successful transition of this phase, we regain our peace and happiness.

Grieving the loss of someone close takes time. There are no

rules and no schedule, just a process we need to go through. The loss of a partner, for example, is not simply one loss, as there are daily reminders of the loss. We go to bed alone, and we wake and have breakfast alone. We are reminded each time of one of the little things we used to do together that we are now doing alone. It is important to accept this as a part of the process of healing. Slowly, however, if we allow ourselves to grieve, we find we begin to remember the good things with warmth and affection. It is as if we carry the loved one around with us and our memories become a celebration in time, encouraging us to let go and move on.

Grief is not only about death, but a grief for things such as the loss of health, a job, etc. I recall when I first had to inject insulin. I kept my test kit and needles in a man bag, so it was convenient when going out. I would sometimes forget to take my bag with me, then feel angry because I had to go home and get it. I was sad about having to avoid some foods I particularly liked, and I bargained with myself about sometimes cheating with those foods. Eventually I adjusted to the new life and now have accepted the new status quo. Not all people are comfortable accepting nurture, and it is therefore important to be aware of this. However, in my experience, those who are expressing sadness authentically need little persuasion to accept comfort from others.

The Healthy Fear Cycle

When we become aware of a threat, or a potential threat, we experience fear. It is the signal to run for cover or to take flight. A threat can only be in the future, even if it is in the very immediate future. This awareness disturbs our peace, and we enter a state of arousal. As our bodies energise for fight or flight, the muscles in the arms, legs and abdomen tense, the heart beats faster, and we become more alert. The abdominal muscles pull tight, and this forces the intestines up under the rib cage for protection. This, in turn, alters our breathing, which becomes rapid and shallow. The rush of adrenaline is intricately linked to these bodily responses. As we identify the stimuli as potential danger, we become aware of our fear. The movement through the initial response of arousal or anger may not be recognised, as it is quickly overtaken by fear.

Some people may experience fear being accompanied by a loss of energy, like a feeling of weakness or trembling in the limbs. This is more akin to the freeze response, which is a primitive reaction to make us remain still in the hope a predator will not notice us.

Fear is also frequently confused with excitement because of the physiological response to the adrenaline rush that accompanies excitement. Many excited people, who lack the ability to discern the difference, prevent themselves from enjoying the adrenaline rush because they allow their fear to overwhelm and incapacitate them. This, in turn, may lead to them preventing themselves enjoying the thrill available in exciting activities.

Relationship Needs When Afraid

If we can maintain our focus on the present, we will energise our human need to seek protection and our capacity to problem solve and look for support from others. We can then communicate with our friends, family or colleagues to find the protection needed to manage the object of our fear. When we are afraid, the basic need is to find protection, covering, safety, alliances and support. Notice the word covering. This is effectively a means whereby others metaphorically provide covering fire to ward off the invasion of an enemy or a predator. As we experience protection and covering, we can reconnect with our anger and focus our energy on facing our fear. We can now return to meaningful communication with those close to us, or our colleagues. By dealing with our anger with the sense that our allies have our back covered, we are free to shift into problem solving. This will involve seeking to achieve the necessary change to promote a return to happiness. An example of this behaviour is seen in small children. When they are afraid, they run to their caretaker, hide, usually behind their legs, placing the source of protection between themselves and the feared person or object. Once they feel safe, they look out from behind the protector and make a face at the person they were afraid of. (Demonstrating arousal anger in their energy to problem-solve and run-in fear, hence their need for protection, and anger again as they mock the feared object.)

I use the word covering to indicate the importance of protective behaviours aimed at avoiding humiliating or shaming the person. For example, telling them, "There is nothing to be afraid of" is akin to saying, "What is wrong with you?" Covering is about offering protection without adding emotional trauma, while also avoiding interventions that may be unconsciously or consciously traumatic.

CHAPTER 9

The Unhealthy Expression of Emotions

Unhealthy Expression of Anger

When anger is inappropriately expressed, we can seldom achieve healthy outcomes. Others may not want to hear us, and we make it difficult to achieve our objectives. This leads to frustration, as we remain stuck in anger. We may then exhibit passive behaviours[28] as displayed through acting out or acting in. Acting out may be seen as agitation, a raised and angry voice, aggressive body language, and violence. This is unconsciously aimed at producing a shift of discomfort.[29] This invites the other person to show the emotion you are avoiding and enables them to avoid expressing the emotion they tend to avoid. For example, if I do not like feeling fear, I agitate aggressively and invite the other person to feel afraid. In other words, the angry person may want to avoid feeling and expressing his or her own fear and prefers the other to be afraid.

Acting in may be exhibited through the passive behaviours of doing nothing, or over adapting, e.g., sulkiness, making a mess or over pleasing. The shift of discomfort is seen in the avoidance of feeling and/or expressing of anger. These passive behaviours are

---

28. Passive behaviours are acts that seem to be reactions to stimuli but will not lead to problem solving. In Transactional Analysis, they are defined in rising levels of seriousness as: doing nothing; over adapting; agitation, i.e., lots of activity directed away from a solution; violence; or incapacitation.

29. A shift of discomfort is an unconscious swap of emotions. It is managed outside of awareness and, for it to be successful, both parties must agree to the hidden agenda. We cannot make another person feel an emotion, but we can make this beneficial hidden arrangement by maintaining the unhealthy status quo. The shift plays into each person's emotion that they want to avoid and is an entry into the expression of cover-up emotions.

external and observable displays, and invitations to unconscious cooperation to achieve negative outcomes. They lead to competitiveness and entry into drama. When as children we observe anger inappropriately expressed by the grownups, we may learn how to be inappropriate ourselves and/or make decisions about avoiding the authentic expression of anger. Because anger communicated in inappropriate ways leads to so much disruption in relationships, anger gets a bad reputation, thus perpetuating the family, cultural and religious processes of avoiding expressing anger.

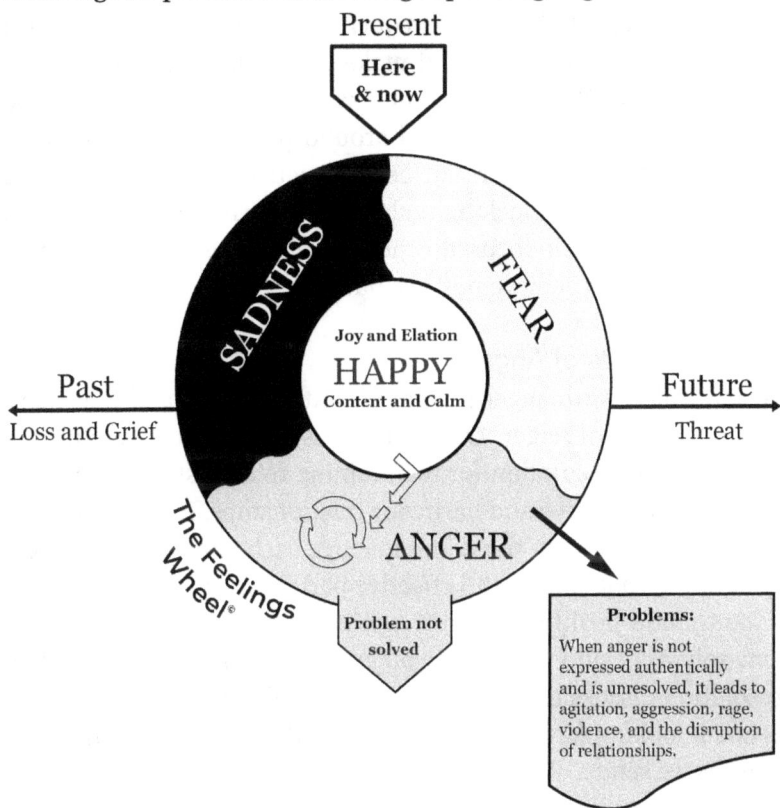

Figure 18: Unhealthy expressions of anger, © John Parr January 1997

Figure 18 shows how we enter anger while losing focus on problem solving. We may simply spin, generating more and more unfocused anger like an angry Catherine wheel with sparks flying everywhere. As a result, we fail to find a respectful resolution. We are looking for an "I win, you lose" outcome. Or we spin with the anger focused internally and we again fail to find a resolution for the conflict and hurt ourselves in the process.

A metaphor for analysing the difference between healthy and unhealthy violence can be drawn from the use of explosives in demolition. The energy from an uncontrolled explosion blasts out in every direction. It can cause a lot of collateral damage and destruction and is generally used when the objective is destruction. However, I can take a small amount of explosive, place it where I want to create a hole through concrete, cover the explosive with a plastic bag full of water and make the explosion. Now the bag directs most of the energy where I want it to go. There is a hole in the wall, some water sprayed around the area, but little or no collateral damage. Anger can be destructive when expressed in unhealthy ways, i.e., lacking real focus and with attack or blame. Alternatively, when focused, and the energy is released under control, we often achieve positive outcomes.

The Four Kinds of Anger

When dealing with anger it is important to understand that there are four kinds of anger. One of them is healthy and helpful, the most important emotion for maintaining relationships. The other three are destructive and harm our relationships. Learning how to differentiate between them and manage each appropriately is key to building cooperative and effective partnerships.

Authentic healthy – anger expressed from a win-win, problem-solving position, where the objective is simply to open a conflict resolution discussion. This is the controlled release of energy and is about looking for a win-win to deepen the relationship. It builds trust as we send a clear message, "If I have an issue with you, I will come to you asking for discussion and cooperation." This is the way to encourage openness and cooperation. It carries no aggression, threat or manipulation.

Explosive anger – expressed in an aggressive and win-lose way, where the objective is to intimidate the other and achieve a win-lose outcome. This will undermine any relationship and even make a relationship fail over time.

Implosive anger – turned in on one's self, where the objective may be to manipulate through offering guilt to the other. This is also destructive, and it invites abuse, encourages manipulation, and can be experienced as punishing through withholding. It destroys trust and relationships.

Indirectly expressed anger – often-termed passive aggressive, where we show our anger indirectly with the objective to invite the other to express anger and then to feel bad about doing so. Again, this is a destructive form and invites others to experience resentment and contempt.

The last three all involve internalising and storing our unhealthy emotional responses, a mechanism where we hold on to resentments and justifications for socially unacceptable behaviours.

Anger indirectly expressed or inappropriately held back often eventually bursts out unexpectedly. This is most likely when we believe we are justified in telling it like it is. It is as if we did not have permission to be authentically angry, so we stored it up until we could contain it no longer. Anger as a cover-up emotion also leads to sudden outbursts of aggressive behaviours that can lead to harming others, self-harm, or depression. The flash point is often signalled when people say, "I have had all I can take" or "that is the last straw" or "enough is enough." These expressions flag that the other person is angry with you, and in addition to the anger you are due, you will receive extra helpings stored up from past unresolved conflicts. Other symptoms of stored, unexpressed anger are loss of energy, loss of motivation, tiredness, tension in the neck and shoulders, and general lethargy and loss of drive.

Working with the Effects of Unexpressed Anger: Andy and Patricia's Story

Andy and Patricia presented for therapy, complaining that they were fighting and emotionally abusing each other. He reported it started because she had "gone off sex." Patricia said the problem was he was not interested in her, wouldn't take time to be together and was always coming home late. They both missed the closeness they once shared and wanted contact. However, they found that when they had time for contact, they would argue over small, unimportant things. Their process was arguing and avoiding intimacy, and it seemed clear no amount of discussion of the content of their arguments would help solve their problem. Rather, what they were doing was expressing their anger in inappropriate ways with no focus on solving their problem. Underlying their fighting was hurt and a sense of rejection. I invited them to take time to review what they wanted from each other. Andy said he wanted to feel loved and recognised for his contribution to the home by working hard. Patricia said she also wanted to feel loved and important and would feel this when he spent time with her, just to be together. Neither of them experienced feeling heard by the other.

Both recognised they lacked a model for expressing anger, having had families where anger was avoided until it spilled over into physical violence. They traced their current conflict back to their first disagreement two years before when he became angry. She felt unloved because he was angry with her for what she saw as only a minor problem. Andy reported having felt unheard by her, whilst at the same time recognising he had been too angry for the actual incident. They discussed this and how slowly they had moved into defensive positions, wanting to avoid fighting, but somehow fighting about unimportant issues.

I facilitated each taking the time to tell the other their feelings by teaching them active listening skills, i.e., using reflecting, paraphrasing and summarising. They practised this over a few sessions and then we added asking and telling each other what they wanted. The next step was experimenting with hearing each other during the week between sessions. This was through exercises where each would take time to speak about their wants and needs, with no expectation of having the other do or say anything. A further step was added which was to occasionally swap seats to see if they could experience their partners' perspective. The intensity and frequency of their conflicts reduced. They began to recognise their anger was about unmet needs and they could talk about these issues without fear of moving into the kind of conflict they had seen in their family of origin. Cooperating to help meet each other's needs followed. They learned how to tell each other about their anger with authenticity, and to listen to each other. Goodwill and finding common ground was central to their development as a couple.

Working with Sadness Covering Anger: Mary's Story

Mary's story is an example of acting-in also expressed as implosive, unexpressed anger, or covering authentic anger with sadness. Mary was a twenty-six-year-old fitness instructor who was married with two small children. She had entered therapy with long-term, low-key depression and was confused why she felt low. She said, "I have all I need: a great husband, two lovely children, a nice home and financial security. However, something is wrong." She had a medical history of suffering from Crohn's disease, an inflammatory disease of the bowel, and 0.5 metres of her small intestine had been removed. Her symptoms had returned, and she was being offered steroid medication. She was on the waiting list for a second operation.

When she was a child, her parents had separated, and she recalls she could get them to be together with her if she was ill. In her family, she had learned it was not good to be angry, so she had swallowed her anger, expressed sadness and somatised her anger in her intestines. She was using her anger to hurt herself because her unconscious belief was that if she expressed anger, she would drive people away from her. As a result, she was storing anger and acting-in, i.e., causing her intestines to become inflamed. She told herself that when she died, "They will all miss me and wish they had been nicer towards me."

During her therapy, Mary learned to spit her anger out rather than swallow it. At first, she would take apples, bite and chew on them, separate the bits she liked and wanted to swallow from the bits she did not want and then spit those pieces out. As she grew in confidence, she told people when she was angry, and ask for what she wanted. Metaphorically, she was deciding what to swallow and what to spit out. She used her symptoms of discomfort in her gut to alert her to when she was swallowing things that were not good for her, and then to talk about these issues with the appropriate people. She was losing her disease and gaining both physical and emotional health.

At the time of the transcript below, she was close to the end of her therapy but had experienced some regression whilst visiting a close friend in hospital.

Legend: T indicates the therapist, and M indicates Mary.

T. "Are you ready to put her on a pillow and tell her how you feel?"

M. "Yes." (Mary is breathing deeply and crying.) "I feel so angry that you've killed yourself. That you're dying, that you haven't taken care of yourself; you've got all these people running around after you now."

T. "Experiment with saying *and I want to cry about this.*"

M. (Still crying.) "I don't. I don't want to cry about it, but I do want to be able to feel it. I want to be able to feel my anger. I think I stop myself because I've got so much anger."

T. "I'm so angry that ..."

M. "I could shake her."

T. "I could shake you."

M. "Shake you, yes. You've got what you want at the detriment of your life. You've allowed yourself to be a victim for so long."

T. "Experiment with saying to her: *You've not dealt with your feelings for so long that they've had to cut great chunks out of you.*" (Reminding Mary of her old process.)

M. "You've not dealt with your feelings so much that they've had to cut great chunks out of you and ..."

T. "And. What did you stop yourself from saying?"

M. "And I hate you for it."

T. "What are you feeling?"

M. "Angry and sad."

T. "This is sad, Mary. Who are you seeing on the pillow?"

M. "It's me."

T. "So, what do you want to say to yourself?"

M. "That you don't ...; that I don't have to die to get what I want."

T. "Great!"

M. "That I don't have to behave like her. I mean I used to have so much respect for her. I saw her as a real role model, my friend. Cos, she had such a ... she's got such a good sense of fun and that's what I really like about her."

T. "Great, so will you keep that memory of her?"

M. "Yes."

T. "Because that's not devalued by things that she's done that you don't like."

M. "Yeah, like when I was training to be a keep fit teacher, she really supported me with that, and she came with me when I did my exam and she was there then, and she actually took me seriously then. I appreciate that."

T. "Great! So, will you take yourself seriously?" (Reminding her of her decision to respect herself and spit out her anger, as opposed to her old way.)

M. "Yeah. I mean, it just really freaks me that l wanted to be like her, and I don't want to die at 34."

T. "Experiment with saying *I will not ...*"

M. "I will not die at thirty-four. I won't!"

T. "What will you do?"

M. "Well, I've found out that the human body can live to be a 150, so I'll go for that."

T. "Great!"

Mary's therapy was over thirty years ago now. She never had the second operation and has not suffered from the symptoms of Crohn's since. She is still happily married to the same husband and is a successful therapist in her own right. Her success is thanks to how she utilised emotional assertiveness techniques and took charge of her emotional wellbeing.

Complexities of Relationship and Responsibility: Examples of a Healthy Use of the Shift of Discomfort

A friend from Paris asked me to host his teenage son, Louis, for a few weeks so he could improve his English. Louis wanted to visit London and especially Leicester Square, as he was very keen to see the buskers. In the square, there was a group of young people playing very well and they had attracted quite a large crowd. He managed to get to the front and sat cross-legged, listening and clearly enjoying the music. On the far side of the crowd, I noticed something that looked like aggression from a small group of youths in their early twenties. These lads were intimidating people in the crowd, who were becoming visibly scared and leaving the group. This presented me with a problem as I was responsible for taking care of my young French charge.

The situation looked potentially threatening and perhaps dangerous, as the group of lads were working their way around the crowd and would soon be upon us. I suggested it was time to go, but Louis resisted—he was enjoying himself and did not see the danger. I had to think on my feet and eventually one of the young men approached me, looking menacing and shouting at me. I took him by the hand, shook it, and smiled at him. At the same time, I placed my left hand on his elbow and turned slightly at an angle of about forty-five degrees to him. I said in a friendly tone, still with a smile, "Yes, the music is good isn't it, but a bit loud."

He again shouted at me, and I continued to hold his hand, still smiling, and said, "Yes, we have to raise our voices, or we would not hear each other." He looked puzzled, clearly not understanding what was going wrong with these manoeuvres. I did not look afraid, and instead was looking calm and friendly. He turned to his colleagues and gave a shrug as if to say, "What do I do now?" They returned the shrug, suggesting, "I don't know?" He looked at me one more time, I waved, and he walked away.

How do I decipher this behaviour? The youths seemed to have some motive for scaring people out of the crowd. I do not know why and do not need to. They were being intimidating. Their behaviour was clearly foul-play as they were not being friendly. They had a plan, even if I did not know what it was. They knew what people were likely to do faced with a group of five or six intimidating youths. Therefore, as they had a plan, they were one step ahead of the situation, driving things the way they wanted them to go. When approached, I did not act as expected and instead was friendly. The plan was going wrong. He tried a second time to get back on track, and again I did not do as he expected.

This confused him, which led to his "what happens next?" look at his mate. Perhaps he thought I did not understand, in which case maybe I was crazy or dangerous, or he thought, "This guy knows something I do not know, in which case he could be dangerous." He and his friends no longer had control. Instead of me accepting a shift of discomfort, I handed it back to him, and now he felt uncomfortable. What were the risks? Well, they could have escalated the aggression and become violent. In that case, I could have seriously injured his right arm and offered him some pain. I may have been able to persuade him to tell his friends to back off. Or I could have been injured, although this was mitigated as there was a crowd and there would have been police somewhere nearby. Indeed, as Mike Tyson says, all boxers have a plan, until they get hit.

Roger Daltry offered another philosophical position when dealing with bullies in the movie *McVicar* when he played John McVicar. When several prison officers came to his cell to beat him up, he broke a chair, took a leg and said, "I know I'm going to lose here, but I'll be the best second you ever saw." In the Leicester Square situation, my first option was to take flight. However, the time to persuade Louis to come with me mitigated that. I therefore needed option two. I was quite scared, but used the fact I was not alone to provide me with cover. I had unarmed combat skills and also trained in Karate. In addition, I knew my fear provided me with adrenaline for the fight and flight, therefore, I had increased muscle power. These were skills the aggressor was not aware of.

The most important takeaway from this example is that not following the aggressor's demands, not doing as expected or told, alters the balance of power, sometimes for long enough to enable an escape. There is no shame in escaping, and ignoring one's fear is to lose sight of the benefits it offers us. Adrenaline can heighten our awareness and make us more capable of surviving. Unfortunately, if we allow it to overwhelm us, it can also dampen our capacity to think clearly, and problem solve. Managing our breathing and grounding ourselves will help us regain our critical faculties. Threatening behaviour does not necessarily leave us with only the two alternatives of fight or flight. We can remain calm, think and problem solve and to do this effectively, we must manage the potential limbic hijack.

Unhealthy or Learned Expression of Sadness: The Unhealthy Sadness Cycle

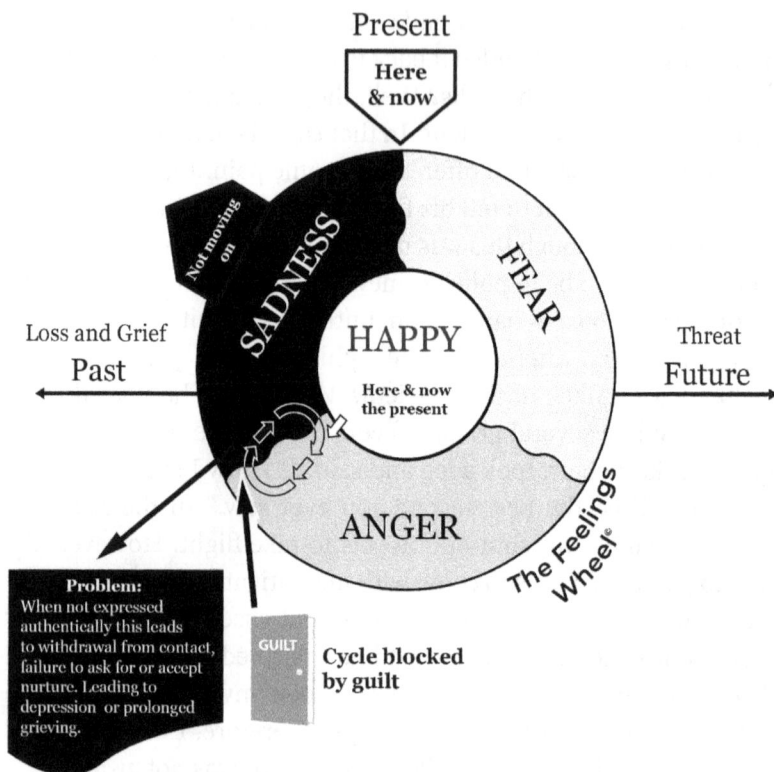

Figure 19: Unhealthy expressions of sadness, © John Parr January 1997

In the Unhealthy Expressions of Sadness in figure 19, we see that a failure to process our grief cycle leads to us not being able to move on and recover. The diagram also shows the two parts of the unhealthy process that cycle between sadness and anger. Disruptions to the natural flow of authentic expressions and communication of our sadness may lead to our failure to bring a resolution to our grief. Unresolved grief may take many years to resolve, and some grieve the loss of a loved one for the rest of their lives.

I find that the most common block to the healthy expression of grief is guilt. I define guilt as belief based and as a cognitive process, not simply a feeling. Guilt is based upon the belief, "I have done something wrong." In the case of loss, it is common for the survivor to be angry at the lost one for dying. This is a natural part of the process. However, as we know they did not intend to die at the cognitive level, we turn our anger back on ourselves through guilt. We then tend to become blocked in the process and are unable to move towards recovery. We exhibit behaviours that block the healthy expression of relationship needs; that is, we do not look for comfort.

The belief I have done something wrong is only of use when I have done something that breaks my moral or ethical code. In the case of genuine guilt, we can either put the matter right, if this is achievable, and then forgive ourselves, or let go of the guilt, if there is no possibility of reparation. In the case of sadness blocked by guilt, we may feel guilty because of our anger, e.g., "I'm mad at them for dying, but it wasn't their fault and so I'm a bad person." We then block our natural expression of sadness and fail to communicate our needs to others. This results in us deciding we do not deserve to be cared for and, therefore, do not accept or seek nurturing. Or we may refuse nurture when offered and close ourselves off from others who care for us. This may eventually lead to others showing unhealthy anger. (They feel hurt and cover that up, replacing it with anger.) As you see in the diagram, we then become stuck cycling between sadness and anger. Our anger can then become focused in on self. This can also result from others not giving us appropriate responses to healthy requests for nurture at times of family loss. Other family members may be in need themselves and become competitive for nurture. We feel sad, do not get our needs met, feel angry, focus the anger internally because of our guilt, and recycle sadness. I often find this is the basic underlying mechanism in reactive depression and depressive illness. In depression, libido declines, energy is lost, nurture and kindness are rejected, and so the unfinished grieving continues. I think an inherent fear of depression can cause avoidance of sadness. This is often the case in adults who observed depression in a family member during their childhood. Unfortunately, the process of avoiding experiencing or expressing sadness can lead directly to depression. Sadness is a natural and healthy process; it is the avoidance of sadness that is unhealthy.

In my work, I facilitate recovery from depression through helping the person to uncover their belief, "I have done something wrong." This is then followed by supporting the healthy expression of anger, healthy requests for, and acceptance of nurture.

Because of the associated libidinal loss in depression, I find raising levels of endorphin and adrenaline helpful. I discovered that getting the depressed client to engage in safe, scary activities aids the healing process. These activities included going on scary rides at a theme park because the fight-or-flight response is activated with a release of adrenaline and positive neuropeptides, i.e., arousal of the limbic system. This increases libido and opens the path to examining the emotions that the experience arouses. Such activity is followed the next day with therapy to focus the client's feelings in the direction of healthy expression of emotions and the resolution of the emotional block. This includes invitations to express anger, along with offers of positive nurturing by demonstrating care while discussing any sadness component.

The feelings wheel is used to help the client find their way through their internal process, so they can continue integrating the learning outside of the consulting room. Central to the process of moving on from unexpressed sadness includes working with guilt. Where there is more serious depression, working with a doctor or psychiatrist is important. They can offer medication to help take the edge off the depression. Where depression is very profound, I view withholding medication as persecutory, especially if done because of the therapist's personal prejudice against medication. However, once the depression begins to lift, I begin the work as described above, later linked with controlled withdrawal from medication.

Working with Sadness and Depression: Michael's Story

Due to illness, I had to cancel a client's appointment at short notice. Michael was in therapy for long-term, low-key depression and relationship problems. During the next appointment, he reported feeling more depressed during the week since he had last seen me. I asked him when he noticed feeling more depressed and he told me soon after his missed appointment. I then asked him if he could remember what he felt when I called to cancel our meeting.

He shrugged his shoulders and replied, "Nothing." He then dropped his shoulders, adopting a depressed posture. I drew his attention to his first response, i.e., to lift his shoulders, followed by slumping forward. I invited him to raise his shoulders again and experience how he felt in this position. As he drew his shoulders up, he identified he felt slightly angry. I asked him to remember taking the telephone call and notice any trace of feeling. He again shrugged his shoulders and now experienced irritation (low-level anger). I asked him to tell me what he was angry about. Michael said he'd wanted to have his appointment and was angry when it was cancelled. He then immediately said, "But it wasn't your fault," expressing guilt, because I was not to blame for being ill. His guilt led to him wanting to protect me from his anger and sadness. In the process, he then discounted his feelings and needed to withdraw into depression. This caused him to avoid being fully in the relationship with me. His guilt also led him to avoid seeking nurture for his sadness and expressing anger at the loss of contact. His process led to an unresolved feeling cycle and his subsequent return to depression.

I invited him to express his anger and empathised with him regarding the loss of our contact and his personal time in therapy. I explained it was natural to feel angry, even if I was not to blame for causing the loss. That I too was angry and sad to cancel, and that whenever we have a feeling it is OK to express it without looking for who was to blame. I reassured him that letting out his anger was a normal reaction and his feelings were OK by me as was he. I also helped him to understand where this process began. We discussed his belief that if he felt angry, someone had to be blamed, and if no one was to blame, then he must be at fault. I affirmed that when people feel angry, no one has to be responsible and anger is simply a feeling. I reassured him that he also had the right to feel angry, even if he couldn't find someone to be responsible. I accepted I was the object of his anger without withdrawing my relationship and without feeling bad. This led to work on archaic material relating to losses of childhood excitement due to his mother's prohibition against his expressions of anger towards her. There had been one significant loss that she denied responsibility for, although it was something she had initiated. She then accused him of being an ungrateful child. He gained awareness of how often she scolded him for being ungrateful for all she did for him and how he learned to suppress his anger and sadness. After some work on this awareness, his depression lifted, and he became animated.

For homework, I recommended he go to a theme park with a close friend or trusted family member the next weekend, and take as many of the scary rides he could. Whilst doing this, he was to record his feelings and come back on the following Monday to continue this work.

In the first session after the homework, he reported he had gone to the theme park with his son. They had gone to the restaurant for lunch, and he had ordered a salad and chips, asking for the chips to be on a separate plate. When the food arrived, the chips and salad were on the same plate, causing the salad to wilt. He expressed his anger to the waiter, something he had never done before. He reported excitedly that the waiter apologised, took the food away and returned later with his order as he requested it. However, his son said, "Dad, you shouldn't have complained to the waiter, it wasn't his fault." He noted he had begun to teach his son the message he had received from his own mother. He was glad to be able to tell his son what he had just learned for himself, and they had a good discussion about it.

After a few sessions to integrate his newfound permission and ensure good boundaries and safety to avoid becoming inappropriately angry, as well as finding ways to manage his sadness, Michael left therapy with a spring in his step.

We can become stuck in feelings if we fail to manage them effectively. In the case of sadness, Charles Darwin said, "He who remains passive when overwhelmed with grief loses his best chance of recovering elasticity of mind."[30]

There are potentially two negative cycles in blocked sadness.

30. Darwin, Charles. *The Expression of the Emotions in Man and Animals.* 1872.

When stuck in one of the cycles, the depressed individual acts in, i.e., using anger against self, through obsessively punishing themselves by going over and over the loss, feeling depressed and refusing nurturing from others. This can in some cases lead to suicidal ideation or actual suicide and is a recognised process in deeply depressive individuals. The shift of discomfort[31] is the avoidance of accepting their sadness and grief, so indirectly the significant others in their life are punished and they feel sad and/or angry as a result. By punishing others because of their depression, there are renewed reasons to feel guilty in the subconscious of the depressed person. Therefore, they stay depressed, while their friends or relations continue to feel sad, angry and helpless about them. In the other cycle, the individual acts out in the form of passive aggression, sulking, or misdirecting aggression, as is common in passive aggressive individuals. The shift of discomfort here is their anger, so others become angry and punish them, thereby briefly assuaging their guilt while also giving them renewed reasons to feel angry and sad. Such behaviours are rather more common than you may imagine.

It is quite common for people to be confused between sadness and depression, often avoiding being sad because they are afraid of becoming depressed. However, this strategy is flawed, as the process can lead to depression.

Way back in the early 1960s, well before I was trained as a therapist, I was in a relationship where there was a clearly identifiable shift of discomfort. My wife was not a person who easily expressed anger, whilst I was often much angrier than was necessary. I came home one day to find my wife crying. When I asked her why, she said, "I bought a piece of topside of beef today and it is almost all fat." I took the meat back to the butcher and complained angrily. I got a good replacement and an apology. However, I now know I was rescuing my wife and persecuting the butcher. In the process, I also kept my wife in the victim position by not supporting her to go

---

31. A shift of discomfort describes how two or more people can unconsciously trade emotions with, for example, one party suppressing their anger and the other expressing excessive anger or hurt. While the angry person denies their sadness, the other displays excessive amounts of anger.

complain herself. What did I get by doing this? I had someone who would do the family sadness so that I did not have to, while my wife was facilitated to avoid using her anger and experience her own power. It may look like a good deal between us, but it kept us both stuck in unhelpful processes. Such behaviours are described in the theory of the Drama Triangle, a topic we cover in more depth later.

Inappropriate or Unhealthy Expressions of Fear

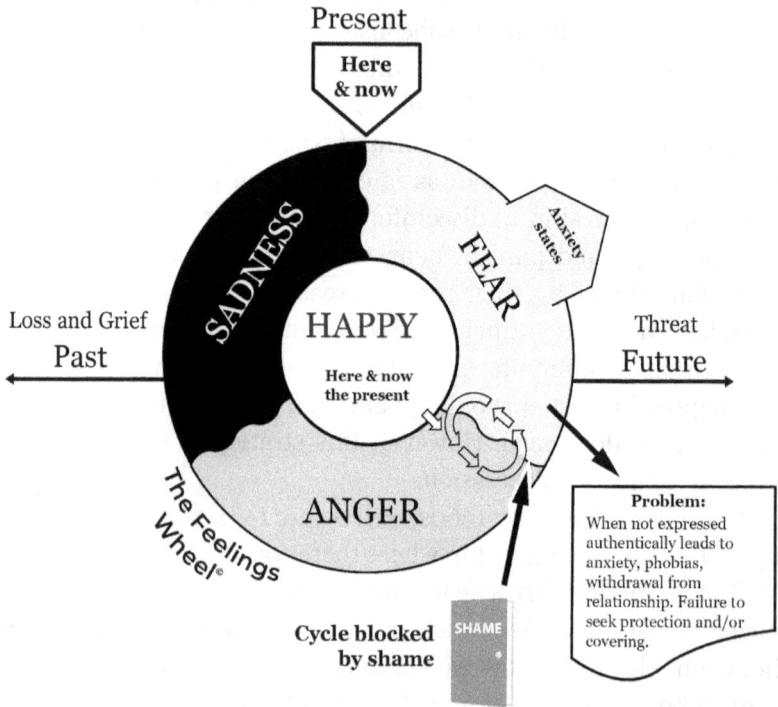

Figure 20: Unhealthy expressions of fear, © John Parr January 1997

Disruption to the healthy process of dealing with fear can lead to a failure to find protection and a blocking of the problem-solving process, together with recycling around anger and fear. My observations and clinical experience have taught me that shame blocks the healthy expression of fear. Like guilt, shame is not a feeling but a cognitive process, based upon the mistaken belief "there is something wrong with me." Shame is a disavowal of anger in order to protect us from the potential loss of an important relationship. When we dismiss our anger, a valuable aspect of the self is lost. We are, in effect, attempting to appear to be the person we imagine the other person wants us to be. As we look upon our own vulnerability, we experience being exposed and may begin the process of experiencing shame. We attempt to hide our shame, metaphorically go into hiding, do not ask for or accept protection, and internally become cowed. Perhaps because we fear others seeing our defect, we cycle between anger and fear. In this internal state of anxiety, we cannot directly ask for protection or covering and we display behaviours that suggest we are a victim that needs rescuing. This may attract those who like to feel good by doing things for others, but the process has a negative outcome, in that it keeps the victim feeling small and insignificant and creates dependence. Nurturing, intended to help, becomes unhelpful, where protection could provide safety, e.g., acts of setting firm limits and expressions of protection. We may hear the other say, "Hey, there is nothing to be afraid of," in a kindly but slightly patronising voice. This often leads to the fearful one becoming stuck, because if there is nothing to be afraid of and yet they feel afraid, it is proof there is something wrong with them. Hence, we continue cycling. Experience has led me to conclude this is the core process in anxiety states.

Helpful covering is achieved by not drawing undue attention to the client's shame, at least until they are ready and feel safe enough to open the subject. Once again, I see two variants of this negative cycle, acting out from this position we display agitation, aggression, and violence. By shifting the discomfort away from their fear, the person invites the other to feel afraid. This, in turn, invites the other to be angry and aggressive and maintains the cycle of unfocused aggression, i.e., it attracts the persecutor's response. Or if we are acting in, we show passivity, timidity, anxiety and avoidance, agitation and incapacitation; the response seen in anxiety states and phobias. This invites the other to feel sorry for them and invites the rescuing response.

The illuminating bible story of Adam and Eve in the Garden of Eden explains this process and shows how a caring individual can avoid shaming the fearful person. If we take a close look at the story, we find a number of really odd events. Before I describe these and link it to my narrative, it is important to look at the writer's perspective, especially about the person of God. Biblically, God is thought of as being omnipotent, (all powerful) omnipresent, (existing everywhere at the same time) and omniscient (all seeing). If we bear these qualities in mind *prima facie,* the storyline does not seem to hold together. It starts by God putting the pair in the garden and forbidding nothing other than they must not eat the fruit of the tree of the knowledge of good and evil. Next, we are told they tasted the fruit, and became ashamed when they knew they were naked. Now the storyline appears to deviate from the basic premises about God. It tells us they hid in the bushes to hide their nakedness and shame. Who were they hiding from? God is all seeing, all knowing, and everywhere. A slight deviation. However, the deviations do not stop there. It says God calls to them and asks where they are. He asks even though he knows and is there with the couple (omnipresent). They tell Him they are hiding in the bushes. He then asks why they are hiding—yet another deviation. They tell Him they are naked. He knows this, doesn't He? Then He asks them who told them they were naked? Come on God, have you forgotten about your superpowers? Well, He knows the answer to this, too. Finally, we get to what this is all about when He provides them with covering. How did He provide covering? Let us assume He really is all the things the bible says He is, then why does He ask these questions? The story tells me that God has empathy for them. He sees they are ashamed and knows that shame is a relationship deal breaker. He wants to recover the relationship and have them remove themselves from drama, so does not want to take the role of a persecutor or a rescuer. He does not use His superpowers to protect them from deeper traumatising, or to protect them from themselves but instead to empower them. By providing the covering, they can return to being seen and the relationship issues can now be addressed openly.

This is a powerful metaphor for not shaming and not drawing attention to shame. Shame causes a breach of relationship, and whilst a relationship is broken, the possibility for authenticity is reduced. Once covered, we can return to the relationship, with shame no longer an issue.

The story is not telling us the naked human body is shameful. They were naked before eating the fruit and had no issue at all. What the story tells us is that shame leads us to hide in the dark to avoid the thing we believe is wrong with us and keep it out of sight. By not drawing attention to what is wrong, God is able to reconnect. Where shame is exposed, we risk re-traumatising the shamed person and making matters worse. However, when they do feel safe enough to bring the object of their shame into the light, it melts away and their anxiety with it. In the story, Adam and Eve do end up being banished from the garden, but not before they re-establish a relationship. Although they no longer live in the garden, they still have a relationship with their God. Once they experienced covering, they could come out of hiding. Sadly, humans tend to use shame as a means of controlling others. We make shame-inducing statements, and the other becomes compliant to avoid being banished. The best relationships are not shame-based, but trust-based.

Working with Fear: Paul's Story

Paul experienced a debilitating fear regarding committing himself to a new relationship. He reported, "When my partner asks for nurturing, I feel afraid I will not be good enough. I don't know what to do." As we discussed this, he recalled how his mother sought nurturing from him and how she then shamed him by telling him he was stupid, could never get things right, and was not good enough. Through therapy, he saw that it was unreasonable to expect him to know how to take care of his mother as a child. And that he had the right to expect she would take care of him as he was the child. He recognised he felt exposed and vulnerable when asked for support because he thought he lacked something (and felt shame because he thought there was something wrong with him). He decided he could tell his partner how he was feeling and thinking when taking care of her needs (bringing the object of shame into the light through self-disclosure). He could ask for feedback and information about her experience of his nurturing, and he could decide if he had the energy and was willing to take care of her needs. He could also ask for his needs to be met in age-appropriate ways. He let go of his anxiety and felt relaxed, reporting that he and his partner were enjoying being together again. Later, he worked on his anger towards women, starting with his mother. He also dealt with issues of loss, relating to the loss of childhood freedom and fun. As we shall see later, quite often we experience more than one emotion at a time, as in the case above. It is then essential to communication to identify each primary emotion and what it is telling us, and then to address them one at a time.

Working with Excitement Mistaken as Fear: Elisa's Story

Elisa had a fear of heights. She wanted to go on a park slide with her small son, but was afraid to climb to the top. I first checked if there was a life experience that had predisposed this fear, but she could recall none. I asked her to report her bodily experience when she felt afraid, and she listed them. Then I asked her to recall being excited. She recognised the two lists were similar. I explained to her the processes involved in generating her bodily sensations in both fear and excitement and then agreed to do some desensitisation work on her fear of heights. We took care to clarify the purpose of excitement, i.e., to prepare us for a safe thrill and of fear, and to alert us to danger. We also looked at how to make an exciting experience safe.

At the time, I had builders in the house and there was a ladder up to the roof space. We contracted to play with climbing the ladder. First, I demonstrated to her how to safely climb to the top and step from the ladder to the loft space over a small gap. Then I came down the ladder and asked her if she would like to climb herself. Elisa said yes but was feeling anxious. Through breathing exercises, coupled with checking what she was afraid of and what she needed, she reduced her anxiety and got in touch with her excitement. She asked for my support and protection by climbing behind her to help her if she slipped. It was a healthy request for an ally or covering. I agreed to do this. She stopped at the bottom of the ladder and again recognised her excitement. She clarified that whilst she was a little fearful, her excitement was greater. She climbed the first two steps, and I followed, close enough to steady her. She made it to the top and stepped across the gap. Whilst in the loft, I encouraged her to look through the gap between the loft space and the ladder, and differentiate between her fear and excitement. She asked me to descend the ladder first and then climbed down alone. Elisa immediately wanted to climb up again, this time with no help. During the next session, she reported with pleasure how she had enjoyed going on the slide with her son.

The Fear Cycle and Providing Self-Protection: Greta's Story

Greta reported feeling fearful of failure in an examination and could not remember an important diagram. On enquiry, she recognised she believed to fail was shameful. As a child, she had been regularly criticised for not being good enough academically. Her father and elder siblings had teased her about her performance and shamed her about what they perceived as low performance and a lack of commitment. Now, as she prepared for the exam, she was increasingly anxious. She could not think clearly about the subject and the more she read, the more her confusion grew. Greta was sure she would not be as good as the other students and had begun to block her capacity to think clearly regarding the subject. I invited her to look at how she could create a positive image of being in the exam and remembering what she needed to know. We also sought to find an adult from her past who had been supportive and protective of her. She remembered a caring grandmother who had intervened on one occasion when her father was criticising her. Greta recalled hearing her grandmother's voice supporting her. This helped to strengthen her inner resource of a positive parent figure so she could apply that for self-protection whenever she needed it.

As she remembered the event with the grandmother's intervention, she became angry and expressed her anger towards her father and siblings. At first, Greta's anger was full of revenge and rage. However, once she had expressed her anger in this way, she calmed, and we agreed to do some integration of her learning. She needed to find within herself a protective strength for when she was fearful in similar situations. Greta also needed to learn how to use her anger in a healthy way, so she could manage her anger and apply it in self-protection. She imagined herself telling her father that she expected him to protect her from ridicule and not to be the source of it. Greta told him she would confront ridicule from others from now on, and not be shamed by it. She also told him she was not stupid if she made mistakes (in this way, she was shifting her belief system). She then began to laugh, and I asked her what she was laughing about. "I have just remembered the drawing I was having trouble with," she replied.

"Great, so tell me about the theory now," I said. She went to the flip chart in my therapy room and demonstrated she could recall the model well and draw the diagram. She could also explain how the system worked. Effectively, Greta had used her internalised image of her grandmother to protect her from the fear of confronting her own fears. She also gave herself the permission to use her authentic anger appropriately.

Working with Compound Emotions: Melissa's Story

Compound emotions call for closer examination to uncover each primary emotion and their associated interpersonal needs. Only in this way can we assertively express our mix of needs and have a cooperative conversation to move the relationship forward. As described previously, compound emotions are built from a mixture of emotions and are often misleading, as we all put our own spin on them. What I may mean as I express a compound emotion may be quite different from what others mean by it. The example shared here illustrates how we can navigate them with more precision.

Melissa came to one of my group sessions after her boss said her team was facing redundancy. She said she was upset and flustered. These are compound emotions. People use them in different ways—some to avoid anger, some to avoid sadness and some to avoid fear. (A glass of milk gets upset, people experience emotions. Upset is avoiding naming an emotion and tells us nothing.) In the situation she described, it would be normal to experience anger, because she did not like the announcement, fear, because it left her uncertain about the future and sad, because of the loss of her role and her team.

When asked to examine what she felt when she was upset and flustered, Melissa found it difficult to be specific. She wanted to tell the group about how she was told (angry) and wanted time to organise her feelings so she could decide what to do next (fear). She knew she would retain a job in the company, which was a possible denial of her sadness. Melissa said she was worried she and her partner would not be able to afford the mortgage payments to their new home now. I saw this as evidence supporting my hypothesis that a part of her compound emotions was fear for her future security and some premature sadness at losing her new home.

Melissa frequently placed her hand on her abdomen as she spoke. I asked her to notice what she felt as she stroked her tummy. She said, "I feel scared." I asked her, "What are you scared of?" She replied, "I'm scared because I don't know what is going to happen to me." (This is all syntonic with the probability that fear was a component part of her compound emotion. Authentic fear is often experienced in the abdomen.)

Whilst appraising our compound feelings, it is important to recognise that the feelings we name have validity and are helpful when decoded. However, when they are not appropriate to the situation, they may be unhealthy expressions, covering something else up. I agreed with her that this was scary and asked her what she needed. Melissa recognised she needed her company to be clear about how they would manage the process. In other words, she needed the protection afforded by clear information and structures.

Melissa began to show signs of sadness, especially in her eyes, and said, "I'm still feeling upset." (This suggested she had not yet dealt with the issues her emotions indicated need to be managed.) She touched her chest as she spoke. I invited her to hold her hand on her chest and feel its warmth. She did this and began to cry. I asked her what she was crying about, and she replied, "It's my team. I have spent a lot of time getting to know them and at last we are working well together and now it could all end." (This is an authentic expression of sadness, linked directly to loss and grief. Although the ending for her team had not happened, it was imminent, so she had already experienced the loss of her security and the familiarity of her life. Therefore, I aimed at helping her to find closure for this.)

I asked her what she was feeling, and she replied she was incredibly sad. Melissa felt loss because her team was being broken up. I agreed this was a loss and feeling sad was appropriate. She asked to hold the hand of a group member as she continued working. (Seeking appropriate nurture.) As she settled a little, she began to become more animated and spoke of how angry she was at her boss, not because of the proposed changes, but because of the rather glib way he had informed her. Also, because he was planning to keep her waiting for a week to clarify the situation. (Now we see the core of her emotional state: anger. She did not like what her boss was doing and how he was doing it. The next step was to find healthy ways to use her anger appropriately.)

I asked her what she wanted from him, and she replied, "I expect a more respectful way of telling me as a manager about such things. I expect to be given information so I can plan how to discuss this with my team. I will talk to him again in the morning and ask for clear information." I asked her, "Are you still feeling upset?" (I wanted to check what impact this discussion had had upon her.)

Melissa said, "No, I feel angry, sad, and a little scared. I know what I will do and what I want, and I will ask my friends for support." She appeared more relaxed. In the next group, she reported she had spoken to her boss, and he had given her the information she needed. He also apologised for having sprung the news on her and not taking time to brief her properly. (We now see she has clarified her issues and decided upon her priorities and needs so she can address and solve them. She knew she needed to deal with all of her emotions separately rather than to remain stuck with the vague feeling of being upset. Each emotion needed different actions and interventions.)

This case study is just one example of how we can work through compound emotions. This is evidence that supports the hypothesis that our emotions are based on four primary emotions—happiness, sadness, fear, and anger. Our reaction to circumstances around us will often be a combination of these four. However, the difficulty is that compound emotions can be very difficult to process. They don't directly alert us to a clear course of action and therefore take longer to work through. Indeed, frequently, we fail to make a complete closure. Not only does the other person not necessarily know what you want, you may not even be fully aware of it yourself. By refining the compound back to the primary emotions, we clarify our needs and how to get them met. We can also see that taking a few moments to appraise our compound emotions can pay off. As we get back to our basic emotions, detect what they are telling us and focus our energy upon solving our problems cooperatively, we empower ourselves to regain our happiness.

Conclusions About the Feelings Wheel

The wheel indicates how one can think about one's emotions, differentiate between authentic emotions and unhealthy learned emotions, and then use it to decide how to communicate to others what you need. It will also help you to decode the more complex compound emotions and refine them down to their basic parts.

By clarifying your emotions, you can use them as essential information for problem solving in communications with anyone—partners, children, friends and work colleagues. Communication using emotional assertiveness assumes all humans are worthy of respect, including yourself. The built-in default emotion is happiness; we are designed to be calm, content and relaxed when all is well, and our emotions are there to help us achieve and maintain this state. We have all learned through life how to misunderstand both our own emotions and those of others, and we can actively improve our EQ by learning to recover our innate emotional intelligence. Whilst this takes practice, time and energy, the results are priceless.

Drama, the Drama Triangle, and the Existential Triangle

Non-Authentic Expression of Emotion

Dr Stephen Karpman developed tools so that we can understand and better manage our relationships from an OK/OK position. This life position says that by me, both you and I are OK and worthy of respect. Dr Karpman originally saw the triangle as a compassion triangle, a tool for finding compassionate ways and means to exit behaviours disruptive to relationships. His model has become popularised as the drama triangle.

When we do not express our emotions authentically, we enter drama, as the emotion we are expressing is unlikely to bring cooperative resolution to conflict. We are therefore likely to move away from the existential I am OK and You're OK life position, and display damaging behaviours that result from psychological stressors.

- When we do not express emotions in a healthy way, we enter drama.
- Drama leads to a disruption in relationships.
- Drama recreates old, defective patterns of relating.
- In turn, this strengthens these disruptive patterns.
- There is a way out!

There are three positions on the triangle: rescuer, persecutor and victim. They are defined below:

Rescuer (R): Offers unsolicited advice, does more than fifty per cent of the work. Unconsciously defines the other as a helpless victim. In the guise of rescuing, creates dependency.
Victim (V): Claims to be victimised or helpless when they are not.
Persecutor (P): Establishes over-rigid or punitive boundaries. Unconsciously sees others as helpless, pathetic or undeserving.

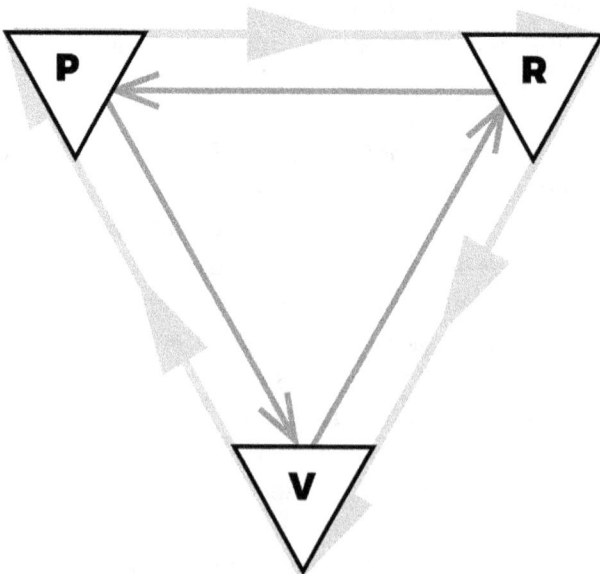

Figure 21: Drama triangle

Note:

1. This equilateral triangle is drawn base over apex, showing the inherent instability of the roles.
2. The arrows show movement in all directions.
3. The three positions represent unhealthy behavioural roles, i.e., the false self and not the real self.

The Existential Triangle

Dr Karpman suggests the compassion triangle as an alternative to the drama triangle. In this, the roles are replaced with authentic behaviours. He diagrams this inside the Drama Triangle, adding a + to each position to indicate the ++ life position. His compassion triangle positions are not roles, they are based upon our existential position and are OK/OK.

I have adapted his work and call my version the Existential Triangle[32] (see figure 22). I turned it the right way up to show the inherent stability available through exercising respectful OK/OK behaviours and renamed it the Existential Triangle to indicate these are our basic healthy human attitudes, showing mutually respectful behaviours. The three positions on the existential triangle are: respect for boundaries and contract, sharing resources; offering appropriate levels of protection by delineating and maintaining boundaries; and expressing vulnerability by asking for help directly and appropriately.

---

32. Thanks to Dr Karpman for his kind permission to take this liberty with his work. Dr Karpman's book on his compassion triangle, *A Game Free Life,* is available on www.amazon.com.

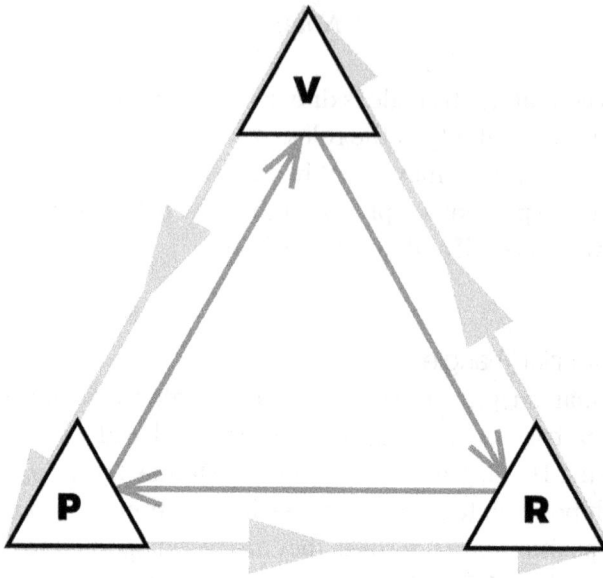

Figure 22: Existential triangle, John Parr adapted from
Dr Stephen Karpman's compassion triangle

- **Respect (R):** Maintaining a respectful relationship (self and others), seeing all as capable of asking for what they need and to offer support if asked.
- **Vulnerable (V):** Acknowledging and expressing their vulnerability and asking openly and without manipulation for what they want and need.
- **Potent Protector (P):** Establishes and manages respectful and agreed boundaries and sees others as having the capacity to self-manage. Shows expectation that contracts are maintained and honoured.[33]

Drama and the Limbic System

When in drama, our limbic system is in a higher state of arousal, leading to a hijacking of the neocortex, and negative behaviours.

---

33. Note: This equilateral triangle is drawn with the base and apex in their usual positions. Therefore, it is inherently stable. These are not roles, just real people exhibiting authentic behaviours.

This, in turn, leads to drama, a failure to communicate and destructive, competitive relationships.

When operating from the compassion triangle, our cortex is available for creative problem-solving, and we are open to build upon cooperative relationships.

Emotions on Stage:
The Model in Action

--- CHAPTER 10 ---

What's Love Got to Do with It?

The English language is very rich and has a huge vocabulary. There are usually several words for everything. However, when it comes to the word love, we seem to have been struck dumb. We do have words describing the intensity, such as fond, but when it comes to describing more complex meanings of love, we are lost for words. On the other hand, the Ancient Greeks had more than seven words for love, each describing different aspects of love. Each of these words is translated from the Greek into English as love. There is an eighth word associated with unhealthy love, Mania, obsessive love. We will not use this word in the exercises about to be discussed. Below are the seven most common Greek words for love:

- **Eros:** Sexual attraction and eroticism.
- **Philia:** Deep friendship as in brotherly love, or love of a person's humanity.
- **Agape:** Commitment or contractual unconditional love. Biblically, the love God gives to humanity.
- **Storge:** Parental love. This is the real unconditional love most parents feel for their children.
- **Ludus:** Playful love, like flirting.
- **Pragma:** Long standing love, as in marriage or a long-term relationship. It is how we feel comfortable with the other. A sense of familiarity.
- **Philautia:** Self-love. This is not egocentricity; it is an important part of being self-confident and feeling good in your skin.

Love and Relationship

When speaking about sexual relationships, partnerships and

marriages, we often use the expression "falling in love."[34] This sounds rather accidental and perhaps risky, suggesting that we have no responsibility, and it is something that just happens, like a relationship accident. We also speak about the act of sexual intercourse as love making, whilst recognising this is often purely physically enjoyable for most of us and holds little meaning in terms of relationship. In this case, do we feel love for the person we had sex with? Is there any deep emotional context in a one-night stand? I would say no. Often, an unfaithful partner will attempt to excuse themselves with the claim, "It meant nothing to me." On the other hand, to their partner, their emotional experience suggests it was anything but nothing. The emotional context of situations like this will frequently be very intense, but none of them can be called feeling love. The emotions are consequences of the dynamics of attachment in relationship, especially where there are clearly agreed boundaries and contracts around fidelity.

And what about "falling out of love"? This sounds an even more scary event, and the expression again suggests a lack of responsibility, and this has just happened to me/us. Does this mean that when we are in a committed relationship, we are continuously at risk of falling out of love? Later, we shall see that staying in love is not an accident, nor is it a matter of luck. Rather, it is about two people being willing to work on maintaining the relationship.

How does falling in love or out of love connect with emotion? Falling in love is a process that involves multifaceted components. Many, if not all, of the Greek descriptive terms for love are involved. Hence this is my definition of love: "Love is a word defining the nature and quality of a relationship. It comprises several aspects of behavioural and psychological influences that describe how we relate to people and things."

I can say from experience that starting and ending committed relationships have often been a roller-coaster ride of extreme

---

34. At this initial stage of a relationship, healthy people experience the nearest thing to Mania, obsessive love. It is normal and we usually get past it in about six months as we develop a more reality-based view of our partner.

emotions, of both highs and lows. None of these emotions are conveyed in terms of love or hate.

When we love, we experience a wide range of emotions and often very intensely. Similarly, when we end a relationship acrimoniously, we feel and display equally strong emotions, but none of them define love. Feeling love for something or someone does not mean that love is an emotion, but the connection is rather circumstantial. I love watching the sun go down, and I love watching the stars on a cold winter night, but does this mean I am feeling love? No, I look at the stars and I feel happy, I experience awe and wonder, and I ponder the meaning of life. I enjoy the activity; I do not feel love. Awe[35] is linked with fear and this fear is often unconscious. My experience of looking out into the depths of the universe certainly contains an element of existential anxiety about the meaning of life. The universe is so vast and I am so small and have so little control. This is awesome.[36]

I love my wife. What do I mean by this? I find her sexually attractive (*eros*). I love who she is, including things I may not always like or appreciate in her, and accept her as she is (*philia*) without needing her to change. This is about recognising that no one, including me, is perfect and that is OK. She does not need to change to be a part of this relationship. She is free to be herself, to dress as she wants, to like the things she likes, etc. Within the context of relationship, this freedom is usually bounded by contracts and agreements. *Philia* is not a license for abuse in either direction. Rights come with responsibilities and healthy relationships are contractual. We shall look at the subject of contracts later.

I am committed to her, so actively put energy into maintaining our relationship. When there are differences, or conflicts, we commit to resolving them; this is *agape*[37] in action.

Within the context of our mutual support and care for each

35. J. Keble: "There is an awe in mortals' joy. A deep mysterious fear."
36. As a side note, I am amused by the commonly used term "awe-sum," to mean "that was great." The universe is awe-sum, the Grand Canyon is awe-sum, giving someone a small gift is nice or generous, but ... ? Here endeth my little rant!
37. Note, *agape* is a conscious decision; it does not just happen; we make a commitment.

other, I show my love through acts of support and nurture; this is akin to *storge*. I do not see her as my child. However, I am available to take a parental role (caretaker) when needed, for example, in sickness.

We are often playful with each other, like flirting and having fun (*ludus*).

I feel completely at ease with her and comfortable with her in any situation (*pragma*).

I love her even as I love myself (*philautia*). Therefore, as I love myself, I treat her as I want to be treated. In my philosophy, this is as good as a relationship gets.

Note the importance of *philautia*. It all starts here. If we do not love ourselves and accept ourselves as we are, warts and all, we are not fully available to love anyone else. If you take a moment to run through the list against any of your relationships, you have a rule of thumb with which to analyse the nature of the love you experience for the other person.

Many experience being swept away with *eros*, and there is nothing wrong with that. However, if you make a relationship solely based on *eros*, it is unlikely to survive. For relationships to become more permanent, we need to develop them beyond sexual attraction if they are to last the test of time. I have friends who I love dearly, and I feel *philia, agape, ludus* and *pragma* for them. I have other relationships, for example, working relationships, where I feel *philia* and *agape*. All relationships can be examined through these lenses. As a result, I can comfortably tell my friends I love them, and I recommend this to you.[38] There is a lovely line in a song by Joan Armatrading called *Shapes and Sizes*. The lyrics say, "Don't wait until it's over before you say it's all been fun, obituary columns are filled with love." It goes on to say, we should tell those people whilst they are still alive or still with us. I recommend the act of being more open with the other people in your life. Take the time to question what you feel about them. Ask yourself what is the nature of this relationship, and what does it mean to me? Check out what actions you take consciously to show your love and humanity.

---

38. Be gentle with this expression. Some people, unaware of the meaning, experience discomfort when told their friend loves them.

Managing relationships is an essential process to experience peace and satisfaction in your life. It is risky to push the envelope of your comfort zone, and the rewards of doing this are immense.

From the above descriptions of love, you can see that none of them relates specifically to an emotion. I hope I have successfully demonstrated my assertion that love is not an emotion. We can link love to feeling, as we do experience physical sensations within the context of the Greek definitions; for example, *eros* is attached to physical sensation. The nearest emotion we can find for love is happiness, but that is an oversimplification. I love my wife, my children, my grandchildren and my great grandchildren. However, I can feel angry towards them, and often do. If love is happiness, then do I stop loving them when I am angry with them? No, I do not. It is because I love them even when I am angry, and because I am committed to them (*agape*) I speak to them respectfully about my anger and what I need. I listen to them when they respond, and as anger begets anger, their response is likely to be angry. Because I love them, I want them to express their anger towards me, also in a respectful way. Because of our commitment, we stay together and resolve our conflicts in a spirit of love and cooperation.

From the above, I conclude love is not an emotion, it is a word for defining the quality and nature of the relationship. With Emotional Assertiveness, when we love we will express our full range of authentic emotion and seek to avoid disrespectful unhealthy expressions.

A simple method to review any relationship

Below is a self-help tool to offer a rough guide to how any relationship feels to you. It is based only upon your own frame of reference and is therefore subjective. It is not an academic or precise measure, but rather a snapshot of the energy one experiences towards the other. It is also how this compares against your personal experience of the balance in the relationship, from your personal perspective. You can use it to make a unilateral assessment of the relationship as you see it. This can help to clarify what it is you need. Used sensitively, by sharing your results with the other person, it can also provide a framework for discussing what would help you each to gain mutual satisfaction. For example, how you both could cooperate with each other to develop specific dimensions of your relationship or explore what you each may want more or less of from the other. We often know there is something we want but may not find the words to explain it clearly. One may begin by saying, "I want more playfulness between us." (*ludus*) The other can then refine this request by asking for clarity about what that would look like, i.e. "What does playfulness look like for you?" or "What can I do to share in more playfulness?" or "What do we both need to do more or less of?"

This is not an opportunity to criticise nor to take the feedback as criticism, but a way to avoid unproductive conflict by thinking clearly about what we feel and need to facilitate good communication by inviting open, authentic, and respectful discussion. Talking with care and good will as a basis, we demonstrate that the relationship is important enough for us to be willing to take a risk. This is an act of love, a means to contribute to the maintenance of the relationship. Being open is to demonstrate how much the relationship and the other person means to you.

Each partner takes time to speak about an area of the

relationship they would like to bring more equality, respect and love to.

The blank score chart in figure 31 is intended to help you make a subjective analysis of your relationships. It is generic, so the seven types of love are not relevant for all relationships. You chose the types you will cover for the relationship you wish to analyse.

The scale is from least through to most. When using it as a couple, remember this is not an objective measure. Each person is doing this subjectively, so the aim is not to achieve maximum scores; rather, it is to be in balance, so that each partner experiences their needs being met. Do not ponder as there is no need to be precise; simply use each dimension intuitively. Make a mark on each line with a cross where you estimate it to be on each scale. The scales do not have graduation marks to reduce the potential to attempt to be precise; there is no machine that can be calibrated for accuracy.

Where a relationship seems to be 100 percent the way you want it to be, I recommend you ask yourself if it is real or idealisation? In my experience, relationships generally have a degree of tension. However, at the start of most relationships, idealisation is quite usual, and this slowly develops to the place where each is aware of areas where they are less comfortable. This is normal and safe where the degree of love on each scale can be the glue that holds the relationship together. On the other hand, where there is little mutual love, the relationship is at risk. This is when an open OK/OK discussion can help. With a healthy respectful win-win approach, couples can either decide to negotiate for a relationship that works for them both (I am OK and You are OK, let's cooperate for the relationship to be OK), or agree that I am OK, and You are OK, but the relationship is not OK and we need to find a healthy way forward.

There are two scales taken from different vantage points:

1. How you would rate the extent of your love for the other person.

2. How you would rate the relationship in comparison to your ideal.

There are no right or wrong responses, just how it seems to you. It is not an opportunity to find fault nor to catch the other out. It is important to remember we are each responsible for our own health and happiness. No one can make us feel good or bad.

The other person may also complete an analysis of the relationship from their perspective. You can then share and compare your scores. This will provide a starting point for discussing anything you both want to develop, grow, or maintain in your relationship.

Each scale is based upon one of the seven Greek words for love. Take a little time to reflect upon them; there may be some that would not be likely to score highly depending upon the nature of the relationship. For example, I love my children (*storge*) unconditionally, and there is nothing that would induce me to disown them. I just love them. Even if they do things I do not like, I will always be there for them.

On the other hand, whilst I love my wife with a degree of *storge* love, it is not totally unconditional. Rather, I love and am committed to my wife (*agape*) and this is partially contractual, based upon agreements and understandings we have made. Some of these agreements are so important to us they can be dealbreakers, though there are not so many of these. An *agape*-based relationship where the key dealbreakers are not kept is likely to end or become intolerable. There would then be no relationship as before, though sometimes we establish a new relationship. For example, a husband and wife may divorce, and no longer have the marriage relationship. However, if they have children, they continue to have a relationship as parents, and hopefully manage that respectfully for the sake of their children. So, I would not score my relationship with my wife anywhere as highly on *storge* as I do my children.

Table 6: The Greek words for love: a reminder of the meanings of the Greek words

Eros	Sexual attraction and eroticism. It may be experienced and not acted upon, e.g. we find an actor appealing. We see someone in the street who is good-looking and do nothing about it, etc. Or we may develop the attraction and act upon it. Respect remains the key as agreement to enter a sexual relationship is bounded by contracts, both personal and social.
Philia	Deep friendship as in brotherly love, or love of a person's humanity. We love who they are as a human being. Ideally this kind of friendship is based upon mutual respect, openness, and warmth. The degree of philia determines how close we feel to the other.
Agape	Commitment or contractual love. (This is contractual by decision and often by agreement. As there are conditions to a contract, is unlikely to be unconditional. Contracts and agreements must be kept and breach of contract can result in a rupture of the relationship. For example, for many people infidelity can be a deal breaker in a marriage or partnership.)
Storge	Parental love. This is the healthy unconditional love most parents feel for their children. (It is independent of their behaviour; you simply love them whatever, even if you do not like what they do).
Ludus	Playful love, like flirting. (This includes being playful with a partner or being playful with other people. It is innocent fun and not intended as a prelude to anything else, although it may often have a sexual energy. To enjoy ludus, it is important to maintain healthy boundaries.)

Pragma	Long standing love, as in marriage or long-term relationship. (It is about feeling familiar and comfortable with each other. A sense of being able to relax and be oneself, being at ease. Sitting together, just being, is one of the possible outcomes of pragma. I am comfortable to simply be myself.)
Philautia	Self-love. This is not egocentricity or narcissistic; it is an important part of being self-confident and comfortable in your skin. (It is not possible to love others in a healthy way if we do not love ourselves. Even strictly religious people are called upon to "love your neighbour, even as you love yourself." This line is in both the old and New Testament.[39])

The blank score charts in figures 31, 32, and 33 are for use as a self-help tool. Please see the next section "Example relationship chart from an individual perspective" and figures 23–30 for a more detailed example of these scales and their use. Note: It is not the objective to score a maximum on each form of love. Rather, the intention is to help the couple to reach a place where their needs are met.

Example relationship chart from an individual perspective
To use this tool for a personal analysis of how you experience your relationship, you can use the following score sheets. Note the scales are not intended as an accurate measurement but are just how you intuitively experience the type of love in the relationship. Therefore, there are no lines or gradients. Neither is it about any value judgement, so the aim is not to reach a 100% score on each form of love. Rather it is to be a guide about your personal perspective.

39. Leviticus chapter 19 verse 18 and Matthew chapter 22 verse 39. Many other religions have similar messages about *philautia*.

Greek word for Love	Score my love towards my partner
EROS (Erotic Sexual Love, usually physical; arousal, often unconnected to personality)	LEAST ⊢————————————▶ ┤ MOST
PHILIA (Acceptance of & love for the other person as a human being)	⊢—————————▶ ┤
AGAPE (A conscious contract or commitment to the other)	⊢————————————————▶ ┤
STORGE (Unconditional, instinctual love, like the love for one's children)	⊢——————————▶ ┤
LUDUS (Playful love, warm & friendly teasing & flirting; fun and humour)	⊢——————————————▶ ┤
PRAGMA (The love that comes with time; comfortable with the other; contentment)	⊢—————————————▶ ┤
PHILAUTIA (Love & respect for self, glad to be you & comfortable in your skin, confident)	⊢——————————▶ ┤

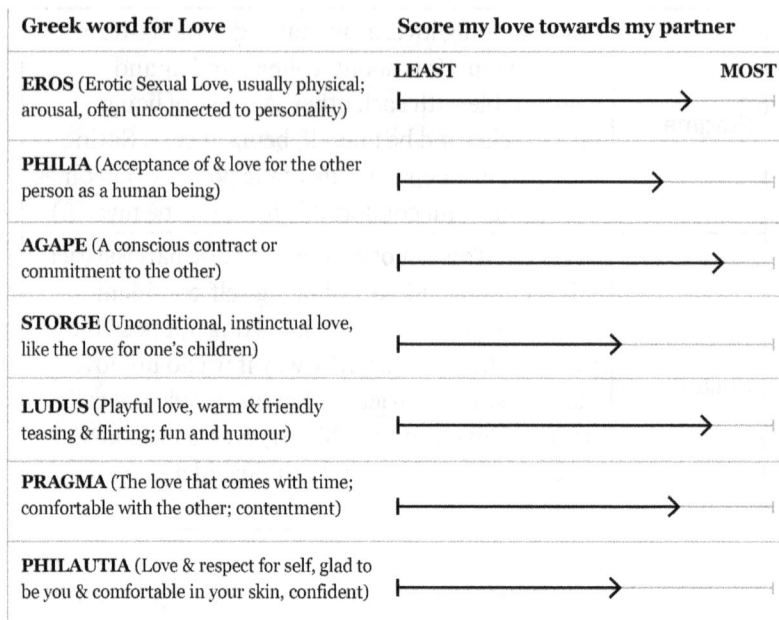

Figure 23: Subjective/intuitive sense of my love for my partner

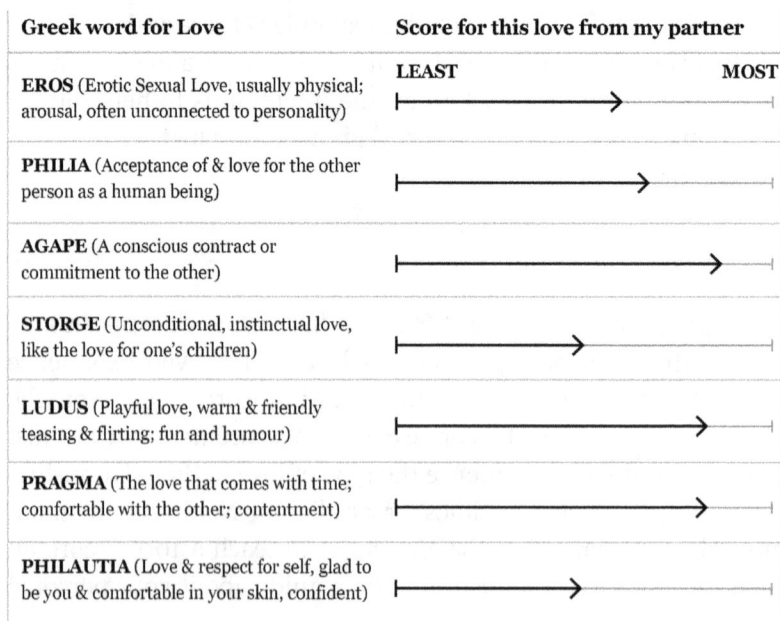

Greek word for Love	Score for this love from my partner
EROS (Erotic Sexual Love, usually physical; arousal, often unconnected to personality)	LEAST ⊢——————————▶ ┤ MOST
PHILIA (Acceptance of & love for the other person as a human being)	⊢———————————▶ ┤
AGAPE (A conscious contract or commitment to the other)	⊢————————————————▶ ┤
STORGE (Unconditional, instinctual love, like the love for one's children)	⊢————————▶ ┤
LUDUS (Playful love, warm & friendly teasing & flirting; fun and humour)	⊢———————————————▶ ┤
PRAGMA (The love that comes with time; comfortable with the other; contentment)	⊢—————————————▶ ┤
PHILAUTIA (Love & respect for self, glad to be you & comfortable in your skin, confident)	⊢——————————▶ ┤

Figure 24: Subjective/intuitive impression about
how I experience love from my partner

In the subjective/intuitive 'feel' towards my partner example in figure 23, this person says they experience relatively high levels of erotic love towards their partner (*eros*), i.e., they are sexually attracted and want to have physical contact.

They also love and accept the other person for being who they are. Whilst they are aware of things they may not like, they accept their partner (or friends) warts and all, without trying to change them (*philia*). This represents a high degree of the love they experience towards their partner. Note this is their personal experience and not dependent upon what their partner may experience about how much they believe that they are loved.

They give a high rating on their sense of commitment (*agape*). They have clear agreements and a strong intention to honour them.

They rate medium+ for their degree of unconditional acceptance (*storge*). Note: a maximum rating would likely indicate idealisation.

They rate above medium for how much fun they contribute to the relationship (*ludus*).

They rate above medium for how comfortable they are with their partner (*pragma*).

They rate medium for how much they experience themselves loving and caring for themselves (*philautia*). There is room for self-discovery in this dimension.

This person is likely to express a strong love for the other person, and at the same time there are important areas where they see room for growth and development in their contribution to the relationship. They are also asking for more from their partner than they experience receiving. Comparing these results with the chart in figure 24 about how they experience the relationship reveals the areas where they could work things through as a couple. Eros is the obvious area where there seems to be dissonance.

These self-reflective perceptions reveal how this person experiences their relationship. It does not show the actual relationship, just one person's impression of it. What it provides for this individual is a method of clarifying their level of satisfaction and areas where they may benefit from an Emotionally Assertive approach, i.e., a respectful, discussion of their wants and needs. It is of extreme importance to remember that one's impression is not the truth, it is simply your personal truth. Until you and your partner discuss your needs, they may be unaware of them. That they do not give you what you want may be because you do not ask clearly to get your needs met. For example, this individual seems to have some issues of low self-esteem. Note they score themselves only medium for *philautia*, self-love. This may well express itself in a reluctance to ask for what they want for fear of rejection, or a belief they are unworthy. That they score only medium however, is not remarkable. We seldom love our life partner as much as we love our children, though this is not usually a topic for discussion. On the eros scale, there is a gap between wants and experience. This would be a beneficial topic for discussion.

A third chart that can prove helpful for discussion between partners is shown in figure 25. This is not taken from life, it is simply an example. Note: On this chart the lines are drawn to where the individual experiences the relationship. It is not a comment upon the other person, and is rather a way of saying how they experience their relationship. It can also be a way to discuss what areas one may wish to develop more of.

Where the line ends with an arrow, it denotes aspiration for development; where it ends with a line, it reports satisfaction with how things are. The numbering is ranking priorities for development; it is a wish list. Used sensitively by each sharing their own perspective, a couple can seek cooperative, win-win ways to strengthen and energise their relationship.

My subjective/intuitive sense about our relationship and what I want	
Greek word for Love	**Score my love towards my partner**
EROS (Erotic Sexual Love, usually physical; arousal, often unconnected to personality)	LEAST ⟶ ① MOST
PHILIA (Acceptance of & love for the other person as a human being)	⟶ ④
AGAPE (A conscious contract or commitment to the other)	
STORGE (Unconditional, instinctual love, like the love for one's children)	
LUDUS (Playful love, warm & friendly teasing & flirting; fun and humour)	⟶ ②
PRAGMA (The love that comes with time; comfortable with the other; contentment)	
PHILAUTIA (Love & respect for self, glad to be you & comfortable in your skin, confident)	⟶ ③

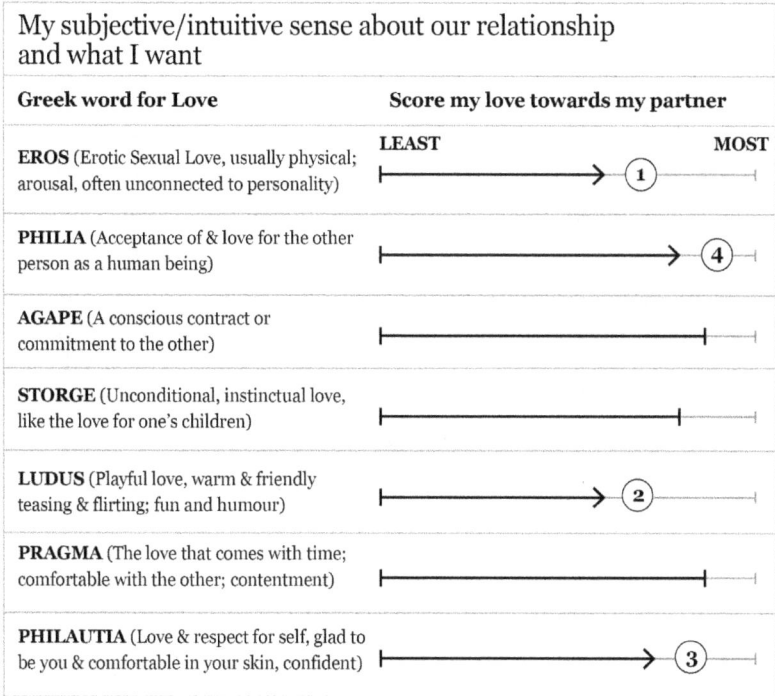

Figure 25: Reflective view of how I experience love in my relationship

Now let's look at how a couple might use this tool. A couple who are open to respectful discussion about how to bring life back into their relationship would benefit from completing a chart of how each one experiences their relationship. The simple way to do this would be for each to fill a chart of their personal take on the various dimensions in their relationship. If they wanted to go even deeper, they could fill in charts as above, and include this to take their discussion broader and deeper. You can also use the charts by changing the headings to what it is you want to explore, such as giving and taking, etc. The hint of caution is not to do this when one or the other is in distress, or there is a high level of tension in the relationship. Sadly, when we are under stress, we are more likely to use the tool as a battering ram than as an oil can. Stress often leads to disrespectful communication; respectful communication can help oil the wheels of relationship.

Example of an imaginary couple using the scale
Cassandra and Michael

Michael and Cassandra met at a party and were immediately attracted to each other. This powerful physical attraction was a feature of their ongoing relationship (*eros*). As they developed as a couple, they found that they shared many things, a love of art, the opera and travel. They enjoyed these activities and most of their holidays and spare time were taken up following these pursuits (*ludus*). However, throughout their relationship they often had arguments and rows that ended in periods when they would not speak to each other. These fights were about the areas where they could not agree and were often personal.

Michael did not like his partner's habit of tidying away his belongings, often to places where he had to search to find them. He decided to teach her a lesson by becoming even more untidy and disorganised. "Two can play at this game," he told himself. He also decided to ruin her well-organised shelves, by putting things of his on them and thus disturbing the neat and orderly system she had of lining up her bottles and jars. He was also annoyed about her tendency to snap at him when he had done something she did not like. He was angry and scared about this and often felt hurt. However, there were many things he liked about Cassandra. For example, she was loyal, logical, and determined. They had similar political allegiances and he had decided that whilst he did not like his partner when she behaved 'badly', he knew on balance he wanted to stay together (A mixture of *philia* and *agape*).

Cassandra had a strong reaction to Michael's habit of 'dumping' his clothes on the bedroom floor, "for me to tidy up" she told herself. She decided to train him by putting his things away, especially things she knew would annoy him, and she was careful to find places where it would take him some time to find them. She also resented his love of golf and felt lonely when he went off to play a round with his pals. However, she loved his intellect and his ability to find exciting and interesting things to do with their holidays (*philia*). They also enjoyed nights out to the opera or the theatre on a regular basis (*ludus*) although of late, these activities seemed to be becoming more and more difficult to arrange. On balance, she decided the things she found irritating were something she could live with. She was also impressed with his commitment to her and to his political beliefs. She knew she wanted to keep this relationship, even though it was not perfect for her (*agape*). As a result of their arguments, their times of having fun together seemed to be less frequent, and sex had become almost a ritual. Avoiding discussing minor tensions as described between Mike and Cassy often surface in areas like *eros* and *ludus*. It is therefore important to be emotionally assertive in order to address such issues and not to leave them to fester and cause discontent.

Each produces two charts, one for how they feel towards their partner, the other for how they experience their relationship. The relationship charts are then mapped onto a spider diagram, to compare the two views of the relationship. The 'how I feel about you' charts can be shared to help look for how areas of want and need are experienced by each partner. For example, if I feel high levels of philia towards my partner and she towards me, whilst the relationship spider diagram shows a gap, what can we do to grow and develop in this area?

Example relationship chart from Cassandra's perspective

Notes:

1. This is not a competition to find who scored lowest on the scales but simply where growth would be helpful and both would benefit from sharing and cooperation. They can each find movement on the scales.
2. The three scales indicating a gap in their perceptions are the areas where they can work together to take their relationship to a more mutually satisfying place.
3. Having taken time to share your charts with each other, allow yourself time to assess your emotions. What do you feel about your perspective and what you have discovered about your partner's perspective? Be aware of what your four emotions show you about your needs. You will benefit by having a clear

vision about your emotions, backed up by clear thinking and structuring.

4. During the exercise, if either of you begin to feel so angry you abandon the ability to speak respectfully, agree time out to calm down. During time out, do not think about all the things the other has done that you have become angry about. Rather, focus on what it is you like and love about them, and why it is important to you to develop this relationship. This is the time for asking yourself, "What benefit do I gain by controlling my emotions and being cooperative?"

My subjective/intuitive sense about our realtionship and what I want

Greek word for Love	Score my love towards my partner
EROS (Erotic Sexual Love, usually physical; arousal, often unconnected to personality)	LEAST ——————→ (1) ———————— MOST
PHILIA (Acceptance of & love for the other person as a human being)	————————————→ (4) ——
AGAPE (A conscious contract or commitment to the other)	⊢————————————⊣
STORGE (Unconditional, instinctual love, like the love for one's children)	⊢————————————⊣
LUDUS (Playful love, warm & friendly teasing & flirting; fun and humour)	————————————→ (2) ⊣
PRAGMA (The love that comes with time; comfortable with the other; contentment)	⊢————————————⊣
PHILAUTIA (Love & respect for self, glad to be you & comfortable in your skin, confident)	——————————→ (3) ——

Figure 26: Reflective view of relationship from Casandra's perspective

Example relationship chart from Michael's perspective

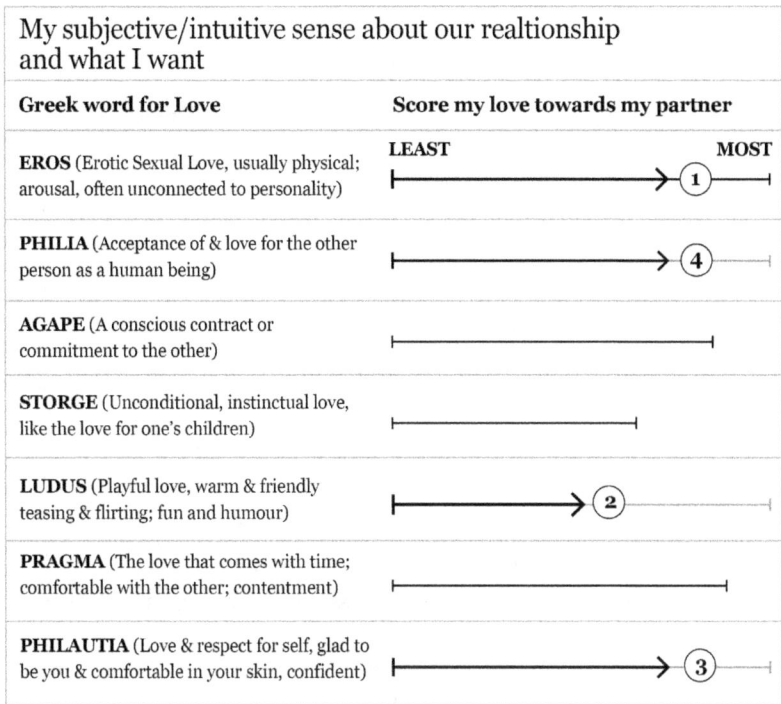

My subjective/intuitive sense about our realtionship and what I want	
Greek word for Love	**Score my love towards my partner**
EROS (Erotic Sexual Love, usually physical; arousal, often unconnected to personality)	LEAST ⟶ (1) MOST
PHILIA (Acceptance of & love for the other person as a human being)	⟶ (4)
AGAPE (A conscious contract or commitment to the other)	
STORGE (Unconditional, instinctual love, like the love for one's children)	
LUDUS (Playful love, warm & friendly teasing & flirting; fun and humour)	⟶ (2)
PRAGMA (The love that comes with time; comfortable with the other; contentment)	
PHILAUTIA (Love & respect for self, glad to be you & comfortable in your skin, confident)	⟶ (3)

Figure 27: Reflective view of relationship from Michael's perspective

The Analysis stage

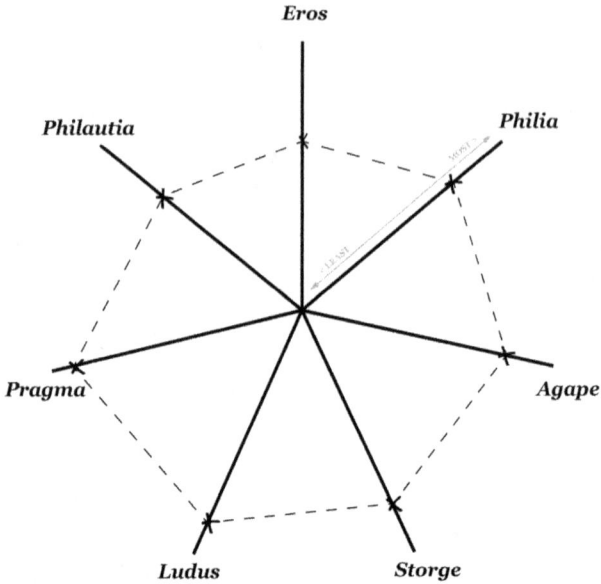

Figure 28: Analysis using Cassandra's examples

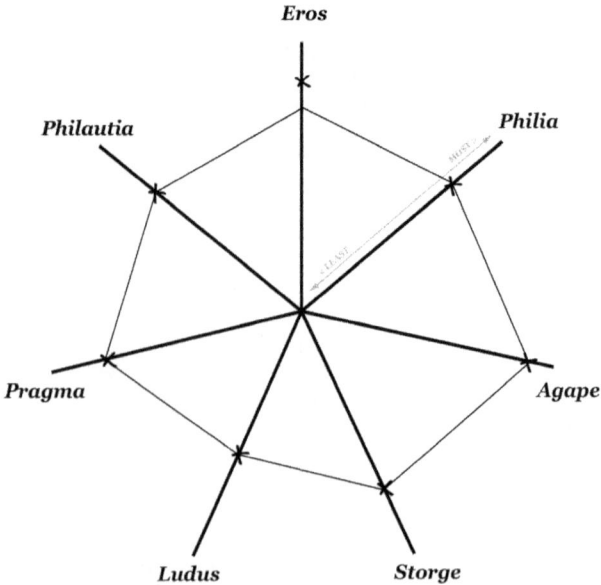

Figure 29: Analysis using Michael's examples

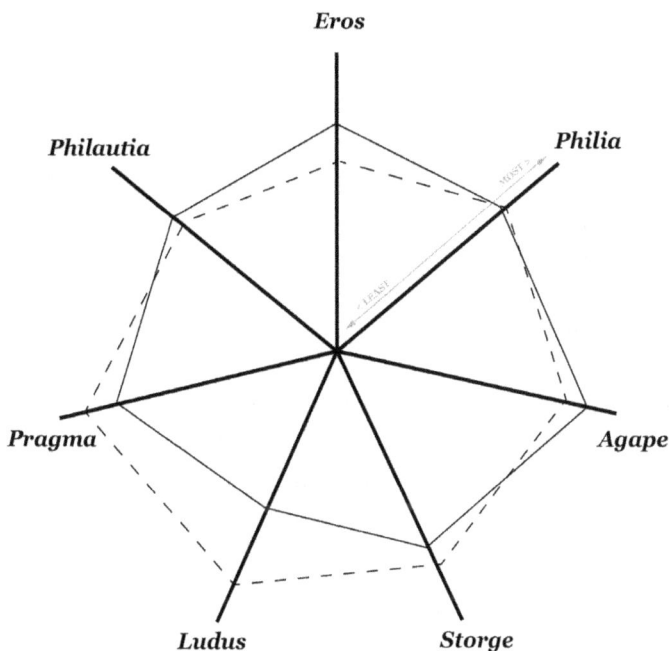

Figure 30: Spider graph displaying comparison between Michael's and Cassandra's perspectives. The dotted line represents Cassandra, and the solid line represents Michael.

It becomes apparent for this couple that they are broadly in agreement with the areas of their relationship where they think there is room for development. It is also clear that both are committed to the relationship and each other, (agreement on *philia, agape*) and that as they are comfortable and settled together *(pragma)* they are likely to have the goodwill to work this out together. They both see room to manoeuvre on the *eros* scale, however Mike is less concerned about this than Cassandra. They also both score this as their highest priority, though for Cassandra it seems more of an issue than for Mike. Given their energy for commitment and staying together it is likely that they will negotiate a satisfactory outcome. They have also made similar disclosures on *the ludus* scale. *Eros* and *ludus* together gives them fertile ground to plow. No pun intended, (my little bit of ludus apparent there) 😊. Where *eros* and *ludus* are both scored as areas for growth, this is an encouraging sign as the two areas complement each other, fitting together well.

As the scales are not measurements, but rather indicators of areas in the relationship where their relationship will benefit from attention, the objective is not to bring each scale to the maximum. Rather, the spider diagram offers them a way to clarify each individual need. On *eros* and *ludus* for example, there is no universal truth about how much fun or sex a couple should have. The relationship is the area for the service to be carried out, much as a Ministry of Transport (MOT) test on a car shows what safety concerns exist and need attention to keep the vehicle in a roadworthy condition. The relationship in this example is still fit for purpose. However, if the areas where the couple are not experiencing mutual satisfaction remain unaddressed, they may experience destructive forces at work between them. Talking about their needs openly, with goodwill and the explicit willingness to meet each other's needs, will help them demonstrate love and keep the relationship on track. Having a problem is not the problem, the difficulty comes from not being emotionally assertive and talking about needs openly.

Why had they avoided doing this? Their discovery:

As they begin to open discussion on these two areas, sex and fun, they uncover underlying tensions that reveal why they have been avoiding intimacy. At the root is that neither one pays sufficient attention to their individual needs. Rather than speaking openly and cooperatively about their anger, they cover their anger up with irritation. Irritation is inappropriately expressed, persistent, low-grade anger. This unexpressed emotion shows in their acts of vengeance in disrupting the order each likes. Therefore, whilst they initially thought that their priority was sex and fun, their actual priority needs to be to gain in self-awareness and love of self, *philautia*, so they liberate themselves to talk openly about what is important to them, even if it seems insignificant. By attending to these little things, they allow energy to return to the things they find important. There is a lovely line in the bible, "It is the little foxes that spoil the vines."[40]

It is important to see your relationships as the invisible third party and to make servicing it a priority. Neglecting the dynamic of a relationship is as bad as neglecting each other. Whilst *pragma* can be a comforting and satisfying form of love, it can also be the

40. From the Old Testament, Song of Solomon 2:15

cause of decay. Sitting together in a cozy room is very comforting and endears us to each other and to our home, however, the fire, the house and the contents still must be kept in good order. Unattended fires, i.e. our relationships, can go out and the room is no longer comfortable. Remember to maintain your relationships. This metaphor tells us that often it is the small things, often overlooked, that can lead to disruption and damage. This is especially the case in relationship. When we do not respect ourselves sufficiently to be open about small irritations, we can build up a head of steam that leads to blowing our tops. Yet it seems so easy to swallow our emotions and not bring them up, because we think this will 'only lead to trouble'.

Step #1 – The analysis begins counter-intuitively by a joyful discussion of the areas where there is a good fit. In the case above, these areas are, *agape and philia.* We start here because in conflict resolution it is always best to begin with the areas of mutual agreement and benefit. By celebrating how, where, and why we are connected, we build a sound argument for finding solutions to reduce the areas of conflict. It is important not to gloss over this stage; rather, to spend time both celebrating the satisfaction these areas provide in our relationship and developing our skills in asking for more of what we like and want. (Practising the mutually beneficial aspects of *philautia*) Also, talking about things that many find difficult to speak about, such as our fantasies and desires, is how we can prepare ourselves for discussing our unmet needs in the other areas of our relationship. This first step is aimed at finding the answer to the question, "Why are we having these discussions?" The answer to this question needs to be, "In order to deepen and strengthen our relationship. It is to heighten our awareness of where and how we can put more energy into maintaining the relationship." Maintenance is an ongoing task in any healthy relationship. If we neglect our house, the fabric begins to crumble, and the same is true of all our relationships.

Step #2 – Do not begin this step if you are tired, stressed or have recently had an argument. It requires both parties to remain respectful and empathic. When your partner is speaking, listen, do not interrupt, and do not ask questions. It is a time of mutual exploration and discovery. The step begins time for each to share their feelings about the gap in their impression of the relationship. In the case of Michael and Cassandra, it is in the three areas of *eros, ludus* and *philautia.*

This discussion is best focused on "I feel" openings. Speak about yourself, what you need and what you may need to do differently. Avoid finger pointing "you are" or "you do" statements and abandon hope that all will be OK if only the other person will change. The only thing each of us has power over is ourselves, how we manage our feelings and our behaviour, so look for information on how you can help each other get needs met.

In the case of Michael and Cassandra, I suggest that the first discussion would be to share about self-love, *philautia.* Gaining awareness of how they each may unconsciously sabotage themselves by not being open about their needs, etc., is likely to be the basis for any avoidance of intimacy. Whenever we do not love and value ourselves, we will tend to show behaviours that are not authentic. It is important here to keep it in mind that defensiveness is very common and not a sign of a lack of goodwill. They have the information that they have goodwill towards each other because they both have a vision of remaining together, the areas of agreement, the common ground, are where goodwill is plentiful. Sharing their areas of vulnerability will offer a means to develop growing empathy. Misusing knowledge gained in this exercise as a form of manipulation is a breach of trust and will be extremely counter-productive. At the end of the exchange, share recognition, support, and affection. Do this for each area where growth would be good for the relationship.

The object of the exercise is not to force the other to change. Rather, it is to seek ways where each can offer workable compromise. No one can tell you what that will look like; it is something for both partners to be imaginative, creative, flexible, and generous about. If you find it difficult to conduct this exercise as a couple, this may be the time for you to go to a skilled professional and ask for help. In that case, show them the work you have done and ask them to facilitate you completing it.

Exercise: A rough guide to the relationship

A blank score chart for feelings of **love towards your partner**

Greek word for Love	**Score my love towards my partner**
EROS (Erotic Sexual Love, usually physical; arousal, often unconnected to personality)	**LEAST** ——————————— **MOST**
PHILIA (Acceptance of & love for the other person as a human being)	———————————
AGAPE (A conscious contract or commitment to the other)	———————————
STORGE (Unconditional, instinctual love, like the love for one's children)	———————————
LUDUS (Playful love, warm & friendly teasing & flirting; fun and humour)	———————————
PRAGMA (The love that comes with time; comfortable with the other; contentment)	———————————
PHILAUTIA (Love & respect for self, glad to be you & comfortable in your skin, confident)	———————————

Figure 31: A blank score chart for feelings of love towards your partner

A blank score chart for feelings of **love in your relationship**

Greek word for Love	Score my love towards my partner
	LEAST MOST
EROS (Erotic Sexual Love, usually physical; arousal, often unconnected to personality)	⊢————————————————————————⊣
PHILIA (Acceptance of & love for the other person as a human being)	⊢————————————————————————⊣
AGAPE (A conscious contract or commitment to the other)	⊢————————————————————————⊣
STORGE (Unconditional, instinctual love, like the love for one's children)	⊢————————————————————————⊣
LUDUS (Playful love, warm & friendly teasing & flirting; fun and humour)	⊢————————————————————————⊣
PRAGMA (The love that comes with time; comfortable with the other; contentment)	⊢————————————————————————⊣
PHILAUTIA (Love & respect for self, glad to be you & comfortable in your skin, confident)	⊢————————————————————————⊣

Figure 32: A blank score chart for feelings of love in your relationship

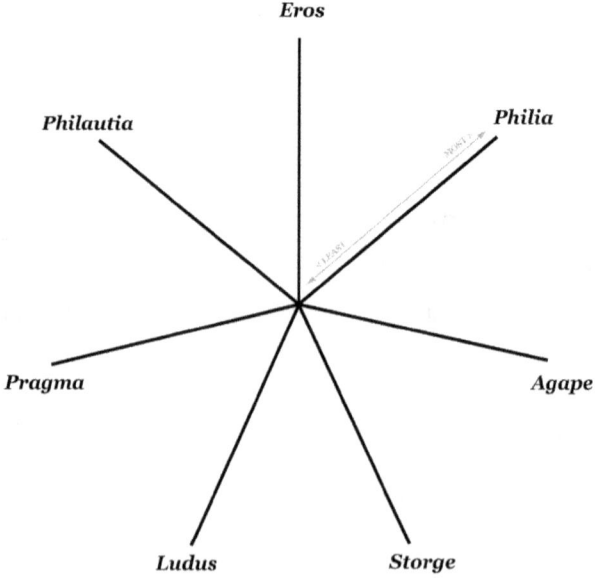

Figure 33: Blank spider diagram for you to complete your results

Note on the *storge* scale: it would be unhealthy to love our life partner unconditionally in the way we love our children. Love between adults is at its best when bounded by clear contracts and agreements about how the relationship will work. We need a vision for the relationship, shared plans, common goals, etc. To achieve this, we need to be thinking about these things before we get fully into commitment. When we do not do this, things we had taken for granted may be found to contain personal differences, ambitions, and dreams. Where there are agreements and contracts, there are usually consequences for breaking the agreements. A partner may become an ex-partner, our children are always our children.

CHAPTER 11

Pick and Mix Emotions (or Compound Emotions)

When we face situations where more than one emotion is activated due to multifaceted issues, we may experience compound emotions or a mix of emotions present at the same time. When this occurs, as it frequently does, we give the blended emotion a name, such as jealousy or envy, much in the same way we name blends of primary colours. However, this may lead to problems in relationships, as we assume the other person will know what our problems are and what we want. Sadly, this is frequently not the case as how we identify these emotions may differ depending upon our family of origin, cultural and religious influences, etc.

Simply naming the compound can lead to frustration for both parties because we expect the other to decode them the same way as we do. For example, you may experience jealousy or envy. These compound emotions are real enough, but do not convey to the other person why we feel that way or what we need to help us find peace of mind. Frequently, we are not even aware of the primary emotions and interpersonal needs we have. Even telling the other we feel jealous is left out of the process and we simply act out based upon our feelings. Often, in the case of jealousy, we show anger and blame the other for making us feel bad. In real terms, no one can make us feel anything; we simply feel what we feel as a reaction to changes in the environment. Although *prima facie* it looks like the other made us feel, they have not. It can be demonstrated that there is no direct cause and effect between what one person does and how the other feels. In response to any behaviour, one may feel angry while others feel afraid or sad.

By failing to detect our primary emotions, and share them with the intent to problem solve, we are unconsciously inviting the other to rescue us. They see clearly there is a problem, try to guess what it is and then attempt to fix it. In such cases, it is helpful to identify the primary emotions, name the problem we have for each one and ask for our need to be met directly, without asking the other to guess. Expressing or acting out on jealousy, we are already entering drama. The drama will involve experiencing the jealousy. It is based upon comparing ourselves to the person or object we are jealous of. Then we tell ourselves, "They are better than me." Or I am somehow sub-standard, or my life partner does not think I am good enough and soon will abandon me for a better model, etc. Such evaluations can lead to experiencing shame, blocked anxiety and showing anger to cover our other emotions.

Envy is an emotional manifestation of shame and therefore has a strong component of fear attached to it. Envy is directed at others, wanting what they have. Jealousy involves fear of loss, i.e., loss of attachment, affection, or security. Frequently, it is also a projection. We imagine our loved one feeling attraction to another because we also experience attractions towards others. There is no harm in experiencing attraction. It is nature's way of ensuring we procreate. However, we can experience attraction and choose to do nothing about it. Being tempted is not a sin; the sin is in acting upon the temptation. When we are aware of our own moments of temptation, we experience guilt and project this onto the other, making them the guilty party. In acting out our jealousy, we unconsciously offer them an invitation to respond by doing what we most fear. It can be a self-fulfilling prophecy. This links jealousy with anticipatory loss, and a combination of fear and sadness with lashings of anger. Both jealousy and envy involve comparisons and contrasts.

Whilst jealousy and envy bring unproductive conflict in our lives and relationships, there is some good news. Both compound emotions demonstrate that underpinning them is a sense of value for the relationship. Sadly, acting out on them offers the partner just the opposite.

What these feelings reveal:

- Jealousy is an indicator that the jealous person cares.
- It also indicates they probably have issues with insecure attachment. It is therefore an important marker for the need

for some personal growth and development. With goodwill, the issues of attachment and fear of abandonment can be dealt with.

- One cannot deal with jealousy using denial, e.g., saying, "I was not looking at that man/woman." You probably were looking, and so what? By denying the reality, you suggest you cannot be trusted. Instead, we could say, "Yes, I was looking, and that is all. I am happy being with you." It is not likely to be received well, because it avoids entering the drama as a rescuer.
- The jealous person is the only one who can solve the issue, often through therapy. With all the goodwill in the world, there is little one can do to placate the jealous person.
- Jealousy can be, and frequently is, a destroyer of relationship. It has the effect of draining the joy of relationship. It denies agape. The jealous person does not demonstrate philia and replaces this with mistrust and dislike.

The way forward is to learn how to analyse or break down our compound emotions into the primary emotional component parts. This is not as difficult as it may sound. First, we must create time and space for ourselves to achieve this.

Step #1 – Tell the other person you are aware you are in a bad place emotionally and need time to clarify what this is about. Reassure them you know you are confusing yourself about something and that it is probably not about something they have done but some issue you need to fix.

Step #2 – Relax. There are many good relaxation CDs available. The better ones are based upon square breathing and yoga meditation practices. Mindfulness is also useful for this.

Step #3 – Listen to your body. Your bodily sensations will help inform you of your primary emotions and identifying them is a huge step towards finding resolution.

As a rule of thumb, anger is experienced in the muscles of the back, shoulders, and neck. It is also experienced in the gluteus maximus muscles, i.e., the cheeks of your bottom.

Step #4 – When you have identified the primary emotions, ask yourself what each emotion is telling you and what you need to do to meet your needs regarding each of these emotions.

Step #5 – Plan how you will share your emotions and needs with the other person in a respectful, cooperative way.

Step #6 – Go to them and contract to discuss the issue calmly. Advise them you are still learning how to do this and ask them to hang in there with you. Let them know you do not want to attack or blame them, and neither do you want to be rescued. Also, tell them that because you are learning how to be emotionally assertive and respectful towards them, you may at times return to your old process. At such times you may need to ask for timeout to regain your composure.[41]

Step #7 – Tell them you mostly want them to listen at first, and that then you would like to discuss your emotions calmly. Also, tell them you are willing and available to listen to their emotional responses without judgement. Then tell them your primary emotions one by one and what you need to be able to move forward productively.

---

41. If you take timeout, it is important to use it to cool off. Some tend to spend timeout ruminating about the things they are angry about. This has the effect of blowing on the embers of your anger and confirming you were correct to act aggressively. Rather timeout is to focus on all the things you like, appreciate, and love about the other. Remember the areas of agreement and avoid going over the content or detail of who said what to whom. By focusing on the positive it is easier to avoid demonising the other.

Step #8 – Have the discussion and remember how easy it will be at first to revert to the old way of doing things. Reinforce the importance of not getting into unproductive conflict and agree to focus on the process and not to get bogged down in the content. (Process is how you say things, i.e., tone of voice and body language, whilst content is the things that were said or done and who is responsible. Content is a trap to be avoided and process is often the key to picking the lock that we use to keep ourselves stuck.)

Step #9 – Each time you repeat this sequence, note how you did and what, if any, were the trigger points for you shifting back into the unproductive ways. Then create ways to catch yourself in the future and replace the old with the new.

Step #10 – The safety net is to agree with your partner's reviews of how you were both doing. Your partner cannot stop you from being jealous. However, they can support you in setting yourself free from these destructive behaviours. Another part of the safety net is to agree with your partner that if you find yourself stuck in developing new strategies, you will go into therapy. This can be couples' therapy or your own personal therapy.

If your relationship is important to you, it is worth taking the time and trouble to play your part in maintaining its health. Relationship management is a duty of care you have towards each other and the relationship. Relationships are a dance that requires both parties to be willing to enjoy together.

The Role of Boundaries in Human Relationships

In all our human relationships, it is very important to be aware of their nature and the key role respect for boundaries plays in the management and maintenance of healthy bonding. A relationship is a term drawn from mathematics. It describes how one part of an equation relates to the other side of the equation. When I analyse the nature of a relationship, for example, in couples' therapy, I look closely at how one party relates to the other. A relationship is described in this diagram below:

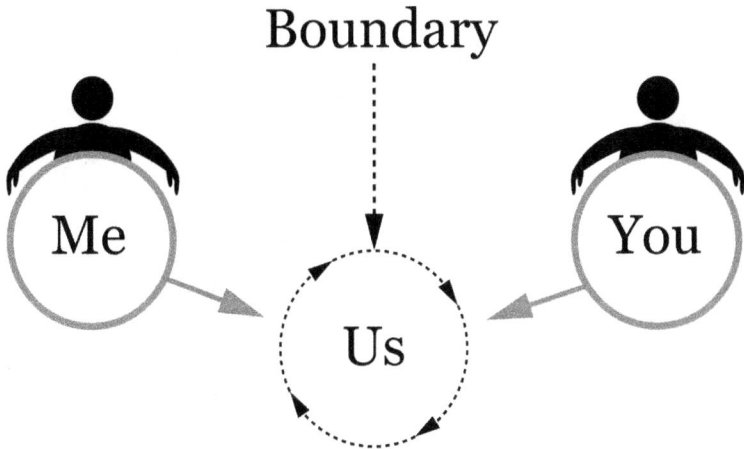

Figure 34: Schematic representation of a relationship.
The relationship is a combination of you and me.

Notice that when we talk about relationship, we are describing how two people interrelate. There is a boundary between the two people. The boundary clarifies that we are separate and different. The relationship is a combination of how the two interact. This produces the third person, us, or we. In other words, a relationship is an equation; I, plus you, equals us. I have never liked the term "my other half" as this suggests an unconscious belief that without the other person, we are somehow incomplete. For the best relationships, we need two whole people who each experience self-love and acceptance (*philautia*) to work together respectfully and cooperatively and form a partnership. There is you, there is me, and the partnership is us. One and one never makes one, except in higher mathematics. One plus one is two, but when we relate together with authenticity, one plus one makes three. Sometimes, one plus one (three) can become four, five six etc. when children are added to the equation. In a family with children, us becomes we. In a healthy family, each person must be aware of the interpersonal boundaries. Committed relationships, such as marriage, living together, etc., are at their best where the boundaries are clear and where there are explicit contracts about what the relationship will be like. Often, we drift into relationship without defining our hopes and needs for the future of the partnership. It is best to be explicit about these things from the outset. I know this does not sound very romantic; however, I see it as a basic essential for having clearly defined rules of engagement. When we are in conflict, we can go back to the contract and use it as a common ground to help resolve the conflict.

For example, when my wife and I became romantically involved, we had some conversations about what our visions for the relationship looked like. One of the important must haves for her was, "It is important to me I have a child." I thought for a moment, as I was approaching sixty and another child was not a part of my view of how my future would be. Having thought about it I replied, "I love children, although I am getting old, I am fine with what you want. So yes, let's build this into our vision." I must say that was one of my better decisions. It has been a source of great happiness to raise our son together and I am proud of him, just as I am of my other three children.

Relationship symbols

When I think of maintaining relationships, I use symbols to help me define the actual quality of the relationship. The symbols I use are basic mathematical indicators of the relationship of two sides of an equation. Any relationship can be displayed using these symbols.

Table 7: Relationship symbols

	Self	Symbol	Other
Healthy	I	=	you
More or less healthy	I	=	you
Unhealthy	I	<	you
Unhealthy	I	>	you
No relationship	I	≠	you

Note: the symbol defines how the relationship works in terms of the dimensions of respect and power.

- Healthy: We each attribute the other as having equal value. This does not mean we are the same, but we are different from the other, yet of equal value. This is a healthy, respectful partnership.
- More or less healthy: There are areas where there are minor inequalities, but they are not significant enough to put an undue strain on the relationship. We can live with this and over time may iron out the discrepancies, especially where there is goodwill.
- I am not as valuable or important as you: I devalue myself. This can have damaging long-term effects that will put a strain upon the relationship and is fundamentally unhealthy. I disrespect myself. Therefore, outside of my awareness, I disrespect the other. I do not believe they are open for equality. By depreciating myself, I act as a victim. This is also unhealthy for the relationship.
- I am more important or of more value than you: I over value myself and devalue the other. This will also place a strain upon the relationship. By overestimating my importance,

I act disrespectfully to the other and am likely to act as the persecutor. This is also unhealthy for the relationship.

- There is no relationship: This is often the outcome achieved when living in the two unhealthy states. After prolonged, unproductive conflict, relationships struggle and one or the other or both want out.

CHAPTER 12

Emotions and Psychological Energy in Work and Private Life

The Year of the COVID-19 Invasion

A pandemic began to rage across the planet in 2020 and is still wreaking havoc at the time of writing. The impact upon humanity has been immense. Life has changed and everyone has been impacted emotionally, economically and socially, and both work and home life are almost unrecognisable. My focus here is on the emotional and psychological problems the social changes have had upon our relationships, stability, and mental welfare.

Studies of human behaviour and psychological stability have demonstrated the importance of social engagement. Eric Berne, the founder of the Transactional Analysis (TA) school of psychotherapy, coined the term strokes to illustrate a process of how we exchange psychological energy in our social interactions. Berne based his concept upon the research of Rene Spitz. Spitz observed very small babies raised in a variety of children's homes and found that where the babies had reduced contact with their caretakers, the incidence of infant mortality was higher. In homes where the babies received more physical contact, the survival rate was significantly higher. He called the lack of physical contact social or maternal deprivation and concluded that socialisation was an important part of child development. In short, deprived of physical contact, babies are more likely to die than are children who have a high level of social contact. Eric Berne noted that even negative physical attention, i.e., being slapped, was preferable to total denial of contact. He coined the terms positive stroking and negative stroking and recorded that in childhood we establish a pattern of expected positive and negative strokes we require for survival. He proposed that we spend much of our lives collecting our quota of strokes and if deprived of positive strokes, we unconsciously seek out negative strokes to maintain sufficient levels of psychological energy. In adulthood, much of our strokes are acquired through social intercourse rather than physical contact, though physical contact remains an important source of strokes. As infants, other people frequently touched us. The contact with our skin or stroking produced stimuli for our central nervous system and assisted in the development of our brain. Without these stimuli, babies fail to flourish despite being given adequate food and warmth.

Spitz's studies of children brought up in children's homes show that though the subjects of his studies were fed, kept clean and warm, they were still more prone to physical and emotional difficulties than children brought up by their natural mothers. Indeed, many of them did not make it. He concluded the children were at risk in the homes where stimulation was low, especially physical contact.

Eric Berne described our need for stimuli as stimulus hunger. As we grow older, the amount of physical contact exchanged with others diminishes, although our need for stimuli does not. The stimulus that grown people require is both physical and emotional. Berne coined the expression stroke[42] to denote the stimuli we require and noted that we gain our strokes by largely substituting physical contact for recognition from others. This recognition may be given in the form of smiles, waves, compliments, and so on. Berne used the term recognition hunger to describe this need for social intercourse with others. Strokes may be verbal or non-verbal, positive, or negative, conditional or unconditional. Verbal strokes range from single exchanges, for example, "hello", to lengthy conversations. Positive and negative strokes are in the content, i.e., "I love you" or "I hate you." Conditional or unconditional strokes are differentiated by strokes for being (unconditional) to strokes for doing (conditional). Therefore, "I love you" is an unconditional positive stroke and "I liked the last report you submitted" is a

---

42. The term is a metaphor for gaining stimuli, much in the way we do when we stroke a dog or cat. When our skin is stimulated, we experience a release of positive neuropeptides like endorphin. Receiving verbal recognition has a similar effect.

conditional positive stroke. As children, we knew that the absence of strokes was unhealthy, and we would rather receive negative strokes than no strokes at all. As a result, if we needed strokes and could not get positive ones, we learned to seek negative strokes.

Stroking can reinforce behaviour, and this is important to bear in mind as a manager. If you give more negative strokes than positive strokes, you may contribute to increased stress in your department. You may recall people who have repeated their negative behaviour to the point of dismissal from their posts. Perhaps these were people who had come to expect negative strokes rather than positive and went looking for them. In very real terms, negative stroking reinforces negative behaviour. In other words, what we stroke is what we are likely to get.

Take a few minutes to complete the stroking profile in figure 35 below. If you wish to make changes, use it to decide how you will bring the changes about.

Positive strokes

	Give	Take	Ask for	Refuse to give
Always				
Very frequently				
Frequently				
Often				
Seldom				
Never				
	Give	Take	Ask for	Refuse to give
Never				
Seldom				
Often				
Frequently				
Very frequently				
Always				

Negative strokes

Figure 35: Personal stroking profile

Completing your regular pattern of giving and receiving strokes will facilitate a means to examine how the pandemic has altered your regular stroke routines. A vast majority of people will discover a reduction in daily receipt of positive strokes and an increase of negative. This pattern change is damaging to our psychological stability. At the time of writing, data shows a nationwide increase in the UK in the rate of infant deaths of nineteen per cent and of infant injuries by over twenty per cent. This phenomenon has been labelled a toxic lockdown or COVID pressure cooker. It is thought that the cause is due to the stress of financial problems, poverty, housing conditions and many other social ills. However, in real terms, the pandemic has not significantly increased these social issues. I believe the major cause is to be found in the reduction of social contact. Working from home means we meet fewer people. We spend a lot of time in Zoom meetings, on the telephone or just watching TV and gaming. The net result is a massive change in the pattern of our stroking.

As well as figures for infant mortality and harm rising, so has the incidence of domestic violence. It is also evident that despite the clear information available regarding the risk of infection due to social contact, thousands of people go out and congregate in groups. Although there were tough fines during 2020 and 2021 for being caught breaking lockdown regulations, people still went out and met, ignoring even the basic social distancing rules.

I also attribute this to greatly reduced levels of stroking, leading to an increase in behaviours seeking negative attention. This is not to say that people who are victims of violence have asked for it. Rather, it is a call for us as a society to recognise the damaging impact that altering stroke availability can have on human behaviour. Footballers still cling together in groups to celebrate a goal. In Leeds, thousands of young people congregated in a park to play snowballing, running into each other, hugging and generally having very close contact. Why? To gather strokes.

From this we can extrapolate the importance of relationship, socialising and friendships, i.e., the proximity of other people. We can also see the role of emotional assertiveness in the service of our need for the exchange of strokes. Fore-play provides low-level stroking, fair-play provides high-level positive stroking and foul-play is a source of intense negative strokes.

Another study that equates to the role of stroking in organisational situations is H. B. Hurlock's research to determine the effects of recognition on motivation and performance. In his experiment, four groups were asked to perform identical production assembly tasks and their output was recorded in terms of numbers of accurately assembled units. Group A were given feedback on their positive achievements and mistakes were ignored. Group B were given feedback on their reject rate and their achievements were ignored. Group C observed the feedback process for the first two groups, and was given no feedback at all. Group D was segregated, not even able to see what the other groups were doing and given no feedback. The results are demonstrated in figure 36 below.

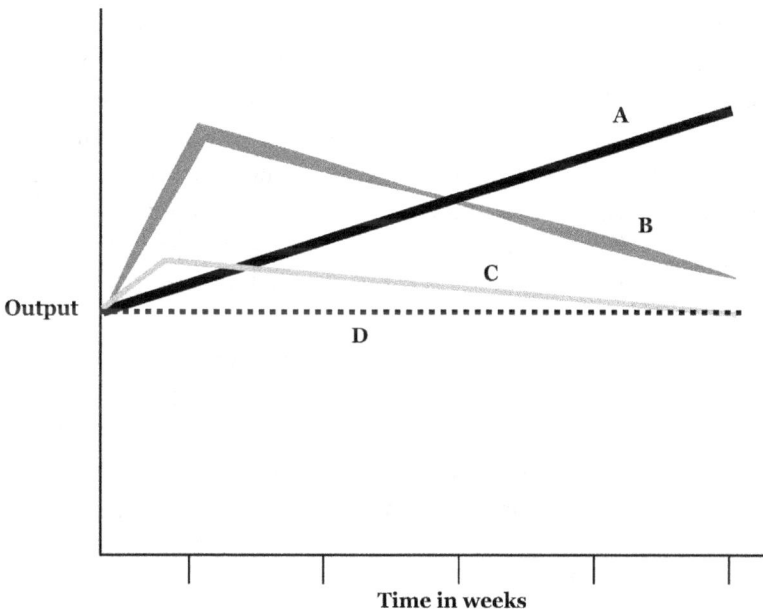

Figure 36: Stroking and motivation graph. From H. B. Hurlock: The effects of recognition on motivation and performance.

From the graph, it is clear the impact positive recognition has on motivation and performance. Some people conclude from this study that the best approach is to first provide high levels of negative recognition, followed by sustained positive recognition. However, this is an erroneous conclusion. It can take a lot more positive recognition to overcome the damaging effects of negative recognition. It is more important to provide regular, sustained, and honest positive recognition. To paraphrase Blanchard, another researcher: "A good manager catches someone doing something right."

Positive strokes are vital for our health and self-esteem and people who receive few positive strokes may actively seek negative strokes as an alternative. But if we focus on people's positive attributes and stroke them for what we appreciate them for, we will encourage more of this positive behaviour. Being positively charged is energising and motivating. Where there is poor performance, we need to be sensitive about how we deliver the feedback. Information about negative attributes can be given in a way that invites the recipient to develop to their full potential. When giving negative feedback, remember, where possible, to include positive strokes and encouragement. Make it clear you believe the individual can reach the required standard and you are available to offer appropriate levels of support and encouragement. Give your criticism clearly, stating precisely what it is you want to change. Avoid making personal comments; criticise the output and not the individual's character.

The pandemic has seriously altered the patterns of social contact and available strokes. Therefore, we need to find ways and means to redress the balance to protect the mental health and quality of the social contact between all our citizens. Failure to take steps to redress this imbalance can have a serious, long-term, negative impact upon society. At the time of reading, this aspect of the pandemic has yet to be widely recognised.

Couples

Falling in love is easy. I've done it hundreds of times! *Emophilia* is the name for frequently and easily falling in love. In most cases, this is love from the Greek word *eros*. There is nothing wrong with *eros* love, and it is probably the most common thing that attracts us into long-term relationship. However, *eros* alone will not sustain a relationship for any length of time. For that, we need to open the way for the other forms of love. Not much is said about how to achieve this and sadly, the result is many relationships end in separation or, even if those involved do not separate, without forging deep and meaningful bonds of attachment and these relationships may be unsatisfying for those who remain in them.

Emophilia is a form of romantic love and, as well as being based upon physical sexual attraction, it frequently has a psychological component called transference.[43] Transference is basically triggered when there is something about the object of desire that preconsciously or unconsciously reminds us of an important figure from our past. When this phenomenon occurs, it is as if we place a cinema screen in front of the other and then project images of the person from the past onto the screen. These can be both negative and/or positive images, and in the case of falling into erotic love, the transference will usually start as positive.

When we fall in love, there is a period when it seems like the two of you are in a bubble, as if you are shielded from the world and reality. During those heady days, it seems the object of our love is perfect and can do no wrong. You almost merge as one entity. This is reminiscent of both experiencing a form of regression back to our early days of child development. In a healthy relationship, this slowly gives way to reality, where you do notice the things you don't like, but the things you do vastly outweigh the things you don't. You are now beginning to shift towards feeling free to be yourself and comfortable with the other. At its best this is how a healthy adult relationship reaches a position where each is of equal value and the relationship deepens and strengthens. Later we will examine this process from a psychological perspective when we discuss development using Kaplan's model in Chapter 13. As well as attachments, the couple develops healthy boundaries each are aware of through open and intimate discussion. Emotional assertiveness skills are

---

43. For those interested in transference and relationships, the following books are informative: Ellyn Bader and Peter Pearson, *In Quest of The Mythical Mate*; Harville Hendrix, *Getting The Love You Want*; and Harville Hendrix, *Keeping The Love You Find*.

the tools we use to achieve this. As we show each other respect, we can develop the relationship based upon equality. It is a partnership to which each contributes their diverse gifts and abilities, and neither one experiences any threat as a result. We make explicit contracts, and we discuss the collective vision of the relationship. This is not a romantic fantasy, but an exchange between mature and stable individuals. We accept each other for who we are, and love is based upon *philia*. We show commitment and our love has *agape*. Eventually we become comfortable with each other, and we have *pragma*. We continue to share *eros* and playful flirting, which is *ludus*. All of this is based upon each having a healthy love of self, *philautia*. Unless we truly love ourselves, we cannot truly love another.

The relationships that prove most satisfying are those where we can be open, vulnerable, honest, and respectful of one another. Whilst it may appear counterintuitive, your anger, expressed respectfully, without an attack of blame, or experiencing being the victim, is central to this. Remember, if you cannot be truly angry, you will find it extremely difficult to be happy. Therefore, learning how to be angry in a healthy way is pivotal to having a sound relationship. In a healthy relationship, all authentic emotions are shared and worked through. Equally, all non-authentic, unhealthy expressions of emotion are to be avoided.

Rob and Priya's Story

Rob and Priya had been married for twenty-five years and had hardly a bad word pass between them. They had developed many rituals over the years, one of which was their breakfast habit. As a part of their morning meal, they shared a bread roll, neither wanting a whole roll for themselves. Each morning, Priya would cut the roll in half, give the crusty half to her husband, and take the soft bottom half for herself. For their twenty-fifth anniversary, they decided to return to the hotel where they had stayed on their honeymoon. In the morning, they arrived at their table to find one bread roll each on their side plates. They both cut the roll in half. He proceeded to spread butter on the soft bottom half and she the top crusty half. They paused, exchanged glances and exclaimed,

"But I thought you preferred the other half!" They had a lightbulb moment. Discussing this, they came to understand that for twenty-five years, they had each been eating the half they did not really want. At first glance, their willingness to make this sacrifice for the other could be seen as touching. However, the reverse of this coin is that they could have been open with each other and found workable compromises, so each got what they wanted.

It is OK to speak about such things and to talk it out, and sorting it out is a great way to commit more deeply. This is a relatively simple and harmless behaviour, although it is likely to be replayed in many scenarios in such relationships.

Families and Childcare

In this section, I want to share a few words about my experience of how not to be a healthy parent. My first son was born when I was twenty-two and in the Royal Navy. My wife was the same age and neither of us had any experience or knowledge of taking care of a small child. When he was born, we were both excited and loved our small son, as do most parents. There is no doubt that he was wanted and welcome in our family. However, we lacked experience and made many mistakes. When I look back on this time, I can clearly see the areas where we did not provide our child with the parental support he needed. Our first problem, that led to much anxiety on our part and a lot of distress to him, was around feeding. After several days of attempting to breastfeed him, my wife was advised to put him on compound powdered milk. Each time we fed him, he projectile vomited and cried persistently. We did not know why or what to do. We tried different formulas, but none seemed to suit him. The district nurse/health visitor also did not seem to know what was wrong and told us to persevere. We took him to the GP, who also advised us just to persist. We did as we were told and we asked our friends who had older children. They were also baffled. After what seemed a long time, we discovered he was lactose intolerant. However, he had a tougher time than us. My wife and I were very afraid he may die. We did all we could, but he must have experienced our anxiety as we held him, attempting to get him to swallow something his body wanted to reject.

Both my wife and I had been raised in the tough love school of our parents. Rigid time routines had been used on us regarding feeding, being left to cry in the pram at the end of the garden, and so on. Therefore, we thought this was good parenting and followed suit. Indeed, back then, many of the user manuals gave the same advice about such things as the importance of getting them into a feeding routine, or not picking them up each time they cry as you will spoil them. Since my training as a psychotherapist, I now know much of what I had been advised to do back then was not helpful to my child. I think it was also not helpful to us either, and we all missed out on a lot of the bonding and play we could have shared.

Later, we experienced a Christian conversion, and this was also not good news for my son, who was by now in school. The teaching in our church was based on the principle of sparing the rod and spoiling the child. So, our son had to deal with the same form of harsh parenting as had been my lot. The basic premise that children need clear boundaries is a good one. However, boundaries can be established, managed, and reinforced with love and kindness. Children do not need the heavy prejudicial parenting dealt out in Victorian times. Thankfully, I have found a way to rationalise my beliefs. I no longer follow blindly what religious teachers and preachers say and instead use my capacity to think clearly and take responsibility for myself. What I have learned through this is tolerance and understanding of parents who do not know how best to raise their children. I believe that most parents love their children, want the best for them and would fight a lion to protect them. However, we can only give what we have. Having had a harsh parenting myself, I did not have sufficient awareness to know my skills were sadly lacking.

My other children were more fortunate as they had an older, more stable father who also knew about child development needs and healthy parenting. My main takeaway from these experiences is that our societies need to do more to support and guide new parents. I would recommend that a knowledge of child developmental stages and what each stage demands from the parent be taught in schools. Parenting skills are not innate, we must learn them. It is often by raising one child that the ones that follow get a better deal. Let us prepare our parents to raise emotionally assertive children for the future. The happy ending is that my eldest son has developed in his own way. He has children of his own and cares for them. He has the courage to be a self-employed entertainer and I am proud of how he has played the cards that life has dealt him.

I am proud of all my four children and love them very much. I am also proud to be a grandfather to eight boys and a great grandfather to two girls. I love that these days my children will ask for some tips about being a parent, and sometimes even how to cook something. My family is a blessing.

The Terrible Twos and Teenagers

There is a period in child development often labelled the terrible twos. This is a time many parents feel like tearing their hair out in frustration. It begins around the age of two and lasts for about twelve to eighteen months. You will know when this period is beginning when your little one first gets the hang of saying "no." Other expressions common to this age are "why?" and "me do it." As you try to put on their second shoe, the first one is kicked off. If you have been there, I am sure you will have many other examples. What is this all about? It is the time when the child is attempting to discover what it is responsible for, what decisions it can make for itself, and what is not negotiable. I discovered that when there is resistance, it is futile to oppose it. This will heighten the conflict. Rather, we need to gain skills in distraction, and meet unwanted behaviour with playful confrontation as opposed to rigidity. The bottom line is for them to figure out what can they have the power to decide upon and where your boundaries lie. Indeed, boundaries are the issue.

My youngest daughter had always been a cuddly child. She loved to jump on my lap and sit with me. One fine day, she came to the door of my office, and I said, "Hi Suzie, come and sit on my lap." She placed her hands on her hips, looked me in the eye and said firmly, "No." I said, "That's OK, you don't have to if you don't want to." She then giggled, ran to me, and climbed up onto my lap. She had discovered she had control of if she had contact or not. This is very important for learning.

On other occasions, I would ask her to come to me, if, for example, she had done something she knew not to do. If then she refused, I would repeat firmly and gently, "Suzie, come here." She would look sulky and make one small step towards me. I repeated the instruction, and she again made a small move. I would repeat this and add, "Will you come all the way towards me?" Eventually, she did as she was asked. She learned there are times Dad really means it.

When she had her first son and he hit the terrible twos, she called me and asked how to manage her son when he did these things. I asked her to remember what I had done with her, that is to be firm, non-confrontational, playful where possible and, above all, consistent and persistent. She remembered and recognised the importance of allowing behaviour that the child can take responsibility for and to be clear about boundaries when necessary.

These difficult behaviours are replayed again around puberty. The common expression flagging this period up is, "It's not fair." I understand these rebellious behaviours are about the transition from childhood to adulthood. They seem to need an authority figure to struggle against. The key to managing this period is to pick your battles with care. Remember, their battle cry is, "You can't make me." I therefore gave my children little battles about things that were of little or no importance to me and avoided mentioning things that were important to me. For example, I would complain bitterly about piercings, strange hair colourings and so on. I would never tell them, don't take drugs, don't smoke, don't get pregnant, etc. Being oppositional over important things is an invitation into rebellion, and they are right, we can't make them unless we chaperone them 24/7. The outcome was that they did none of the things I did not want them to do and most of the things I was not really worried about. They were able to rebel safely.

At Work

In the workplace, it is as important to develop interpersonal skills as it is to acquire technical skills. Working together in teams, or connecting with our customers, we achieve better results when we establish healthy, cooperative relationships. I recall hearing a consultant say to a training group, "You don't come to work to make friends, but to make things." I believe that this comment totally misses the point; when we make friends, we are more efficient and effective. Whilst this takes energy, the investment pays off when our teams become synergistic.

Respectful Attitude Towards Self and Others

Regarding respect for others and self, there is no difference in either the home or the work setting, and mutual respect is always the starting place. Self-awareness and sharing of authentic emotions are the keys to building trust in any relationship. The more we share, the more we know the other and the more we cement our interpersonal bonds. By using our authentic emotions as opposed to phony cover-up feelings, we are in the right place to begin any win-win negotiation.

Self-Awareness

Self-awareness is having a clear perception of yourself, including your strengths, weaknesses, thoughts, beliefs, motivation, and emotions. It allows you to understand other people, how they may perceive you, your attitude, and your responses to them.

- Know your strengths and cope with your weaknesses. This will help you improve self-awareness;
- Ask for feedback and listen to it;
- Develop intuitive decision-making skills;
- Know your emotional triggers and find strategies to avoid entering destructive emotional patterns;
- Set boundaries and respect;
- Practice self-discipline; and
- Keep an open mind.

Self-Management

Self-management is about finding the self-control and the mastery needed to take control of one's work (e.g., to manage one's time, workflow, and communication.) It is also important to express your emotions in a healthy way, showing situational awareness.

Below is a list of self-management skills that can give managers the confidence to lead their teams and for followers to work together cooperatively. It also applies to any interpersonal relationship:

- *Stress management:* Does your blood pressure shoot up when you experience conflict? Remember to control your breathing;
- *Organising skill:* Do you organise yourself based on the management of your own emotions?
- *Problem solving:* Do you use your emotions as a moral compass?
- *Decision making skill:* Do you take account of both how you feel and what you think?
- *Confidence:* Do you encourage yourself and summon up your self-confidence?
- *Self-protection:* Do you use your skills and knowledge as self-protection, building healthy alliances when necessary?

Social Awareness

Social awareness is the ability to understand and respond to the needs of others. Understanding other people's feelings is central to emotional assertiveness. Emotional assertiveness provides the means to actively engage in demonstrating your social awareness. In more practical terms, social awareness is the ability to know and feel the people around you and to interact with them in the most effective and humane manner, i.e., empathy.

Here are some tips on how to build social awareness:

- Pay close attention to interactions with others;
- Develop your listening skills;
- Identify other people's emotional states. Remember to watch for facial expressions of emotion;
- Pay attention to the potential for unconscious cover-up emotions and do not accept invitations into blaming, attacking, or experiencing being a victim as a response;

- Think about your emotions and what information they are providing you about the relational temperature;
- Be aware of how you feel about the thoughts you have when listening;
- Think before you answer and respond with clear answers.

Relationship Management

This relates to your ability and willingness to engage in a relationship. It means to take your share of responsibility for staying in an OK/OK position and avoiding the Drama Triangle. It is about seeing a relationship as a partnership and paying attention to partnership agreements that are both explicit and established by the group. This means seeking to maintain the equals sign between you and operating from a position of mutual respect. Relationships are partnerships, and, in any partnership, we have rights and responsibilities. Maintaining relationships is a constant task; we need to keep our focus on the relationship to ensure maximum energy to complete the task. This applies equally at home and at work, therefore, it is essential to do your share. Use your emotions in a caring way, confront with care and not with the intent to catch the other out. Gaining the moral high ground may feel good, but it can become lonely up there.

> "No man is an island entire of itself; every man is a piece of the continent, a part of the main." (John Donne, 1624.)

To Whom Do I Owe this Emotion?

Many of us experience times when we have very intense emotions, and it feels like we are caught up and just cannot stop until we have won or scored our point. What is this all about?

Here is another example from my family. My sixteen-year-old son once told me at the dinner table of a conflict he got into with one of his teachers during the day. (We must remember that even though the protagonists are both in the same conflict, both will view it differently as both have differing frames of reference.) To set the story in context, he was in the runup to sitting his GCSE exams[44] and had been working very diligently, often until quite late. He expected to get very good grades in all his subjects and always did well in his exams. He had been taught to be assertive about his needs and emotions.

The class had done a test in preparation to answer a particular question. My son had answered accurately, in his opinion. This was a question worth only one mark in the exam, so not very important in the scheme of things. His teacher told him that his answer was not OK, and he disagreed. They argued, and both became very frustrated. When he told us about the event, he again showed he was still angry. I listened and helped him to look at the situation from both sides, though he was clearly not yet ready to let the matter go.

The next morning, as we got into the car, I told him how much I loved him and how proud I felt of him. I was not thinking about the story of the day before at the time. Rather, as I watched him come out of the house, I felt a surge of pride towards him and reminded myself how much I loved him. I wanted to tell him.

On the drive to school, I raised the topic of his argument with his teacher again, asking, "Would you like to hear my thoughts about it?" He said he did. I told him I understood why he was angry and thought he was rather angrier than the situation warranted. He agreed and asked me why I thought he had done this. I explained how sometimes we have unfinished business with someone from the past. That at times when people in the here and now behave in ways that remind us of the unfinished business, our subconscious seizes this as an opportunity to get back into the old business. It is as if we somehow think this is an opportunity to get a better result this time. We are unaware we are unconsciously making a link between the past and the present. Some of the anger we then feel towards the person in the room now does not belong to them, but to the other person. Then, when the person we are now in conflict with sees we seem angrier than the situation calls for, they can become triggered

---

44. In the UK the General Certificate of Secondary Education (GCSE) is a series of examinations taken at age sixteen, at the end of secondary education. Some children leave school after this, whilst others go on to further education and then university.

to go back to their unfinished past conflicts. Now, neither one is really dealing with the current issue, but there is no simple way out. What we need to do is to step back, count to ten breathing deeply, and think clearly, so we can calm our limbic hijack.

I explained that not only did continuing to fight not help, but it could be damaging, as the chemicals released in our bodies at such times are harmful, especially to the brain. I asked him to think about times when he felt the same way towards his mother and I when we had conflict and he recognised this. We had talked about the transference phenomenon before, so he understood. He agreed, saying, "I was way angrier than the thing was worth." He then asked how he could manage this in the future, so we had a very full and rewarding discussion during the drive.

The mechanisms involved are complicated, but can be reduced to these basic principles:

- Any unfinished business remains unfinished unless the emotional charge is dealt with authentically;
- Authentic expression of emotion needs to find closure;
- Closure is not only achieved by finding a solution, sometimes, especially if a solution is not practicable, we can choose to simply let things go. This is a skill worth learning;
- There are some things that are not negotiable, and this is OK. In such cases, it is important to evaluate what you will do to manage the situation in a healthy way. Then we need to remember that a relationship is the third party. You are OK, the other person is OK and perhaps this relationship is not OK by one or both of you;
- Unfinished emotional business, especially that which is repetitive, leads to learning unhelpful patterns of relating and has a nasty habit of biting when we least expect it;
- The more we follow these unhealthy patterns, the more we repeat the patterns;
- When in relationship with others, irrespective of the kind of relationship, the emotions we feel towards the other should be impacted by this relationship. If we love them, it is an act of love to deal with conflict. The more important the relationship

is, especially where there is strong attachment, it is our duty of care to present the other with our authentic emotions; and

- Sharing emotions is only effective when we show respect for the other.

Duty of care
Maintaining healthy relationships takes energy. We may well fail to achieve the high road each time. Few of us are free of unfinished and unconsciously stored conflict, however, the more we succeed in managing these issues, the easier it becomes.

Remember, whenever conflicts spiral, they become unproductive. It is highly likely both parties are following an unconscious negative pattern, and therefore are outside awareness. This is not a deliberate act of aggression, although it may look like that. Rather, it is a display of someone out of their emotional depth and drowning. They are not waving but drowning.[45] If one of you can find dry land and seek to find a win-win outcome, this is a positive result.

It is in our nature to look for who started this, or to claim, "It is not me; it is them." There is no point in this approach; it is simply a continuation of the destructive process. At times, when we regress to these behaviours, it may sometimes seem, "If I lose, it means I am mad. Winning is all that matters." If you recognise thoughts akin to this, stand back and look at what the issue is about, and what you would like to achieve. In my view, winning the relationship is more important than winning the war.

Emotionally Effective Relationships
In any committed relationship, it is natural for individuals to grow and to develop. However, change may alter the dynamics of the relationship. I invite you to remember that relationships are generally based upon contracts and changes need to be negotiated. Demonstrating a willingness to listen to the other, and to negotiate where a change or development affects the other, are vital aspects in achieving balance. Whilst this can be time-consuming and may

45. "Not Waving but Drowning" is a poem by the British poet Stevie Smith, published in 1957.

not always be easy, it is essential. Remember to respect each other and take time to self-disclose. Be creative, whilst at the same time holding on to those things that are important, i.e., your bottom-line issues. Healthy relationships are rewarding. Life in the twenty-first century is stressful; healthy relationships are the single most important contribution to resisting stress.

Chapter 13

Communication and Emotions at Work

Brief Introduction to the Theory of Group Development: Emotional Assertiveness in Teams and Groups

Until now, we have looked at one-on-one interpersonal relationships, although I have also drawn attention to the importance of emotions and attachments to humans as a species. For our ancestors, belonging to the group was a matter of life or death. It therefore follows that there will be dynamics and behaviours we need to explore to understand the role of emotionality in the context of being a part of a tribe, team, or group. This chapter will therefore look at these dynamics, focusing on both group leadership and group membership.

Much is written about the role of the group leader and leadership behaviours in the process of developing a functional team. Little has been written about the importance of followership, i.e., the behaviours of group members participating in and contributing towards group effectiveness, sometimes called alignment in business settings. As we examine the psychodynamics of group growth and development, we will look at some models that throw light on both aspects of group dynamics. We will also make links to emotionally assertive behaviours in both the leader and the followers, and draw parallels in how group dynamics and child developmental processes impact the leaders and members of any group.

Being emotionally assertive in the context of group membership requires not only the healthy management of the expression of our emotions but also calls for flexible and emotionally intelligent management of interpersonal boundaries and leadership and followership boundaries. We will examine the concept of group dynamics from a psychological perspective and from a behavioural science perspective. We will also see how these models can be analysed by noticing how the stages of child development and attachment are mirrored in group development theory. The developmental models will also cover the behavioural dynamics of how we approach and withdraw from one another as the life of a group becomes more and more functional.

Three theorists will be used as the grounds for comparison: Dr Eric Berne from TA; Dr Bruce Tuckman from stages of group development; and Dr Kalman J. Kaplan, consultant psychologist for the child development and concomitant adult behavioural positions. If this theory is not interesting to you, please feel free to skip this chapter. If, like me, you get very excited comparing different models to dive deeper into comparative theories and conceptualising to enhance understanding around various models, then please read on. I find it satisfying when models look at situations from different perspectives, offering more depth and breadth to our understanding of the whole. When working with understanding human behaviour, I find that when one model does not seem to provide an answer, a different model, looking at the same situation, may throw light upon what had previously been difficult to see. A model of human behaviour is really like a map of the world. A cartographer must decide what projection to use to provide a map suitable for the purpose it is intended for. This is because the world is a globe shape and can only be accurately seen in three dimensions, whilst a map is two dimensional. Only by metaphorically peeling the surface of the earth, like one might peel an orange in segments, can the surface be represented in two dimensions. This is known as an interrupted projection, as seen in the Orange Segment Map on the following page. However, this map would prove useless for navigational purposes.

The four basic map projection properties are area, shape, distance, and direction. Each of these map projection properties will be accurate for the purpose intended, but slightly distorted if you want to use it for a different purpose. Of the four projection properties, area and shape are the major properties and are of themselves mutually exclusive. If a map shows the area accurately, the shape will be distorted, and vice versa. In the same way, a psychologist or therapist needs to be clear about the model they use, its strengths and its shortcomings. Sometimes we need to use as many projections as possible to gain an understanding of the whole. For example, an architect will draw three basic projections of a building: front, top, and end, plus sometimes an artist's impression to pull each projection into a virtual reality.

I hope, like me, you will find the comparisons with the three models of group and personal dynamics interesting and useful. They are part of my attempt to take a wholistic view of human psychology. However, even this remains a two-dimensional representation, and the human psyche is multifaceted.

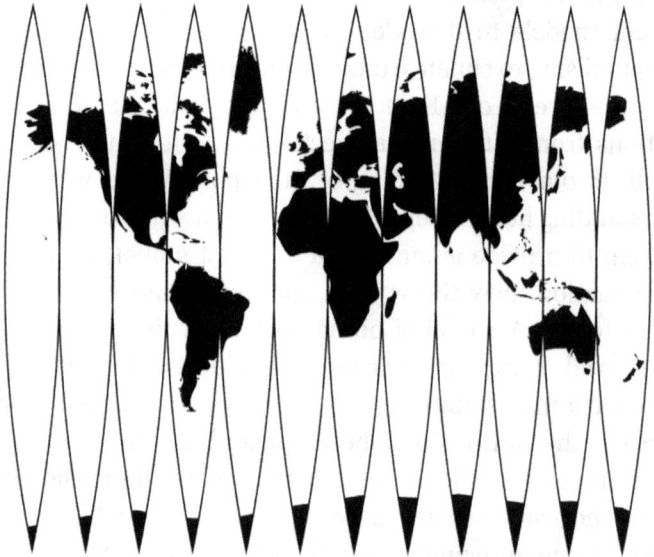

Figure 37: Interrupted projection map

Individuation, Attachment and Group Dynamics

Psychiatrist Dr Berne used group therapy as a major part of his treatment methods. His position on groups is chiefly a developmental one. He proposed that we enter groups with the following needs:

- Biological needs for stimuli; in TA, this would mean the stimuli we obtain in interpersonal exchanges with others.
- Psychological needs for time structuring, meaning we need to structure our time to obtain the above-mentioned stimuli.
- Social needs for intimacy, indicating the importance of intimate social connections.
- Nostalgia needs for patterning transactions; our unconscious need to recreate familiar behavioural patterns.
- Provisional sets of expectations based upon experience; our unconscious expectation this group will be like other groups we have joined.

He called these internal unconscious constructs about the group our Group Imago.

As we join a group and become an active member of it, he said our task is to adjust our needs and expectations to actual reality. In other words, we must abandon our unconscious beliefs about the group and discover how to be us in the group we are in now. He saw the adjustment as taking place in stages, relating to our preconscious or unconscious imago, or shifting frame of reference about how the group will be, how we will behave in the group, how the leader will behave, and who else will be in the group.

Berne's Research on Group Dynamics:
In his book *The Structure and Dynamics of Organisations and Groups*, Berne describes what he called "an experiment in Social Psychiatry". He attended a group led by a spiritualist that had been established to conduct séances led by a psychic. Berne used his membership of the group to observe what happened when he made various inputs. His observations led to his constructs about group boundaries and how people operated within them. He researched the following boundaries:

- The external boundary (who is in and who is not in the group)
- The major internal boundary (between group members and the leaders)
- The minor internal boundaries (between each group member)

See the boundaries diagram in figure 38:

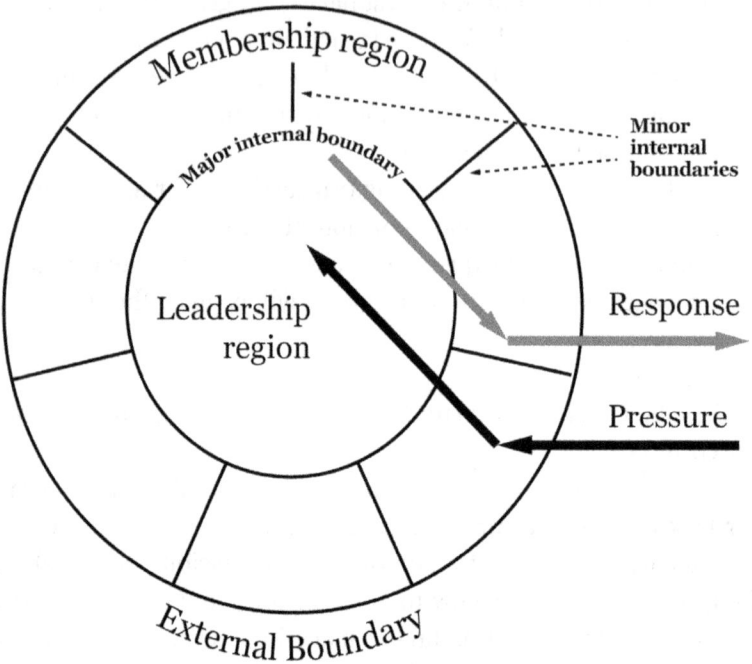

Figure 38: Boundaries diagram

The major external boundary is represented symbolically by the walls and door of the room where the group or team meets. At the interpersonal level, it defines who is in the group and who is not. An experienced trainer will indicate the group is starting by closing the door to the meeting room. This indicates to outsiders their presence is unwelcome and they may only enter when invited. However, the major external boundary is also an unconscious boundary that is established over time. It is about how we come to feel safe and protected within the sphere of influence of the group or team. It is the primary role of the leader at the coming together of a group to define this boundary and the task of followers to defend it and help maintain it.

The major internal boundary is about the clarification of leadership and followership roles within the context of group roles. In corporate teams, leadership is appointed, although not always.

However, there are seldom leaderless groups. If no leader is appointed, someone will emerge and assume the role. Similarly, in some groups, leadership may change, and the only basic norms are that there will always be a leader and a leader is only a leader where there are others following. When there is no clear leader, it is like a vacuum, and someone will be drawn into the vacuum to fill the role. An appointed leader who cannot influence the team to follow them will soon be replaced, if not physically then psychologically. In many cases, the group members will look for an informal leader to show the way. In a very real way, leaders usually get the kind of followers they deserve, and followers get the kind of leaders they deserve. In other words, good sound leadership usually inspires good followers and vice versa.

The minor internal boundaries refer to the boundaries between each of the group members. We each have an unseen physical area around us that subconsciously defines our personal space. In the UK and much of Europe, this extends about a half a metre all the way around the person, i.e., as if we have a territory about one metre in diameter around us. If you notice, when we stand next to someone, especially someone we do not have a close relationship with, we can stretch our arm out and barely touch the shoulder of the other person with your fingertips. However, in Spain, for example, this physical space is about one third of a meter. At a party, if an English person meets a Spanish person, there is an unconscious tension, as they each want a different distance between them. The Spaniard will want to move closer, whilst the English person will want to retreat. In an hour or so, they will be shuffling around the room together seeking their own comfort zone.

Whilst a person's personal space is about their boundaries, these are much more than simply physical space. They are about things like how we feel about physical contact with others, what is and is not OK by us, our values, etc. How do we feel with the amount of personal information we will freely share and how much are we available for others to share with us? By observation, we can quickly determine a person's physical boundaries, whilst discovering the interpersonal boundaries require gathering information and trial and error. Discovering who new people are takes time and the exploration period can be anxiety provoking for some.

Kaplan's Approach and Withdrawal Patterns

In Kaplan's TILT Model (see figure 40 on page 208), an important and valuable tool is the ability to observe behaviourally where a person is situated on the TILT reparatory grid at any time. This enables those aware of the model to adjust their behaviours to match those of the other person they are relating to. It is as if the emotional and relational approach and withdrawal act like the poles of a magnet. When the polarity is aligned, then there is attraction and when not, there is repulsion. This is graphically presented in Dr Kaplan's model in figure 40 on page 208. On various positions on the grid, individuals experience differing needs regarding attachment (attraction forces) and need for alone time and space (repulsion forces). These forces are unconsciously manifested and are clear indicators of how to achieve sympathetic distancing behaviours to enhance healthy relationship development.

As the group moves through developmental stages, the approach and withdrawal behaviours of each group member changes as if they are mirroring the stages of child development. The task of the leadership is to inspire the group members (followers) to act together and support leadership in responding to the external pressure, i.e., to repel the potential invaders. If the leader has established their position and the followers respond to the challenge, the group survives, but if the group leader cannot inspire the followers, the group is disrupted, or fails. We will delve deeper into these issues later in this chapter.

Survival Issues

Berne also drew conclusions about significant unconscious processes and membership behaviours for groups and the members of groups, He called them survival issues. He says that groups have three types of survival issues:

• Ideological survival (relating to the values and norms of the group, often called the canon)

- Physical survival (relating to the group continuing to exist as a recognisable entity)
- Effective survival (the group being able to carry out work, or achieve its agreed objectives)

Ideological survival requires the leadership to maintain the canon of the group.[46] As Berne was Jewish, he used the state of Israel as an example. As a nation, Israel survived for two millennia as an ideological reality in the hearts and minds of the Jewish people in the diaspora who had no practical physical homeland.

The ideology was enshrouded in the Jewish culture and maintained through rituals and strong family and kinship ties. Throughout the world, wherever Jewish people lived, they tended to maintain a recognisable culture.

Physical survival depends upon the ability of the leadership to concentrate group cohesiveness to repel invasion. In other words, it is about defending the integrity of the group by maintaining the major external boundary. He says Israel failed to maintain its major external boundary in the first century and ceased to exist as a state. Historically, this was not the first time the Jews had lost their homeland. They first suffered exile to Babylon in 538 BCE. The Jews' second and longest period of having no homeland began around 70 CE after the Roman-Jewish wars. The leadership were unable to prevent the destruction of the physical reality of a nation within a geographical context. Their temple and capital city of Jerusalem was also lost to them at that time. Nonetheless, they remained identifiable as a group.

Effective survival depends upon the group's ability to discharge its duties or complete the allotted task (its ability to complete organised work.) In the final analysis, this is due to the ability of its leadership to inspire the followers to complete their tasks and the remit allotted to the group. In doing this, they collectively contribute to ensuring the survival and success of the group. Today, Israel is a well-organised state, maintaining physical boundaries, even

---

46. The canon refers to the group's principles, beliefs, rules, ethical codes, and rituals, etc. The canon is a part of what separates one group from another, something that sets it apart.

in the face of external pressures. It is also an economic success and has shown itself to be capable of withstanding threats to its physical boundaries.[47]

What can Disrupt a Group?

Berne concludes that any group or team can be brought to destruction by violating its major group structures. He calls this disruption. He says that to destroy a group as an effective force, you attack it ideologically to induce decay (erosion); attack it physically to cause partial destruction (attrition); or penetrate the major group boundaries to disrupt it (infiltration)—erode or break the integrity of the major external boundary or the leadership boundary. Examples of this are repeated attacks on the personal behaviours, morals, or capacities of the leader to erode confidence in the leadership. We see this whenever politicians of any persuasion speak about their opponents. With great glee they pounce upon any hint of indiscretion, misjudgement, or other issue that can be used to sully the name of the leadership or ridicule the other parties. Another way to disrupt a group is to physically invade the group's space, for example, a crowd invading a football pitch.

Within a group, if a group member breaks a social contract by challenging the persona of another group member in a way that is not permitted by etiquette, such behaviours can also erode the fabric of the group structure. Socially, we call such behaviour rudeness. A rude person is often labelled as an agitator. When agitation is directed at the group leadership, it is called revolutionary.

The need to preserve the major group structure takes precedence over all other work. In other words, groups unconsciously put their energy into maintaining the group structures. Therefore, groups where there are high levels of unproductive conflict and agitation are less successful than they could be. Energy that could have been used towards completion of productive work is lost to the infighting. High levels of agitation lead to dramatic reduction

---

47. No judgement, either positive or negative, is implied in the references to the Jewish nation, Jewish people, or the conflicts Israel has with its neighbours. I use this reference as Berne used it. It is a clear example of the issues involved in group survival.

in the group activity, so the group loses efficiency. The intensity of group process at such times shows an in inverse relationship to group activity (i.e., individuals put more energy into what the group is squabbling about than in working together on the agreed goal or task).

The Health of a Group
Berne says:

1. The principal concern of every healthy group is to survive for as long as possible, or at least until its task is done. This is seen in the reluctance to disband once the group objectives have been achieved. A group established to save the whale, having achieved that, may reconvene to save all aquatic mammals.
2. There are two sets of influences that can threaten the existence of a group: external pressure, and internal agitation.
3. The continued existence of a group as an effective force, depends on the maintenance of its organisational structure, i.e., the generally recognised rules, regulations, and control mechanisms of the group, or how things are done around here.
4. Every failure of a group to maintain its effective existence is due to a failure of the group apparatus (the group's organising management process). Management cannot simply blame others.
5. All the work of any group falls into three categories: the group activity, the external group process, and the internal group process (how members communicate, either cooperatively or with unproductive conflict).
6. The existence of a group is continually in jeopardy if it cannot mobilise enough cohesive force to support all three kinds of work.

In a dysfunctional group, much of the energy is lost to managing internal agitation. Emotional assertiveness offers us ways to manage our interpersonal relationships effectively. Managing the expression of authentic emotion in a spirit of cooperation is a tool to transit the stages of group development so we can achieve synergy.[48] Once we establish healthy relationships with our co-workers, bosses, and subordinates, we become a functional family and achieve a win-win position where we work together for the good of the whole. Berne's work on the psychological forces acting within a group, can help us not only regulate working in groups but also look at family dynamics. Most of us have a spirit of cooperation embedded somewhere within us that is a tool for collective survival. Even reptiles can achieve this. There is a YouTube video showing how a group of small turtles get together to help another who has become upturned. They get around the distressed animal and help tip it the correct way up.[49]

Bruce Tuckman Stages of Group Development:

Tuckman focuses upon the dynamics of the group itself. He was particularly interested in observations of how a team operated from its inception, through working on a task to completion. He looked at patterns of interpersonal relationship management, leadership styles and general behavioural cues spotting identifiable clusters. These are used as indicators that can be classified as distinct group developmental stages. These developmental stages are there for all to see during the formation and life of any group. For the group leader, they are reliable cues to the most helpful leadership style to facilitate the group's healthy development. He first proposed four stages:

- Forming: When the group or team come together for the first time.
- Storming: A period often accompanied by interpersonal conflict, usually between individual members and the group leadership.
- Norming: A time where the group begins to cooperate in establishing their unique way of working together.

---

48. Synergy is where the output of the group is greater than the sum-total of the input. In other words, the group is extremely efficient and can achieve more with less.
49. https://www.youtube.com/shorts/iU_b5xluPnM shows turtles acting collectively as a team.

- Performing: When the group becomes fully functional and efficient. This is when the group finally achieves synergy.

He later added a fifth stage of development and named this adjourning. It is a time when the group has completed its task and is to be either disbanded, changed, or recommissioned.

Previously, when in management roles, I have found Tuckman's classifications extremely helpful to aid understanding and selecting management interventions, especially at times when the teams were showing behaviours leading to loss of group cohesion. Tuckman proposed the stages as if they are linear. However, in real terms, the stages reoccur, but on a forward trajectory as in the drawing below.

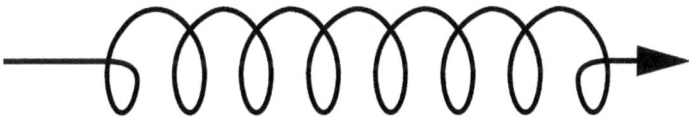

Figure 39: Forward trajectory

Each team meeting may have elements of the stages, but will be transited faster that the first pass through them.

TILT (Teaching Individuals to Live Together) (Kalman Kaplan[50])

Adapted from a group dynamics perspective:
Kalman J Kaplan discovered an extremely useful dimension of interpersonal relationships built upon child development theory that is uniquely applicable to one-on-one relationships. I discovered Kal's work in the early 1990s, and immediately saw its potential for use in psychotherapy, especially with couple's therapy. I later recognised the versatility of his work as the dynamics he describes are evident wherever human beings interrelate. As I frequently

---

50. Kalman J Kaplan: *TILT: Teaching Individuals to Live Together* (Philadelphia, PA: Brunner/Mazel, 1988), and Kalman J Kaplan: "TILT: Teaching Individuals to Live Together." *Transactional Analysis Journal* 18, no. 3 (1988).

worked within organisations, looking at communication, human behaviour, and teamwork, I began adapting Kal's material for use in corporate environments, especially where the development of relationships in a group setting were the focus. The material in this section about groups is therefore based upon his material, with my adaptations. I strongly recommend you read his book.

The model provides recognisable behaviours revealing how we approach and withdraw from others.[51] As such, it is useful for team leaders during the process of facilitating effective group development and steering their group to achieve synergy. Kaplan noticed that amongst the theories of child development, two processes were continually at the fore: those of attachment and individuation. Therefore, we can see two child developmental processes of movement from deindividuation towards individuation (distanced from self to close to self) and detached to attached (distanced from others to close to others).

- Deindividuation is the primitive emotional position for the baby, as it has not yet developed a sense of self.
- Individuation is an awareness that takes time to develop and is an understanding that "I exist separately from others".

If we look at the attachment dimension, we also see a child developmental process where the child begins from an emotional position of having no attachment, towards the development of secure attachment.

- Detachment is the condition we enter the world in. We do not know of the existence of others separate from ourselves, so we cannot be emotionally attached to another.
- Attachment is a condition that develops from healthy contact with caretakers, leading to us forming emotional bonds with them.

Kaplan understood that if we look at these dimensions

---

51. In this context, approach and withdrawal relates to the physical, emotional and psychological distance in human relationships.

separately, they appear to offer us opposing information about healthy child development. In other words, seen as separate axes, the healthy position would have to be moderately attached and moderately individuated. He realised these two seemingly opposing models were in fact not two opposing continua, but two processes taking place simultaneously. As a result, he constructed a model to examine the impact of success or failure on either of the two interrelated tasks; that is of moving towards both individuation and attachment. We will look at this in the diagram in figure 40.

I find this model very useful because it offers clear indicators and markers of the nature of someone's possible internal emotional and psychological conflicts in relating to others.

The diagram forms four quadrants labelled A, B, C, and D, with the centre point labelled E. These letters have no meaning other than to indicate the various quadrants, and they are effectively standard geometric labelling. Examining the TILT model, we can now see there is a third axis on the model, B.E.D., this being the healthy developmental path. It shows how the two developmental tasks influence each other.

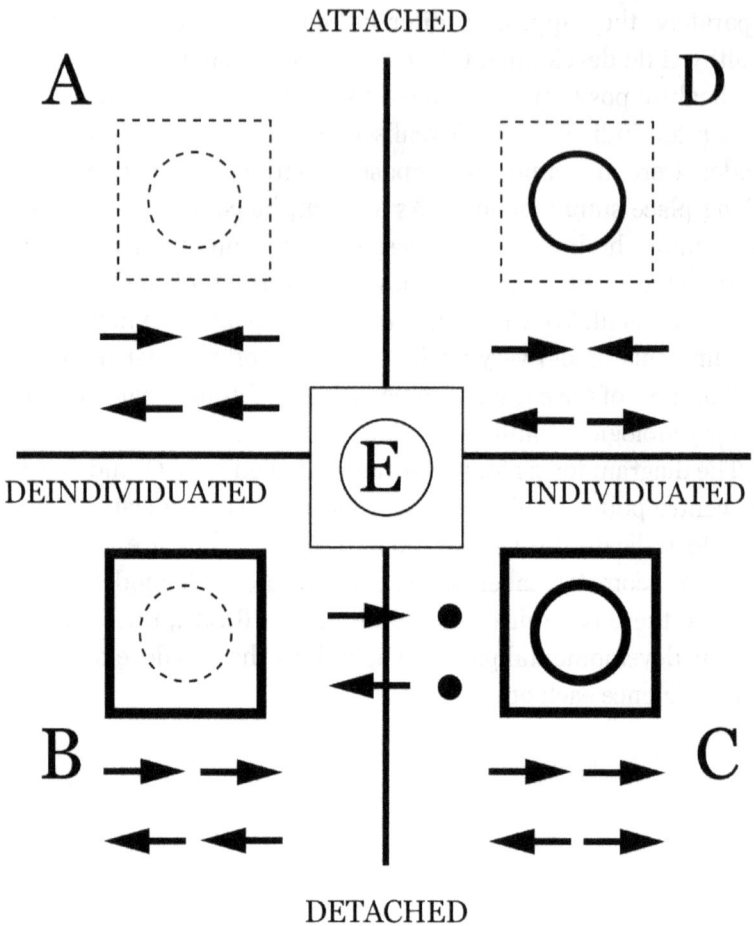

Figure 40: Walls and boundaries. Diagram reproduced with Dr Kalman J Kaplan's permission.

Walls and Boundaries

In addition to the developmental axes, Kaplan draws our attention to the processes by which infants develop interpersonal boundaries and the role of psychological defences, which he refers to as walls. In the diagram, interpersonal boundaries are shown as circles and walls i.e., our defence mechanisms are squares. Solid lines for walls and boundaries represent clearly defined conditions whilst dotted lines indicate permeability. We will see how, at first, we have no awareness of our boundaries, hence the need for parental protection (walls) during child development. The dotted line indicates the reality; whilst the baby is unaware of its boundaries, the parent knows they exist. On the B. E. D. axis, we see the interpersonal boundary developing into a clear awareness of who I am, whilst the defensive wall is replaced by a dotted line. This indicates that because we are secure with our boundaries, we do not need to have the defensive walls constantly up. Note: As adults we generally take responsibility for our own defences, as it is part of the healthy development process.

In the model, he draws our attention to personal approach and withdrawal behaviours, meaning how we behave when others make overtures of friendship (move towards us). We either reciprocate, i.e., move towards them, or we reject the offer and move away from them. These behaviours are shown by pairs of arrows representing the other (left hand arrows) and the self (right hand arrows). By approach and withdrawal, he means how we demonstrate our management of the individuation and attachment continuums, observable in the approach and withdrawal patterns we display in our interpersonal relationships. In other words, behaviourally how we reveal our emotional responses to offers of intimacy and alone time. This last piece of information is very useful in analysing the current temperature of an interpersonal relationship and how to use this information to assist in strengthening connections.

Swapping Walls for Boundaries

Let us examine further the concept of walls and boundaries. A boundary is a definition of who we are, what we will and will not accept, etc. If we think of the formal documents in the deeds to your property, you will see a map and on the map around the buildings and garden is a red line. This is the boundary marker and is only visible on the map. There is no red line around your property. We build walls or fences around our property, and this is built on the edges of what is ours. It is not intended to keep us in, but to keep others out. People may only enter our property with our permission. Relating these descriptions to the model, this is a clear metaphor to look at our boundaries and walls. Others cannot see our boundaries. It is our responsibility to draw attention to them, if or when someone crosses them without permission. When we experience boundaries being invaded, we have our defences to manage this, i.e., we can raise our walls.

At birth, the child has yet to form an attachment to the caretaker and is defined as being deindividuated. The position showing deindividuation and detachment is position B on the grid. We all began our developmental journey in position B, i.e., being deindividuated and detached.

From within the protection of the defensive wall, the child begins to discover the self-other boundary through experimentation, at first perhaps recognising its skin as a basic boundary and later through observation, noticing others come and go. He or she will begin to develop a sense of self and the development of boundaries begins. The parents can therefore begin to lower the wall, permitting the infant to explore its surroundings and the process of individuation is underway, i.e., there has been a movement towards attachment and towards individuation. This is shown as position E on the grid. In this position, the boundaries are partially formed, and the walls are somewhat lowered. Finally, the child reaches a rudimentary sense of self and has also bonded, i.e., clearly formed attachments. The self-other boundary is firm, and the wall can now become more permeable (position D on the grid). Notice that the boundary's dotted line has been replaced with a firm line. We are replacing walls by establishing boundaries.

This process is repeated B to E to D at each of the developmental stages across our life span. Kaplan proposes this sequence of developmental moves starts at conception. The fertilised ovum, which is undifferentiated (position B), must form an attachment to the uterus where it then begins to individuate (position E), until it is ready to separate (position D). During this period, the ovum is protected by the womb (the wall). Kaplan says these movements, B.E.D., occur repeatedly across our life span. Each time we have a new major life event, we experience what he calls a forward regression from the D position to B. This is not a negative, dysfunctional regression, but a move forward in the interest of further personal development. Joining a new group is one of these life events, and we can see that each individual group member will show the developmental process. This underpins why we have the forming stage of Tuckman and the Provisional Group Imago of Berne, and is an important feature of group dynamics. I, therefore, make comparisons between each of the three models, stage by stage.

Dysfunctionality Connected to Parenting Patterns: Over-parenting, Under-parenting and Inconsistent Parenting

There are three potential hindrances to smooth transiting of the developmental process. With healthy parenting, we are facilitated to proceed on the healthy B. E. D. axis.

The three dysfunctional parenting models are over parenting, under parenting and inconsistent parenting. Each of these models of behaviour can produce unhealthy development patterns in the infant and cause it to tilt from the healthy B. E. D. axis onto the unhealthy A. C. axis.

Over parenting is to overprotect the child and to guess what it needs and provide it, without the child asking and even when it needs nothing. The child may become overly dependent and stay small, or, if it experiences this behaviour as smothering, attempt to grow up quickly to find space to breathe.

Under parenting is when the parent is relatively unavailable to support their child's transition on the B. E. D. axis. Effectively, the child must quickly learn to emotionally grow up quickly and take care of itself.

These parenting behaviours can lead the child to decide, "If I grow up, and become my own person, you will abandon me. Therefore, I will cling to you, and give up individuation" (position A on the grid). Or alternatively, "Unless I push away from you and grow up quickly, you will engulf me" (position C). With these two options, the child may develop either an unhealthy level of attachment and avoid individuation, or an unhealthy level of individuation and become rigid in its thinking, highly defensive, and withdraw from contact with others.

The outcome of fear of abandonment can be poor self-other boundaries and poor ego defence (position A). The outcome of fear of engulfment may be rigid boundaries and rigid walls (position

C). Position C may be due to intrusive parenting or even a simply physiological issue such as the child not being able to breathe during breastfeeding. In position C, the person will avoid close relationships unless they have the power. From this position, they exhibit firm, almost brittle boundaries, "It's my way or the highway." As well as rigid boundaries, they also exhibit apparently impenetrable, defensive walls.

On the other hand, when the child avoids growing up, abandoning the move towards individuation and effectively emotionally merges with the other, (position A), it does not develop a clear sense of self, has poor boundaries, and fears being rejected and abandoned.

In the third unhealthy parenting behaviour, the caretaker is inconsistent, swinging from over parenting to under parenting. If an infant experiences inconsistent parenting, they may alternate between the A and C positions. In adulthood, this decision leaves the person to behave inconsistently. For example, one moment they may respond to you as if you are extremely positive and loveable (position A). Then, without warning, they act as if they want nothing to do with you and may even demonise you (position C). As we can observe over attachment, lack of attachment, and inconsistency in attachment in dysfunctional families, we can observe echoes of these behaviours in teams and groups. Unless these behaviours are managed appropriately by the leader and the members of the group, the team may also become dysfunctional.

To be emotionally assertive in a group as either a leader or a follower, it is important to understand how we approach and withdraw from each other. This will depend upon which position we are on the reparatory grid at any time. We can then use this information to help us match the movements of the other in ways that do not invite unhealthy distancing patterns in them. Dr Kaplan's behavioural method for observing the approach and withdrawal patterns is therefore very helpful in negotiating our own behaviours in a team. It is also equally relevant to one-on-one relationships.

Interpersonal Approach and Withdrawal Patterns
Each position on the grid represents a different pattern of managing

interpersonal distance (the arrows below each position indicates these patterns). In position B, owing to the ill-defined self/other boundary, and the rigid ego defence mechanisms (strong defensive wall), the individual's pattern of interpersonal distancing shows non-reciprocity. When others move towards them, they respond with withdrawal. When others move away, they experience anxiety and respond by chasing after them.

In position E, the individual exhibits a degree of passivity, waiting to see what the other will do. If the other approaches or withdraws, the individual displays acceptance. However, they do not initiate movement themselves. This may be a friend or colleague who is chatty and accepting when you contact them, though seldom takes the initiative to call or contact you.

In position D, this person exhibits reciprocity, accepting other's approaches without the need for defensiveness and remains comfortable when the other leaves. They can also initiate taking time alone when they need it without becoming rejective or withdrawn. They appear comfortable in their skin and can manage relationships, being fully capable of attachment and comfortable taking responsibility for themselves. Depending upon the prevailing environmental stressors, any of the positions on the B. E. D. axis is considered healthy. When we become aware of the significance of the approach and withdrawal signals we each send to the other, we are better informed about how to adjust our own behaviours to facilitate healthy connectivity. This model is especially useful to team leaders, as it provides information on the most helpful leadership style in any situation.

Emotionally intelligent individuals are well equipped to notice and respond to the behavioural stress signals of others. The same applies to leaders of groups, as emotional assertiveness is the tool for building and managing effective groups. We will return to this when examining the Emotional Assertiveness Model and applications.

Transiting the B. E. D. Axis Together
Because of the importance of the approach and withdraw behaviours at each developmental stage, relationship development

and group development depend upon us making the B. E. D. steps together. This is where the link between the TILT model and Berne and Tuckman's models can be established. Group dynamics are based upon the transition in unison from the B to E and on to the D position. Movement from one stage to another in healthy developmental steps mirrors the patterns in healthy child development.

Comparisons Between the Three Models

Comparing Bern's Group Imago theory, Tuckman's Stages of Group Development, and the B. E. D. axis on Kaplan's TILT grid. Note: Although with Kaplan's model there are three positions, I propose that movement on this axis are not three steps, but a slow progression along a continuum, i.e., from B to D can be viewed effectively as four movements. We start at B, move towards E, then we move from E towards D. Finally, we arrive at position D. When the group is at position D, we have a clear picture of how we fit in to this group, and our identity as a fully paid-up member of the group. We are clear about how the others, including the leader, fits in and how the group operates. (The group culture.) This is when the group achieves synergy.

Kaplan makes the point when considering using this model with couples, that many interpersonal relationship problems are caused when the couple are operating from different positions on the grid. Any of the B. E. D. positions can be healthy, and are a function of where we are personally, especially regarding managing life-changing events. However, if one part of the relationship is in the healthy B position, whilst the other is in the healthy D position, each of them may experience some dissonance in the relationship. It is as if they are both dancing together and want to be partners in the dance of life. However, outside of their awareness, each is dancing to music playing through earphones from a different iPod. It is almost impossible not to step on each other's toes if one is dancing to the tune of a waltz whilst the other is dancing to a tango.

Kaplan's model tells us that the way to resolve the dancing difficulty and avoid stepping on toes, is for the two to effectively adopt the first healthy developmental position, B. Then together, step by step, move through E to D. In this way, we account for the individual approach and withdrawal needs, encouraging developing together to the healthy position, D.

I propose, that in terms of group development dynamics, the same pattern holds true. The leader's task is to facilitate the process whereby each group member achieves the position D together. In this way, each group member can function in their role in the group. When all members of a group are in position D, the group achieves synergy. We are effectively each in step with the other members of the group. The leader has been a competent conductor, ensuring each instrument in the orchestra is in tune and playing their part in performing the symphony.

Dysfunctional Groups

Positions A, C and A/C describe various group dysfunctionalities observable where leadership tasks have not been adequately preformed or where there are one or more dysfunctional group members.

Position A results from ineffective leadership, being overprotective and failing to shield the group when necessary. Position C is from over controlling, or micromanaging leadership and does not facilitate the group moving healthily on the B. E. D. axis. The A/C is from inconsistent leadership or absentee leadership.

Eric Berne: THE GROUP IMAGO

The group imago is a term meaning the unconscious, often idealised image we hold of a group. The process of adjustment of our group imago involves four different stages.

The first stage of a person entering a group is the provisional group imago. This is a blend of unconscious fantasy and conscious expectations based on previous experiences in groups.

The next stage is a modification of the provisional into the adapted group imago. The modification is a rather superficial first impression appraisal of the other people in the group. This is usually made by observing them during rituals and activities. Berne used these terms to describe behaviours we enter to meet our need for social stimuli. At this point, the member is ready to participate in pastimes (another form of time structure involving polite chat, such as swapping information about families, or the big football game last night). However, he/she will not yet start any games (a term Berne used to describe unconscious patterned behaviours bringing negative and often harmful recognition), although he/she may become passively involved in the games of others.

The operative group imago is the third stage. This transformation works on the following principle: the imago of a member does not become operative until he thinks he knows his own place in the leader's group imago, and thus their place in how the leader views the group. This operative group imago remains shaky unless it has repeated reinforcement. At this stage of adjusting, in one's group imago, group members are likely to play more games.

The fourth phase of the group imago is the secondary adjustment. At this stage, the members begin to give up their games in favour of doing things the group's way, i.e., conforming to the group's culture. If this occurs in a small group or subgroup, it prepares the way for intimacy. More time and energy are available for the team's tasks and less time is lost in the group psychological processes, i.e., unproductive conflict.

The four stages of adjustment of the group imago and their suitability for structuring time are: (1) the provisional imago for rituals; (2) the adapted imago for pastimes; (3) the operative imago for games; and (4) the secondarily adjusted imago for intimacy. Knowledge of this progression allows us to define, with some degree of accuracy, the four descriptive terms: participation, involvement, engagement and belonging.

Tuckman: Four Stages of Group Development

His four stages are focused upon the dynamic of the group, rather than personal unconscious processes and issues. There are clear parallels between Berne's four stages and Tuckman's. This is to be expected, as a group is a collective of the multiple unconscious issues of its members.

Table 8 compares the stages Tuckman, Berne and Kaplan provide:

Table 8: Comparison of Tuckman, Berne and Kaplan

Tuckman	Berne	Kaplan
Forming	Provisional Imago	B
Storming	Adapted Imago	B towards E
Norming	Operative Imago	E towards D
Performing	Secondary Adjusted Imago	D

Kaplan TILT B. E. D. Axis

Kaplan's model of healthy development follows the B. E. D. axis. As you can see, I split this into four steps that align with both Berne and Tuckman's models.

- When we are in position B, we experience uncertainty. We ask ourselves how and where do I fit into this new situation? As a result, we become defensive, and we metaphorically peep over our wall, watching for how to be. We are usually not quite our confident self.
- As we move towards position B on to position E, we lower our defences and gain in confidence. We still spend time observing the lie of the land, seeking to find our place.
- Moving on towards position E then on to position D, we continue to grow in confidence, still holding back a little, but now generally more confident.
- Finally, we reach D, and we are free to be ourselves, we lower our defences and become available for deeper levels of relationship.

Comparing and Combining the Four Stages

Stage 1 Berne: The Provisional Group Imago (a blend of fantasy and conscious expectations)

Berne says that before joining groups, individuals already have expectations of what the group will be like. These expectations are drawn from their frame of reference (i.e., their unique way of seeing the world, built from life experience) and are based upon their previous experiences of groups, starting with their own family group. Time structuring during the early stages of the group will be geared around ritual. Ritual consists of things humans do unthinkingly daily, such as shaking hands when we meet, asking "how are you?" without really wanting to know, and replying, "I'm fine, how are you?" etc.

In this period, group members are concerned with boundaries, e.g., who is in and who is out of the group (external boundary), who is the leader and the members (major internal boundary), and what is the task for the group. Group members are basically concerned with leadership issues, dependency on the leadership and how group members relate to the leader. See the diagram Provisional Group Imago below.

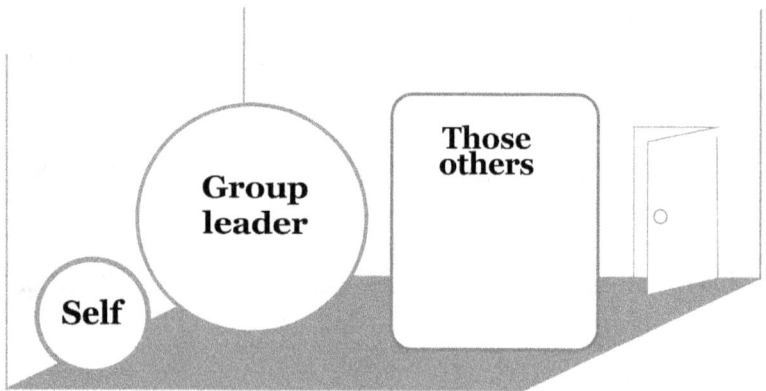

Figure 41: Provisional group imago

The positions act as screens upon which we project our

unconsciously held images of leaders and group members from our past experiences.

Tuckman calls this the forming stage.

This is a time of defining who is in and who is out of the group. He says orientation, testing, and dependence are functions of the forming stage.

Kaplan Position B

Kaplan also proposes that the starting place for a new relationship is in position B. Here we need our defensive walls to allow us time to reorganise our boundaries to match the prevailing reality. Whilst as adults we manage our own walls and boundaries, in terms of team membership there is also a role for the team leader. Their task is to provide clear direction and boundaries, as well as ensuring all the necessary structures are in place to welcome new members into the group. For example, someone joining a new team will need a desk, chair, and other equipment to do their job. They also require an induction program so they learn the ropes, the how things are done around here. This mirrors the role of a parent welcoming a newborn into the family, i.e., being their wall to provide safety for the baby to begin to discover itself. This stage clearly matched both Berne and Tuckman's models, whilst offering a deeper understanding of the issues by linking them to child development theory.

Time Structure[52] in Stage 1 is Ritual

Ritual behaviours fit closely with Kaplan's notion of walls and boundaries in position B. Ritualistic human exchanges are very safe, i.e., are consistent with a need for strong defences. We need

---

52. Time structure is a concept from Berne and TA. He describes several ways we use time to gain recognition, or strokes: *Withdrawal* is spending time in one's head. Strokes from others are not available, but we can offer them to ourselves. *Ritual* is activities one does regularly where strokes are predictable. *Pastimes,* where we engage in chit chat. *Work* is any activity including working, sports, etc. *Games*, which are psychological interactions where we gain negative recognition. *Intimacy,* where we allow ourselves to be open with others.

this to allow us room to discover how we fit into this new situation within the context of predictability.

Leadership Tasks in Stage One

- Deal with the external group process and define major external boundaries. This is then seen as a barrier warding off external intrusions and creating safety, as in Kaplan's wall.
- Make clear contracts between group members and the group leader, also members and each other as in defining boundaries in Kaplan's model.
- Clarify who is in the group, who is not and who is in charge. (Also, about the defensive wall from Kaplan.)
- Maintain optimal levels of anxiety. Encouraging development of interpersonal boundaries (as per developmental needs, from Kaplan.)
- The leadership style is the benevolent autocratic style.

Table 9: Summary of destructive and constructive leadership behaviours at stage one

Destructive Behaviours	Constructive Behaviours
Excessive anxiety in the leader	Clear contracts
The tyranny of failing to provide structure	Clear structure
Hidden sadism, leaders who take delight in inviting others into distress	Building optimal anxiety
Confusion about roles	Clear assumption of responsible leadership, providing clarity
Appears too aggressive or too seductive	Clarity of boundaries and clarity of group task
Too task orientated	Facilitation of group members getting to know one another

Destructive Behaviours	Constructive Behaviours
Too many rules, too authoritarian	Early provision of practical/survival information, e.g., toilets, breaks, food limits
Focus on one person's pathology/acting-out behaviour at the expense of other members	Preparation of the team's area in a manner which demonstrates that group members are expected and welcome

EXERCISE

Experiment for Self-Learning

This exercise can be conducted in your own time. It is best done by taking time to recall a new situation or group you attended.

- Take five minutes and recall when you first joined a new team or group. Identify any thoughts you may have had about what the group would be like, or what the people may be like.
- When you first entered joined the team and noticed people beginning to join the group, can you recall any thoughts you had about who they were, how they looked, etc?
- Finally, go back in your memory to the first morning in the new post or situation. Can you recall how the early moments were? Also, recall any emotions you were experiencing. How do you feel emotionally about these memories?

Stage 2: Berne Adapted Group Imago

This stage is arrived at through superficial appraisals of the other people in the group. It is made through observations during rituals and activities. Group members are now ready to participate in pastimes. However, they tend not to start games (psychologically motivated behaviour and communication, intended to replay old defective patterns of relationship). The time structure in this stage is pastimes. This stage is typified by agitation across the leadership boundary.

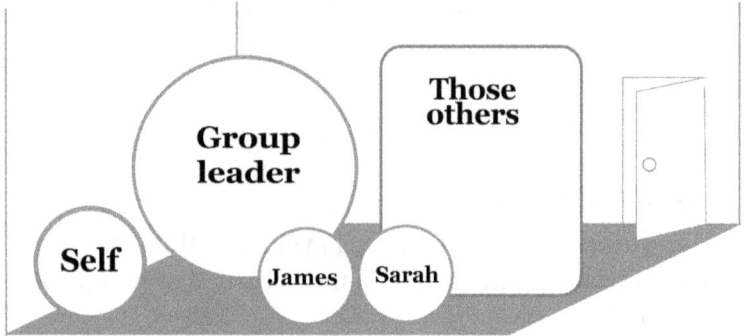

Figure 42: Adapted group imago Berne

Tuckman Storming

Storming is characterised by conflict and polarisation around interpersonal issues, with emotional responses mainly in the task sphere. These behaviours act as resistance to group influence and task requirements and are labelled as storming.

In this stage of the group, we see conflict with, or rebellion against, the leader, i.e. agitation across the leadership boundary. There is resistance to group influence and to task requirements.

On the surface, storming appears to be about the nature of the task, but psychologically it is about the ability of the leader to be effective and remain respectful. In other words, the OK/OK life position of the leader is being tested. Can the leader take the pressure and remain respectful towards others?

Kaplan's model says:

Partial movement from B towards the E position, still showing lack of clarity about boundaries. Demonstrating dissonance around defences, occasionally being inappropriately angry or overly passive at others.

Time Structure: Pastimes

At this stage, we begin the process of feeling our way around the group, tentatively finding out how things work and particularly how we fit in the picture. We still have walls and are still discovering who we are in this new situation. Metaphorically, we begin to peek out over the defences.

Leadership Tasks in Stage Two

- Keep leadership boundaries and group tasks intact whilst still allowing individual group members the maximum opportunity to test them.
- Take feedback seriously.
- Do not respond to perceived attacks and dissent by offering a counterattack, but remain firm, holding boundaries in a respectful way. The leadership style is democratic.

Table 10: Summary of destructive and constructive behaviours at the adapted group imago stage (storming)

Destructive Behaviours	Constructive Behaviours
Leader who deflects or denies examples of aggression and tries to syrup over conflicts	Taking people's feedback seriously without collapsing under perceived criticism
Leader interprets anger and rebellion as a sign of the individual being dysfunctional, or speaks in a way which invalidates/patronises members	Does not give in to blackmail threats and demonstrates respectful communication
Group leader looking fragile, sick, or appearing hurt. Invitations for members of the group to protect them from attack	Validating people's right to their feelings, thoughts, opinions and concerns without giving up their own rights

Destructive Behaviours	Constructive Behaviours
Taking any of the drama roles (victim, rescuer, or persecutor)	Remains demonstrating the I'm OK-You're OK life position
Ignores the conflict – pretends it doesn't exist	Ability to negotiate issues – to be flexible about negotiation for the group to form its own unique culture
Supporting polarisation or scapegoating	Discriminating between compromises/negotiations which would facilitate or handicap a group task
No sanctions or unjust sanctions	
Abandoning group	

EXERCISE

Experiment for Self-Learning

- Reflect upon the last exercise, and recall any time soon after joining the new group, where an individual or even yourself appeared to be somewhat aggressive towards the leader, especially about the definition of the goals and tasks. Can you recall any examples of when individuals opened some form of conflict with the leadership? For example, disagreed with the best way to do something, argued about objectives or deadlines, etc?
- Do these memories fit in with the storming phase of the group?
- How did the leader manage the conflict?
- What was the outcome?
- How do you feel emotionally about this?

Stage 3 Berne: The Operative Group Imago

In this stage, the group member has further modified their imago according to their appraisal of how they fit into the leader's imago. The time structure is now games. An imago does not become operative until the member thinks he/she knows their place in the leader's group imago, and the group is not fully in this position until this applies to all members.

Tuckman: Norming

Resistance has been overcome, and more feeling and cohesiveness develops. Group standards evolve and new roles are developed and adopted. Intimate, personal opinions are expressed about the task. It's a time when group members may gain insights, feel safe in the group, have an investment in its future and can share emotions and offer each other support. A group at this stage has a clear sense of "this is how we do things around here". Shared norms and values have developed.

Kaplan Movement from E towards D

We see movement away from the passivity of the E position towards the proactivity and maturity of the D position. We have not yet fully reached D, but are showing more signs of the gradual swap from walls to well-established boundaries.

Time Structure: Games

Games is a concept from Berne and Transactional Analysis. Psychological games are about gaining predictable, negative strokes. This enables us to confirm our belief systems. At another level, games with relatively low intensity are a way of testing relationship reliability, and especially exploring how win-win we can be and how safe we are to lower our defences. We are beginning to explore how safe it is to lower our walls further and how we can clearly define our interpersonal boundaries.

Leadership Tasks in this Stage

* Facilitate the development of interpersonal skills and

modelling behaviour that will support the development of group norms.

- Foster the healthiest forces within the individual and the group; those oriented towards individuation and self-actualisation.
- Set rules and contracts as well as sanctions.

Table 11: Summary of destructive and constructive behaviours at the third stage

Destructive Behaviours	Constructive Behaviours
Encouraging rigidity	Members get recognition for making explicit queries around establishing group norms
Reluctance to let the group move to the stage where group members make more autonomous movement and where the group leader loses centrality	As a group leader, encourage norms to maintain flexibility and state clearly there is not "only one way to do it"
Rigidity concerning rules such as "there are no exceptions", no allowance for individual differences and individual needs	Facilitate the group developing their own norms – norms become the group's personality
Unhealthy or malevolent destructive members are allowed to stay and destroy group cohesion, tasks and processes	Flexibility around norms
Carry one's expectations; group norms based on experience, thus perhaps interfering with the unique development of each individual's group norms	Focuses on the process of valuing and norm formation or culture building. Allows for new norms, even if different from their own experience

Destructive Behaviours	Constructive Behaviours
Leader tries to make rules instead of norms. Leader expresses own values, allowing no freedom and attempting to repress individual's views	Referral/exclusion of destructive members after very careful consideration of cost/benefit effects on the rest of the group
	Explicit statements of leader's values, e.g., race, sexual orientation, where this is appropriate
	Respect for each group member's uniqueness and value

EXERCISE

Experiment for Self-Learning

- Reflect upon past group membership. Have there been any examples of the group establishing norms, for example about timings, or other issues?
- Consider how this went and how the leader managed it.
- How do you feel emotionally about this?

Stage 4 Berne: The Secondarily Adjusted Group Imago

In this stage, the member gives up their agitation in favour of doing things the group's way. This prepares the way for intimacy. The time structure in this stage is therefore intimacy.

Tuckman: Performing

This is the time when a healthy leader reaps their rewards. Interpersonal relationships become the tool of effective work in the task and group activities. Member's roles become flexible and maximum group energy is channelled into the task. Synergy is achieved.

Kaplan Position D

Group members have a clear awareness of their personal boundaries and are willing to assert them when necessary. As an expression of the sense of personal self-worth and autonomy, they show little or no defensive behaviours. They seem to feel good in their own skin.

Time Structure: Intimacy

Intimacy requires a minimum of defensiveness and a maximum of awareness of our own boundaries and how we maintain them. This is consistent with Kaplan's D position on the TILT grid. It is from here we can maximise our cooperative group behaviours, make healthy human connections and have maximum cooperation. Synergy is based upon the low level of group maintenance required to keep the group functional and the concomitant release of energy to devote to working together to achieve the task.

Leadership Tasks

- Allowing group members to perform acts of leadership, for example, chairing team meetings, forming subgroups to investigate options to improve efficiency, etc.
- Offering praise, positive recognition
- Minimising control, i.e., lets go and lets the group get on with doing their work, working together with minimal supervision.

Table 12: Summary of destructive and constructive
behaviours at the fourth stage

Destructive Behaviours	Constructive Behaviours
Criticises destructively, says "I know better" Puts people down, takes the credit for the team's work Deprives group of autonomy	Lets people get on with it, letting go
	Allows people to perform acts of leadership
	Becomes a participant – joining the group
	Minimum control, maintains some safety boundaries – though group will usually do this for themselves (time, refreshments, etc)
Too keen on schedule	Offers praise, positive recognition for the person and for their work
Tells people what they're doing isn't good enough, and finds fault. Notices more of what is wrong than what is right Holds too tight a rein	The leadership slot is vacated to an appropriate person, though they are ready to step in if necessary. Says things like, "Let's experiment with this."
Offers more sanctions than reward	Invites comment and evaluation, allows group to make choices
Stresses task and ignores maintenance. Is cool, impersonal, and distant. Refuses to listen to group members	Within a wide range of open boundaries, says what's permitted and what's not
Invalidates feeling Invokes negative behaviours Is lacking in appropriate permissiveness	Relaxes, enjoys group Gives permission to have fun and work
	Encourages and validates autonomy, immediacy, authenticity, spontaneity, feeling, skills and knowledge

Experiment for Self-Learning

- Reflecting upon past experiences of being in teams or groups, can you recall any examples of achieving synergy, i.e., arriving at the performing stage?
- How do you feel emotionally about this?

Being Open: How We Connect with Others

We all have emotions and, contrary to popular belief, emotions in the workplace need to be welcomed and used appropriately. It is impossible to form healthy working relationships without connecting with others at the emotional level. However, we do not normally come to work to make friends, join a family or find deep relationships. Also, some people, by virtue of their personality type, prefer to make a clear delineation between their work and their private lives. However, the contract for employment usually includes an expectation that we work together respectfully in teams and to do this we need to manage our emotions, and this means use them appropriately as well. Cover-up, non-authentic emotions lead to distressing behaviours and a reduction in team effectiveness.

Sharing Our Resources: The Win-Win Way to Grow as a Team

Working together is all about finding win-win solutions. Respect for self and others is the key to this. Respect calls for us to accept that each is responsible for managing themselves and can cope with healthy workplace relating. We must each take responsibility for our own emotions, their expression, and the consequences of our behaviours. When we do this without judgement, we can move to deeper levels of exploring the win-win position.

What does this mean in real terms? Primarily, we need to allow more room for the expression of healthy emotions in the workplace.

When we listen to each other without becoming judgemental or critical, we make room for developing healthy relationships in the workplace. This is not to suggest we must be unreal or overly polite. Rather, it means allowing room to be human. As we discover each other's real selves, we facilitate team development and reach the level of high-performing teams. We put energy into avoiding the expression of cover-up emotions and entering interlocking dramas where energy is wasted. Interpersonal space is an important aspect of emotional assertiveness. By being aware of how much space your colleagues need, and not invading it, you demonstrate respect for their boundaries. At the same time, be aware of your own limits. Your needs are also important.

Respecting Boundaries and the OK/OK Position: Kenny Everett, We're not Going to Hurt Each Other, Are We?

In the UK, one of our much-loved comedians, Kenny Everett, played a leather clad punk. In one sketch, Sid Snot goes to the dentist, and he takes the dentist by the genitals when he stands next to him, looks up at him, smiles and says, "Now we're not going to hurt each other, are we?" What is this to do with emotional assertiveness? For me this is a wonderful humour-filled metaphor for respecting interpersonal boundaries and maintaining the fair-play relationship. I do not propose to adopt the technique with your dentist, or anyone else for that matter. It is not intended as an example, but as a visual representation of managing boundaries.

There may be times when we meet people who have learned that they feel more secure when they replay negative scenarios. For them it is often as if relationships are all about either win-lose, lose-win or lose-lose. They spend a lot of time engaging in foul-play. It is important to understand that this behaviour is often driven from unconscious beliefs gained through difficult parenting or developmental experiences. They are also frequently motivated by a desire to have warm relationships, and simply blind as to how their behaviour stands in their way. It is at such times we need to be very clear about our boundaries and how we take care of ourselves when others may present a real threat to our personal safety or self-worth. In a crude way, Everett's sketch shows the importance of mutual agreements to do each other no harm. I believe violence is seldom the answer to interpersonal problems. However, if someone does violence to us, we have a basic human right to self-defence. It is, in my opinion, not inconsistent with the I'm OK- You're OK position to use appropriate levels of force to defend yourself. One friend of mine, who was an ex-member of the SAS said, "When in danger, it is always good to have all the options available. Running away is a viable option at times." I think this is wise advice, as violence is a last resort, yet it remains an option. Mike Tyson, once the world heavyweight champion, said, "When we enter the ring, we all have a plan, until the opponent hits you on the nose." This suggests that violent or intimidating people often have a plan in their minds about how their manipulation will work. Whilst the other follows the aggressor's plan, the aggressor is driving towards their desired outcome, i.e., to achieve a win at the other's expense. By deciding for oneself how we will react and not following 'the plan,' we begin to define our own boundaries and limits. This leaves room to negotiate towards an OK/OK (win-win) outcome.

Therefore, always have as many options as possible for emergency situations. Thankfully, most of us rarely face violence. And if you do, remember the moment someone violates your boundary with violence, you have every right to use violence to protect yourself. This is not a denial of the OK/OK philosophy, rather it underpins that way of thinking. Sometimes, we need to enforce our boundaries and self-respect is central to this. I would say, do not breach the other person's boundary with violence, and instead operate demonstrating respect. When dealing with your children, this is critical. If you want to teach your children to respect self and others, respect them. Doing violence to children shows them disrespect, and it violates the basics of what they have a right to expect from their parent. It is the parent's job to protect, love and nurture their children. We need to teach them how to be self-aware, to self-manage and to be aware of others, taking their share of responsibility to manage relationships.

Availability: A Willingness to Share in the Lives of Others

Emotionally literate individuals can manage their boundaries in such a way that they are available for others on a human level. When we achieve this, being ourself in the workplace or at home maximises our effectiveness. In group development terms, this puts us in the right place to contribute to the team, reaching the performing stage of group development. Remember, it takes a team time to achieve this position, so be patient and tolerant of others during the stages of group development.

We are different; we learn our own unique ways to cope with emotions and we all grow at different speeds. Be patient and tolerant of others during the stages of group development and be kind to yourself. When we remain accepting and yet willing to grow, we can make it. The benefits are well worth the effort.

Application in Schools

Corinne McDevitt wrote this case study of an application of the model for use with children in a school setting. An Australian school principal approached Corinne because the school was experiencing behavioural problems following a string of disasters in their area, including drought, fires and floods. Corinne detected an emotional assertiveness issue and asked for my help in designing an emotional assertive response.

Emotional Assertiveness for Schools® case study

Written by Corinne McDevitt. Emotional Assertiveness Master Trainer, of Training Lab Sydney Australia.

Problems in Our Australian Schools

It was February 2020. The Australian fires had devastated so many towns, bushland and animals over most of the country for months. The red glow, day and night, was eerie; then came the floods, and COVID-19 was still to hit Australia.

I was training emotional assertiveness to several school principals and teachers in rural NSW, along with clients from diverse government and corporate industries. The principal of Nana Glen Primary School (ages five to thirteen), Deanie Nicholls, commented on how many of the students were acting out of character. As a result, their negative behaviours were leading to detention and the rate of detentions had grown exponentially. The teachers realised that the students were behaving badly deliberately, so they could stay in with their teachers and feel psychologically safe. That is, by getting into trouble they were then supervised and near an adult. The Nana Glen town was particularly impacted by the fires with families losing homes and livelihood. Although the fires and floods had gone, whenever a fire truck passed the school, the children would be emotionally triggered and start to panic, asking, "Are the fires back?", "Are we going to die?", or "Will you check that my parents are OK?"

On many levels, I felt for the principals, teachers and these communities regarding the hardships they were going through. I was also concerned about the negative patterns the students were forming as mechanisms to feel safe. The students had high levels of fear, panic, short tempers and anxiety; this was across the whole school, as well as amongst parents and teachers.

I agreed with Principal Deanie Nicholls to travel the eight hours north of Sydney to run a pro bono pilot workshop on emotional assertiveness training for the students, parents and teachers. I asked John Parr if we could take the adult program, mostly run for government, clinical and corporate management, and staff, and convert this for children. The objective being to support them in mental resilience and recovery from the national disasters. John generously gave many hours and late nights/early mornings at no cost to either the school or me, so we could deliver the applied emotional intelligence skills to the children. This program needed to be age appropriate and be designed to achieve successful outcomes. I converted the PowerPoint presentation so the children would enjoy learning Emotional Assertiveness®, and learn all about the four main emotions; how to use their fear, anger and sadness in a positive way to regain happiness and calm. John paid to produce animated videos on how schools and parents can support the child to manage stress; plus, a graphic designer, to create the digital workbooks, Time Out, Coaching, Parenting and Conflict worksheets, based on feedback from the schools, along with Emotional Assertiveness ® *Mascot characters: Happy, Angry, Sadness, and Fear.*

Then COVID-19 hit and Australia went into lockdown. All schools were closed, unless a student had a parent in the emergency services. When schools returned several months later, the school principals reported that aggression, disrespect and lack of empathy were high among students, on top of the other issues.

Students as young as eight were telling other students to go kill themselves. Aggression, feeling lost and violence was spiralling in senior schools. This story was being reported by media across Australia.

Although travel was banned due to COVID-19, the school principals provided me with an official government letter to drive the eight hours north of Sydney to train the executive, staff and students in what had now become a Department of Education pilot for the Emotional Assertiveness ® for Schools program. Police were checking travel permits; only necessary work, exercise and grocery shopping was allowed, so my partner spent days surfing to comply legally and get provisions together whilst I worked.

Results From Training the Emotional
Assertiveness® for Schools Pilot Programs:
Message from the principal, one month after training the 130 primary students (aged five to thirteen), staff and executive:

> "Good morning, Corinne. I just wanted to let you know that we had an art therapist at school last week. She gave us feedback on the children and the way they spoke about their feelings. She stated that she has never seen children with the amount of emotional intelligence that the kids at our school showed as a whole group. I thought you'd like to hear that and pass on our amazing feedback. Thanks to you and John, bye."
> – *Principal of Nana Glen Primary School, NSW, Australia.*

Detentions decreased by over seventy-five per cent:
The school had reported on the statistics before the 2019-2020 national disasters, showing six to eight detentions a week due to challenging behaviour. After the fire/floods and COVID-19, this increased dramatically. Since running the Emotional Assertiveness® program, they have reported only one detention in total every two to three weeks. These excellent results have been sustained since June, for the last five months. The students are self-managing their behaviour and expressing their anger, fear and

sadness in a positive way. Teachers are now focusing on developing leadership skills rather than managing negative behaviour.

Autism Spectrum Disorder (ASD) is a developmental disability that can cause significant social, communication and behavioural challenges. The school has several children with ASD. The kindergarten teacher, Tania, used the Emotional Assertiveness Feelings Wheel© on the floor of their classroom. Being the pilot school, the children drew their own Feelings Wheel©. Now we provide scalable digital resources for schools to print out and place on the wall or floors, and for workbooks.

Figure 43: Year 1 (age 6)
Emotional Assertiveness Feelings Wheel: Drawn on the floor in their classroom. The original is in full colour.

Emotional Assertiveness® trains the students and teachers that it is OK to be angry, sad and afraid and, importantly, how to express these emotions in a positive way to help us solve our problems, conflicts and anxiety; enabling them to return to being content and happy. A six-year-old girl with ASD, came to the teacher holding the printed Emotional Assertiveness, Sad Mascot. It was the end of the school day. She said, "I am sad, but know it will be OK, as this is what you will do." The teacher was amazed, as normally she would have had a meltdown. This child's parents have reported that her disturbed behaviour would usually continue late into the night and now she was quickly addressing her needs by asking for what she wanted.

By December 2020, the principal reported that another boy with ASD had started to have major meltdowns again. She said, "He is tired, we are all tired, and it has been a tough year." The principal consulted with the boy's mother, who reported he had been having several episodes at home. The mother made this comment: "After 'that course' (Emotional Assertiveness®), he had very few meltdowns and this has lasted until now."

Future Leaders:
My favourite feedback was from a year five student (age ten). She said, "The Emotional Assertiveness® course will help me with my career, in a couple of years."

Emotional Assertiveness for Senior Schools:
Age twelve-eighteen-year-olds
Kempsey is another rural farming town, about five hours north of Sydney. The area has a high indigenous population. The acting principal, Rob Lyttle, heard of the results we were getting, so Kempsey High School became the first pilot for us to train the senior school's executive, forty-nine teachers and 490 students with Emotional Assertiveness®. For both pilots, I travelled to the school and taught the program simultaneously, face-to-face to students in the library and via Zoom to all the classrooms. I used interactive training techniques, movie clips, the chat, three computers to view all the classes, and played a game where each class earned points for their input. We trained the whole school in three days and achieved the training outcomes.

Student and Teacher Feedback:
One young man showed real leadership skills during the face-to-face training in the library. In Emotional Assertiveness®, we talk about meeting your emotional needs. As I was training them about

fear and the importance of protection, and then about sadness and the need to express sadness without having to look after others, I noticed he resonated with this, nodding in agreement. After we had finished, he came to me and thanked me, saying he had got a lot from the course. In the debrief, the principal asked if I had noticed this student. He then went on to explain that the sixteen-year-old had just lost his father to cancer and his mother and the four siblings were about to be deported, as they were on their father's refugee visa. The Immigration Department and the media had been there that week. Normally, the school students raised money for the end-of-year dance for year twelve. That year, the economically struggling school community raised $7,500 for the young man and his family and had no school dance for the graduating students.

Teacher's Feedback:

The Emotional Assertiveness® for Schools program includes online pre-training for the teachers. One of the staff said how, after the fifty-minute online training session covering sadness, the course had helped her with her own teenage son who did not want to go to school. He had been having problems at his school and was dragging his feet in getting ready. In frustration, she had been cranky with him. That morning it had happened again, but this time she analysed her emotions based on the training and Feelings Wheel and realised she was not actually angry but felt sad he was having a hard time at school. She put her arms around her son and told him she was sad he was having a tough time and gave him a big squeeze. Her comment to me was this action made all the difference for both her and her son.

Student Movie Stars:

As part of the Emotional Assertiveness® course, the students, along with their teacher, write up generic problems they and the teachers are facing at their school, especially around expressing the four emotions: anger, sadness, fear, and happiness.

The students then created mini movie clips about how to address these problems in an Emotionally Assertive® manner. The students and teachers have done an incredible job with this, and the school will use the clips to teach other students (and teachers) about how to manage their emotions and behaviour positively. Our aim is to have a collection of the movie clips developed by the students, when the school and parental permissions have been granted. These educational resources will be shared, for free, worldwide to all schools who complete the program.

The high school executive reported the program was a huge success, and we are looking forward to tracking the results, as the school continues to embed the applied emotional intelligence skills to shift the culture of the school from hardship to collaboration and empowerment.

Practical Reliable Affordable EQ Skills:
As a master trainer, what I find powerful about John Parr's Emotional Assertiveness® course is that it works for adults, children and teenagers. The program is being used in diverse industries and we are having success whether the person is a CEO, or a manager of a corporate or government department, staff member, clinical team member in a hospital, a teacher, parent, or a student navigating the challenges of school.

Where to Next, 2020 and Beyond:
There is a Thai saying "same, same but different". John and I just completed training a private school in England, via Zoom. The headmaster and the psychologist talked about the behavioural problems they were facing with the children since COVID-19. Then, two private schools in Armenia, also expressed interest in the training, due to the students struggling with the impact of online and home schooling during the COVID-19 pandemic and, sadly, this was followed by the experience of the horrors of a war. Although with different accents and from different parts of the world, what all the school heads were expressing was they are all facing the same problems with higher levels of anxiety, disengagement and challenging behaviours displayed by junior and senior students on a mass scale. The teachers are struggling.

The 2019/2020 fires were so intense in Australia that even after the fire was put out, the tree roots were still on fire under the ground. The trees would fall over days or weeks later, and this would start another spot fire causing more problems, cyclically adding to the horrors of the national disaster.

School counsellors and clinical support roles are so important. The pandemic that began in 2020 has brought a world change with countries, government, businesses, adults and youth struggling on a mass scale. More than ever, there is a need for practical, reliable sustainable skills for managing our anger, sadness and fear, so we can effectively deal with the compounded stress from the lockdown, loss of jobs, isolation and uncertainty. Teachers, counsellors and therapists report they are so busy dealing with spot fires, and so much noise, due to the impact of COVID-19, that it is making it harder to work with the students who are self-harming and suicidal. Sadly, within ninety kilometres of where I live, there was a string of suicides in 2020 amongst teenagers and adults.

Vision and Accreditation:
The vision is to support as many teachers and students as possible with these powerful life skills. I would like to thank Lisa Kirkland, the New South Wales Department of Education Principal School Leader official approver. Also, the principals of the schools where the program has been delivered, for their trust for enabling the pilot programs and for the satisfying and exciting results. Their vision, commitment and dedication to their staff and students' wellbeing is evident. Emotional Assertiveness® for Schools is now New South Wales Government Education Standards Authority (NESA) approved and accredited for over 230,000 New South Wales public, private and independent school teachers. Meeting their criteria is not an easy feat. Training Lab is also on the preferred New South Wales Australian government supplier list for training government staff in emotional intelligence leadership skills.

Emotional Assertiveness® for Schools e-Learning App:
We have partnered with Yarno, an e-Learning company. We will be using their advanced e-Learning technology, combined with the Emotional Assertiveness® program, to enable schools to have friendly competition whilst practising applied emotional

intelligence and communication skills to address school and work problems. Business professionals won't miss out on all the fun as they will also have access to the Emotional Assertiveness® e-Learning App, tailored to their industry.

From 2021, the Emotional Assertiveness® International trainers will start to teach the program in schools in multiple languages and countries. The principals and education department staff will also go through The Emotional Assertiveness® Certification for trainers, coaches and therapists.

In Conclusion:

Worldwide, 2020 and 2021 have been hard years. The feedback from all the training I have run using John Parr's Emotional Assertiveness® programs is that it is shifting adults' and youths' lives, as they learn how to understand and apply these priceless life skills in solving their problems, conflicts and improving relationships. I am honoured to learn from and work with John, and proud of what we have achieved with the Emotional Assertiveness® for Schools' junior and senior pilot programs and look forward to seeing what the future brings.

Corinne McDevitt
Founder of Training Lab
Emotional Assertiveness Master Trainer
www.traininglab.com.au
corinne@traininglab.com.au
Sydney, Australia

Ancillary information from John Parr:

In the UK, we have now run the Emotional Assertiveness program in a school in the UK and are in the process of training two members of staff to support the ongoing use of the material in the school. During the pilot program, a six-year-old boy had a light-bulb moment. This child had been showing serious behavioural problems, and was on the headmaster's daily report for extreme misconduct. In the session, he exclaimed, "Ha! Now I know why

I keep getting into trouble!" His form teacher and the headmaster reported that his behaviour had changed and that he was no longer a regular visitor to the headmaster's office. Whilst he was still incorporating his newly gained insight, the improvement in his behaviour had been sustained for several months.

As for the work in Australia, only last week the principal of Nana Glen school contacted me (John Parr) to say that they were still experiencing the positive outcomes from the first seminar run in 2020. They only saw the behavioural problems with newly inducted pupils, and some new members of staff not yet trained in Emotional Assertiveness. She wants the new staff members trained as well as the new students. She also wants some follow-up for the whole school.

Diversity and Race: Emotional Intelligence for the Australian First Nation, Aboriginal Community

By Bonita Byrne and Corinne McDevitt
Email: Bonita bonitabyrne1950@gmail.com and Corinne corinne@traininglab.com.au

A Wiradjuri Aboriginal Elder, Bonita Byrne, was born to an Australian Wiradjuri Aboriginal family in Narrandera, NSW, Australia. Corinne stayed on the Aboriginal reserve on the sand hills, five kilometres from the township of Narrandera, population 5000, with two per cent being Aboriginal. For years, I have worked in various Aboriginal communities throughout NSW. During my studies, including my two master's degrees, I have majored in Aboriginal studies and community. In the course of my work, my studies and my life, I have found that the history of colonisation in Australia has had a devastating effect on our people. Things that have impacted our people are the loss of land, forcing our people to depend on government welfare for survival; and the occurrence of the stolen generation resulting in children removed from their families never to see them again, contributing to the breakdown of families, their language, culture and identity. To this day, Aboriginal people are overrepresented in the criminal justice system, juvenile and prison system. Many of my people suffer with anger issues, unhappiness, sadness and fear as a result of the past, and continuous racism and discrimination. Most of these issues have never been dealt with. Aboriginal people live fifteen to twenty years less than the wider community and many do not live past sixty years old.

An as Aboriginal elder, I have completed both the Emotional Assertiveness course, and the Assertiveness Skills course. I have benefitted personally and professionally in all the emotional areas.

For example, what I have learnt is awareness of my emotions and that each emotion has different needs, but the good news is that those emotional needs can be addressed in a healthy way, so I can live life in a more positive way. I feel that many Aboriginal people like myself have suffered mental and emotional stress and have not learnt to address their emotional needs in healthy ways. Many identify and resonate with the problems we have faced.

In collaboration with Corinne McDevitt, the Australian Master trainer of Emotional Assertiveness, I have conducted a number of programs including one with the Aboriginal Medical and Dental Organisation, plus we were selected by one of Australia's largest banks to train thirteen Aboriginal Emerging Leaders from government and indigenous organisations around Australia as part of their sponsored foundation.

We have had positive feedback from these Aboriginal leaders and medical front-line staff locally and Australia wide. As we move forward with an Aboriginal perspective on this amazing applied Emotional Intelligence Program, I am sure many of our people will be positively affected by the teachings and the tools supplied to utilise to create changes in Aboriginal leaders, adults, youth, families, Medical Centres and our wider community.

"It was a new perspective for me on emotional wellbeing having completed M.NUM.Ser (Mental Health) degree. Group work was good."
RivMed Team Leader and works closely with the Corrective Centres (previously a senior detective police officer). Rate personally 8/10 and professionally 8/10
(Leadership program)

"Great course, very handy to learn about different emotions especially when dealing with emotional clients with mental health and drug use concerns."
Aboriginal Medical and Dental Corporation
Preservation Caseworker.
Rate Personally and Professionally 9/10 and 9/10
(Frontline staff program)

Bonita Byrne Wiradjuri Elder Emotional Assertiveness

I grew up on the mission seeing a lot of pain.

My father taken away to jail, kids away from our families.

As a Wiradjuri Elder I am passionate to empower Aboriginal communities to take responsibility for their emotional and mental health.

There is a gap how the money is being used.
It it not effectively addressing the emotional and mental side of things.

With your help I want to show you how we can heal and put a stop to the effects of intergenerational trauma.

Figure 44: A slide from presentation "Emotional Intelligence" describing Bonita Byrne's experiences as a Wiradjuri Elder.

Emotional Assertiveness for Aboriginal & Torres Strait Islanders

A leadership and applied emotional inteligence program for business leaders, elders, community adults and children.

Figure 45: A slide from presentation "Emotional Intelligence" describing the purpose of the program.

Emotional Assertiveness for Aboriginal & Torres Strait Islanders

The problem

You know how mental health is a hug problem, well the stats show for indigenous Australians it's even worse.

Well what we do is specialise in training Emotional Assertiveness and resilience skills.

In fact we have reports from government and coporate services across the board that Emotional Assertivenss programs are cutting through the problems and making real difference.

We are looking for organisations to help us reduce the crime, suicide and intergenerational hurts that have continued on for year in and year out.

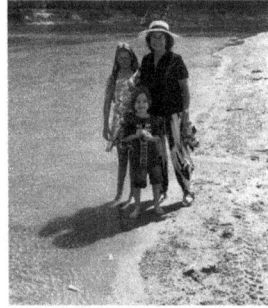

Figure 46: A slide from presentation "Emotional Intelligence" defining the problem the Training Lab is looking to solve.

If we prevent only 1 male, 1 young person & a mum from going to jail we save the government $450,410 per year

The justice system is the fastest growing industry. Costs Australia $14.02 billion a year

Prisons and periodic detention centres £2.4 billion a year

Cost 1 prisioner $305 per day $111,325 per year per prisioner.

Cost $624 per day per youth for juvenile detention $227,760 per youth a year.

80% of Aboriginal women in prision are mothers.

Prision capacity is 90% full. 96% full for secure facilities.

Reference: Austrialian Government Australian Institute of Criminology, Research report 05 page 16.

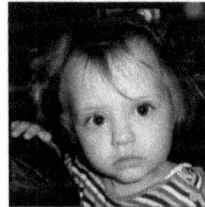

Figure 47: A slide from presentation "Emotional Intelligence" detailing the financial impact on the broader community.

Thank you and we look forward to continuing the yarn with you

Bonita & Corinne

Figure 48: A slide from presentation "Emotional Intelligence" with Bonita Byrne and Corinne McDevitt.

Aboriginal Wiradjuri Elder Bonita Byrne
Master of Research and Master of Education
Deadly Minds
deadlyminds9@gmail.com
Australia

Corinne McDevitt
Master Trainer
www.traininglab.com.au
corinne@traininglab.com.au

Comment from John Parr

Bonita and Corrine have been doing outstanding work adapting the Core Topics Emotional Assertiveness program for delivery to the Indigenous people of Australia. Bonita has not only adapted the delivery style, but she has also recreated the diagrams such as the feelings wheel so they have meaning in terms of how the indigenous peoples use culturally recognisable storytelling graphics. It is heart-warming to see the progress she and Corinne are making to make a real difference regarding Aboriginal issues and doing this in a way that respects their culture and values.

Respect for self and others, along with diversity and inclusivity are high amongst Emotional Assertiveness' core values. Whatever culture or setting we work within, it is our aim to adapt the material and personalise it in terms of cultural norms, corporate values and religious belief systems. I am proud to know you both and be involved in this venture. Thanks for the wonderful work you have initiated.

Summary and the Big Picture

During our lifespan, we meet, make friends with, work with, play with and live with other people. The human being is a social animal by design. At the centre of all our activities, bonding and finding how we fit into social groups is key to our wellbeing. Social behaviours that began with our ancestors functioned as survival mechanisms; modern humans have the same mechanisms, and this lies at the root of our emotional lives. Our emotions serve as important information to aid in how we manage our relationships, they tell us what we need to do to maintain connectivity to our fellows. They also inform us about how to remain psychologically healthy.

Whilst most of us seldom think of the importance of attachment and cooperation in our individual and collective success, we still need each other. We are all, somehow, a part of a greater whole. All Homo sapiens can trace their origins back to the same ancestors, so we are family. Sadly, all too often we seem to treat each other more as hostile aliens than family. Yet, we are each born with the capacity to be able to get along together. We are all capable of being able to empathise, and to understand what it would be like to be in the others' shoes. I think above all this is what it takes to be human. Compassion, kindness, respect, cooperation, and mutual support are amongst the important attributes that are markers of belonging to our tribe. This is all about fore-play and fair-play. These attributes are so important to our species that there is a centre of the brain devoted to encouraging us to cooperate. We derive pleasure from this.

I hope I have made the case for the importance of Emotionally Assertive behaviours in our dealings with one another. It is the single most impactful thing we can do to make a difference in this world. By developing our capacity to use our emotions for the good, we demonstrate the markers outlined above. This is the outworking of fore-play and fair-play.

Sadly, throughout history, destructive conflict has been abundant in our world. We each see daily outpourings of foul-play. It is present in our intimate relationships, in the workplace, in politics, and in international relationships. Most of the ills in our world can be traced back to a breakdown in relationship, caused by a lack of emotional intelligence. A shortlist of the global issues our failure to cooperate brought us to includes famine, where the world has sufficient food to feed all, conflicts abounding on almost every continent, ranging from full on war, terrorism, racial to religious tensions, and pandemics. We even refuse to face the evident risk to the survival of humanity, that climate change is bringing. Rather than uniting to find a solution, we argue about whether climate change really exists, do we really need to control the emissions of greenhouse gasses, the validity of research, etc. As this unproductive conflict goes on around us, we can see the evidence of global warming everywhere: unprecedented floods, whole areas of the globe experiencing water shortages, the ice caps melting, and the highest rate of extinction of other species in history. The list is endless. Added to this, the big powers have stockpiles of nuclear weapons sufficient to make the planet uninhabitable.

War stems from an inability or unwillingness to find a win-win negotiation. It is the ultimate foul-play. Combatants and politicians on each side of a conflict become entrenched and willing to fight to the death, often against imagined threats, or misguided beliefs. Much of these polarising influences can be managed and resolved when we find common ground and talk about how to cooperate based upon good will.

At such times it is normal for observers to draw conclusions and take sides. However, we members of the public only have limited information, and that is through the media and is frequently inaccurate or biased. Our desire to circle the waggons and take positions is most likely fear based, although it generally appears to be about anger. It is as if the disputes draw us into them, as a moth being drawn to a candle. By taking sides however, the danger is we add to the polarising of arguments and reinforce the foul-play. All this leads to an apparent lack of basic human compassion. Demonising is a marker of extreme foul-play. Watching this we want to make our collected impressions fit together so we can understand it. Sadly, we only know a part of the whole story. Is this not very similar at this global level to what we experience when we observe friends in relationship distress? From experience I know how difficult it can be when a couple who we love, fall out, and how lines get drawn and how the wider circle of friends can be drawn in. It is amplified when the conflict becomes so unproductive, they separate. Do we remain friends with one? Do we stay friends with both? Just as they face loss, we too experience loss. So even at this personal level of foul-play we have two people locked in an unproductive conflict and getting nowhere. We see others in their extended network faced with managing the fallout. At all levels our failure to maintain bonds and to show empathy frequently ends where whoever wins the war, one way or another also loses. Further, such situations are most likely to end with both sides being the loser. Where can it go from here?

The answer is in individual responsibility. First, each side needs to grasp that they have a role in maintaining foul-play and seeking to return to fair-play. We bystanders may think we have no responsibility for the conflict, but I do not believe this. I see the underlying issue is about taking collective responsibility for conflict and finding ways to shift away from power grabbing. We share collective responsibility internationally in the same way we do at the personal level. Therefore, we could begin lobbying politicians to find ways to de-escalate from conflicts like NATO vs Russia, East vs West and others. By placing importance on finding friendly ways of accepting differences, being tolerant and seeking where nations could share investments, rather than polarising and competing, we could make a difference. I believe the answers lie in regularly looking at both the macro and the micro levels of the need for human cooperation. The big picture is that our world is in trouble. We are facing unprecedented issues due to overpopulation, global warming causing climate change, and mass migrations to get away from conflict and poverty. There are areas of the world with not enough food or water, whilst others have a surplus. With cooperation, we have enough to feed everyone. At the personal level, we each need to be willing to make sacrifices to bring about the necessary changes to address these critical problems. There is the rub! Every time we choose we lose, and to choose world peace, a true sharing of resources, a reduction of greenhouse gas emissions and so on, we must each contribute. Individually it looks like the problems are just too big and nothing we do personally will make a change. However, if we all contribute a little, the change will be immense. For example, I forget to turn off a light. Does that add to global warming? Well, not much perhaps, however turning of that light multiplied by millions makes the change. We have power, we simply do not get that real power comes in cooperation. Emotional Assertiveness is central to this. By developing and deepening our ability to bond and attach, even to strangers, we can change the world. We simply have to all pull in the same direction. Our aspirations may be different, our personal and collective goals may seem divergent, yet with cooperation we can all get what we want. The concept of shortage is subconscious and archaic, We can overcome this by being aware of just how much we have if we share resources. Then at the global level shortage can be addressed with good will. This is not a communist ideology, rather it is humanitarian.

The global economy is impacted by our failure to manage our resources. At the time of writing, inflation is spiralling out of control, and people are starving because they can no longer afford the necessities of life. The price of fuels of all kinds is going sky high. Our over dependence on fossil fuels is driving climate change etc. As a result of the globally, multifaceted aspects of humans engaging in foul-play, the world is straining at the seams. At all levels, from individual personal relationships to international relationships, foul-play abounds. The fallout is growing; crowds of displaced persons and refugees from all over clamour to find refuge by flocking to the richer countries. These rich economies resist by attempting to stem the tide but do nothing to help the countries where refugees come from. We could be using the money spent on enforcing boundaries to instead help poorer economies become stable and hostile countries a safer place to live. People are suffering. Foul-play does not work; it does not provide the fertile ground where people can enjoy being winners together.

In addition to this we need to account for the impact of over two years of a pandemic. At the time of writing, COVID-19 has killed over fifteen million people globally. The pandemic has also hit the global economy. The pandemic is not directly about foul-play; a virus does not have a harmful motive and just acts as per its design. However, even the pandemic can be the basis for foul-play. How we respond to it and how we react to our fellow humans can be assessed by observing behaviour: do we see fair-play, or not? We are all touched by these issues. What are we feeling when we look at these situations? How are we using our emotions to look for healthy strategies to support all the peoples of the world?

No matter what side of the political spectrum you are on, most people are now aware that the survival of humanity is at risk if we do not work together to solve the issue of global warming, and we have limited time left to solve the problem. Some are very angry about these things, but sadly, I frequently hear the anger expressed in terms of attack or blame. A good idea or intention can be expressed in ways to either invite cooperation or invite competition. As we have seen, there are no bad emotions, and yet emotion may be expressed either in healthy or unhealthy ways.

On the positive side, at least we are being encouraged to face the issues, as even attack and blame can stimulate healthy responses. However, on the negative side, unhealthy expressions of anger create destructive conflict more often than not. It is time for us to all pull together for the same cause. I am sure we can do this, but I am not sure we have yet seen how vital this is. We all live on the same planet. We all share the same resources, and the only solution is a collective one. Winner and loser politics is not an option, as this can only lead to endless conflict. The way forward is cooperation. In the song *Russians*, by Sting, the sentiments are very relevant to today's world:

> We share the same biology, regardless of ideology
> Believe me when I say to you
> I hope the Russians love their children too.[53]

---

53. Sting, "Russians," June 1985, *The Dream of the Blue Turtles*, 1985, musical recording.

We hear in Sting's lyrics his fear for his children's safety, and his search for hope. He finds this in the possibility that between the potential combatants there can be empathy, based upon our love for our children. We share the same hopes for our children's safety.

I suggest we can go further than this. Avoiding war because we fear for the safety of our children is, for me, a sound argument, a great starting place. However, how about using Emotional Assertiveness and seeking to go the extra mile? I suggest that we also love the Russian children and the Russian people. This is the true meaning of a win-win outcome. In 2022, the world has become even smaller than it was when Sting wrote "Russians," and the need for human connection is more and more apparent. It seems, that as a species, we are avoiding the harsh realities we must face to ensure human survival. Beyond survival, perhaps we could even seek advancement, more peace, better relationships and shared happiness, pleasure, and the joy of living.

I have been to Russia many times. I have friends in Russia whom I love dearly. I have found those Russians I have met to be warm, friendly, fun to be with, intelligent and open to connectivity. What then is the animosity between the East and the West about?[54] What could be the motive for engaging in conflict between the East and West? I hypothesise that the emotional need not being addressed is fear. I think our leaders may be experiencing fear of invasion, of annihilation and fear of loss of power, including personal financial gain. Some of this will be authentic, based upon real fears and a need for safety, whilst some may be based upon dishonest motives and even corruption. Therefore, we need to approach solution with caution. This is the role of fore-play.

Our part in maintaining this unhappy situation is to invite those others to be afraid by escalating our belligerence towards them. We probably do this for much the same reasons as do our protagonists. Sadly, anger begets anger, and unhealthy anger even more so. All parties in an unproductive conflict are subconsciously avoiding solving the key issues. This leads to fear and anxiety. It is time to give up demonising each other and start a process of respectful,

54. Note: this question about Russia and the West is only an example. The same argument can be applied to any international hostility.

cooperative relating. This is not to say everyone has pure motives, and that people do not behave very badly, as it is obvious this is not so. That is not grounds for armed conflict, but for managing boundaries in a mutually respectful way. Step by step, we need to find our way back into healthy relationship through fore-play first, rejecting foul-play and embracing fair-play. I am not advocating for the case of those who are passivists, in the time of the Roman Empire I support the saying, "If you want peace, prepare for war." (In Latin this is *Si vis pacem, para bellum.*[55])

War has been a feature of the twentieth and now the twenty-first centuries. The total deaths due to the first and second wars alone are more than triple the deaths COVID-19 has caused. Add to this, conflicts in Vietnam, the Balkans, Africa, the Middle East and so on. The numbers are tragic. Each war has been fought with more and more destructive weaponry. Nuclear weapons, and chemical and biological weapons are a scary reality, so at some level we all have grounds to feel afraid.

The very real issues we fight about is survival, and when we operate purely in terms of the survival of the fittest, the outcome is not good. That line of thought inevitability leads towards destructive conflict with a focus on win-lose outcomes, as opposed to win-win. Within the east/west dynamic, NATO is seen by Russia as a threat, and Russia is seen by NATO as a threat. How about we move towards a de-escalation of threat and an amplification of finding healthy ways to cooperate? Imagine how beneficial this could be to us all. Globally there would be a reduced need to spend on weaponry, which is currently between 1.5 and 6.6 per cent of GDP depending upon which sources we examine. Being able to cut these budgets will release funds to build schools, hospitals and create work for the unemployed. The list of positive things we could achieve with cooperation is truly awesome.

Remember what happens when teams use Emotional Assertiveness skills to achieve synergy? i.e., the performing stage of development. Now, apply that to what we could achieve if the global conflicts were resolved through empathy and humanity.

---

55. Attributed to the Roman general Publius Flavious Vegetius from the book *Epitoma Rei Militaris*.

Global synergy would take our species to a whole new level of thriving, way beyond just surviving. We would still retain small military forces, but they would mostly be used to act in times of crisis to assist when there is flooding, earthquake, etc. Only occasionally would they be needed to enforce boundaries. That is so long as we all agreed to act with fair-play.

What can individuals do to make an impact in our world and be a part of a movement of change for the good of the whole? The good news is that we have all we need to manage these issues and more. The solution is to go back to basics. Just as every journey starts with the first step, so too does this journey. The first step is to look to ourselves. We must recognise the importance of having respectful and cooperative relationships with as many of our contacts as possible. We need to clarify the difference between authentic, open expressions of emotion, aimed at establishing and building healthy relationships, and destructive, unhealthy expression born of going for non-winning outcomes.

By gaining self-awareness, we place ourselves in the starting blocks that begin the race to having happy and helpful connections with others. Add to this the skills of self-management, and our emotions will not take over or control us, rather we manage them. Therefore, the task is to learn how to manage our emotions and to use them in a healthy way. This is based on also giving up the myth that other people's behaviour and emotional expressions somehow swamp us and make us incapable of coping. In the short term, it may feel liberating to blame others for how we feel and behave (foul-play), yet this is enslavement not freedom. This road leads to simply repeating destructive patterns of behaviour and at this point in history, that bodes very ill for us.

When we add to this mix, the awareness of others and accept equality, along with taking responsibility for managing our side of a relationship, we have all we need to make a difference. Finally, as we accept our personal responsibility and assert ourselves emotionally, we commit to the journey. Emotional assertiveness is the engine that drives the machine; empathy and compassion are the fuels that power it.

All this is not only possible, it is our birth right, and I believe is also possible to reclaim. We are designed to get along with each other. It is years of miscommunication and emotional confusion that teaches us how not to get along.

Start by solving the unresolved conflicts in your relationships. Where there are tensions, get to the bottom of the emotional foundations, address them, and move on. For example, make friends with those difficult neighbours, and rebuild relationships with friends that have grown cold due to unfinished business. Above all, if you have children, help them to express their authentic emotions by modelling this to them and by listening to them. None of this will solve the problems of war or global warming, however, it could start a trend that has an amazing and long-term benefit. Then, who knows?

If you find merit in the model I propose in this book, please feel free to look at our website www.emotionalassertiveness.com. On the home page, there are some short, animated videos that explain the thrust of our work. We currently have trainers in Armenia, Australia, Canada, Denmark, France, Kazakhstan, the Netherlands, Romania, Russia, the UK, and the USA. It is our intention to grow this network and make a small contribution to bringing positive change in our world. If you see merit in this, why not join our growing global community?

Bibliography and Further Reading

Bader, E., & Pearson, P. *In Quest of the Mythical Mate*. Routledge, 1988.

Berne, E. *The Games People Play*. New York: Grove Press, 1964.

Berne, E. "Trading Stamps." *Transactional Analysis Bulletin* 3 (1964): 127.

Berne, E. *Transactional Analysis in Psychotherapy*. New York: Grove Press, 1961.

Berne, E. *What Do You Say After You Say Hello*. Great Britain: Andre Deutsch Ltd., 1974.

Bowlby, J. *A Secure Base: Parent-Child Attachment And Healthy Human Development*. London: Routledge, 1988.

Clarkson, P. *Transactional Analysis Psychotherapy: An Integrated Approach*. Tavistock: Routledge, 1992.

English, F. "The Substitution Factor - Rackets & Racket Feelings, Part I." *Transactional Analysis Journal* 1 , no. 4 (1971-1972): 27-32.

English F. "The Substitution Factor - Rackets & Racket Feelings Part II." *Transactional Analysis Journal*, 2 (1971-1972): 23-25.

Erskine, R.G. "Shame & Self-Righteousness: TA Perspectives & Clinical Interventions. *Transactional Analysis Journal* 24, no. 2 (1994).

Erskine, R.G., & Zalcman, M. "The Racket System: A model for racket analysis." *Transactional Analysis Journal* 9, (1979): 51-59.

Goleman, D. *Emotional intelligence: why it can matter more than IQ.* Bloomsbury, 1996.

Goleman, D. *Destructive Emotions And How We Can Overcome Them: A Dialogue With The Dalai Lama.* Bloomsbury, 2002.

Hendrix, H. *Getting The Love You Want.* Simon & Schuster, 1988.

Holtby, M. "Interlocking Racket Systems." *Transactional Analysis Journal* 9, no. 2 (April 1979): 131-135.

Kahler, T., & Capers, H. (1974). "The Miniscript." *Transactional Analysis Journal* 4, no. 1 (1974): 26-42.

Kahler, T. *The Process Communication Model.* Little Rock: Taibi Kahler Associates, Inc., 1996.

Kaplan, K. J. *TILT: Teaching Individuals to Live Together.* Philadelphia, PA: Brunner/Mazel, 1998.

Kaplan, K. J. "TILT: Teaching Individuals to Live Together." *Transactional Analysis Journal* 18, no. 3 (July 1998).

Karpman, S. "Fairy Tales & Script Drama Analysis." *TA Bulletin* 7, (1968): 39-43.

Karpman, S. *A Game Free Life: the definitive book on the Drama Triangle and the Compassion Triangle.* USA: Drama Triangle Publications, 2014.

Kübler-Ross, E. *On Death And Dying.* New York: Macmillan, 1969.

LeDoux, J. *The Emotional Brain: The Mysterious Underpinnings of Emotional Life*. Great Britain: Weidenfield & Nicholson, 1998.

MacDonald, S. P. 2007. "The erasure of language." College composition and Communication, 585-625. Published by National Council of Teachers of English

Mehrabian & Ferris. "Inference of Attitudes From Non-Verbal Communication in Two Channels." *The Journal of Counselling Psychology* 31, (1967).

Mellor, K., & Schiff, E. Discounting. *Transactional Analysis Journal* 5, no. 3 (1975): 295-302.

Moiso, C. "The Feelings Loop." In *TA The State of the Art*. Dordrecht, Holland: Foris Publications, 1984.

Montagu, A. *Touching: The Human Significance of The Skin*. New York: Harper and Row, 1971.

Parr, John. "The Feeling Wheel: A Tool for Systematic Analysis of Feelings." MSc Thesis, Middlesex University, 2001.

Pert, C. *The Molecules of Emotion*. London: Simon & Schuster UK Ltd, Pocket Books, 1999.

Schiff, A., & Schiff, J. "Passivity." *Transactional Analysis Journal* 1, no. 1 (1971): 71-78.

Smith, M. J. *When I Say No, I Feel Guilty*. New York: Bantam Books, Inc., 1981.

Steere, D. A. *Bodily Expressions in Psychotherapy*. New York: Brunner/Mazel, Inc., 1982.

Steiner, C. *Achieving Emotional Literacy*. London: Bloomsbury Publishing Plc., 1997.

Steiner, C. *The Other Side of Power*. New York: Grove Press, 1981.

Store, A. *Human Aggression*. England: Allen Lane, The Penguin Press, Pelican Books, 1974.

Thomson, G. "Fear, Anger & Sadness." *Transactional Analysis Journal* 13, no. 1 (1983): 20-24.

Tomkins, S. S. *Affect, Imagery, Consciousness*. New York: Springer, 1962.

Wordon, J. W. *Grief Counselling and Grief Therapy (second edition)*. Great Britain: Routledge, 1995

Why not become a
Certified Emotional Assertiveness Trainer?

Those with a background in psychology, psychotherapy, coaching, counselling, or training consultancy may find it beneficial to become a Certified Emotional Assertiveness Professional. For information about training and certification contact John at johnparr@psdci.co.uk. Some general information can be found on www.emotionalassertiveness.com.

Emotional Assertiveness International ltd., currently has Certified Professionals in Armenia, Australia, Canada, Denmark, France, Kazakhstan, the Netherlands, Romania, the UK, and the USA.

If you are looking for introductory seminars in any of these countries, contact johnparr@psdci.co.uk and you will be put in direct contact with a trainer in your region.